THE COLLECTED COURSES OF THE ACADEMY OF EUROPEAN LAW

Volume XXXII/1

New Frontiers of EU Funding

Law, Policy, Politics

THE COLLECTED COURSES OF THE ACADEMY OF EUROPEAN LAW

Edited by: Professor Neha Jain, Professor Claire Kilpatrick, Professor Sarah Nouwen, and Professor Joanne Scott

Assistant Editor: Joyce Davies

The Academy of European Law is housed at the European University Institute in Florence, Italy. The Academy holds annual advanced-level summer courses focusing on topical, cutting-edge issues in Human Rights Law and The Law of the European Union. The courses are taught by highly qualified scholars and practitioners in a highly interactive environment. General courses involve the examination of the field as a whole through a particular thematic, conceptual, or philosophical lens or look at a theme in the context of the overall body of law. Specialized courses bring together a number of speakers exploring a specific theme in depth. Together, they are published as monographs and edited volumes in the Collected Courses of the Academy of European Law series. The Collected Courses series has been published by Oxford University Press since 2000. The series contains publications on both foundational and pressing issues in human rights law and the law of the European Union.

OTHER TITLES IN THE SERIES INCLUDE:

Human Rights in Transition
Edited by Nehal Bhuta

The Emergence of European Society through Public Law
A Hegelian and Anti-Schmittian Approach
Armin von Bogdandy

Revisiting the Fundamentals of the Free Movement of Persons in EU Law
Edited by Niamh Nic Shuibhne

Data at the Boundaries of European Law
Edited by Deirdre Curtin and Mariavittoria Catanzariti

Legal Mobilization for Human Rights
Edited by Gráinne de Búrca

The UK's Withdrawal from the EU
A Legal Analysis
Michael Dougan

Justifying Contract in Europe
Political Philosophies of European Contract Law
Martijn W. Hesselink

Contemporary Challenges to EU Legality
Edited by Claire Kilpatrick and Joanne Scott

Reframing Human Rights in a Turbulent Era
Gráinne de Búrca

New Legal Approaches to Studying the Court of Justice
Revising Law in Context
Edited by Claire Kilpatrick and Joanne Scott

New Frontiers of EU Funding

Law, Policy, Politics

Edited by
CLAIRE KILPATRICK
JOANNE SCOTT

OXFORD
UNIVERSITY PRESS

OXFORD
UNIVERSITY PRESS

Great Clarendon Street, Oxford, OX2 6DP,
United Kingdom

Oxford University Press is a department of the University of Oxford.
It furthers the University's objective of excellence in research, scholarship,
and education by publishing worldwide. Oxford is a registered trade mark of
Oxford University Press in the UK and in certain other countries

Published in the United States of America by Oxford University Press
198 Madison Avenue, New York, NY 10016, United States of America

British Library Cataloguing in Publication Data

Data available

Library of Congress Control Number: 2024947420

ISBN 978–0–19–894031–9

DOI: 10.1093/oso/9780198940319.001.0001

Printed and bound in the UK by
Clays Ltd, Elcograf S.p.A.

Table of Contents

Notes on Contributors

Richard Crowe is Head of the Institutional & Budgetary Law Unit at the Legal Service of the European Parliament. He provides legal advice in EU legislative and budgetary procedures and represents the Parliament in litigation before the EU courts. Prior to joining the European Parliament in 2011, he worked at the Legal Service of the European Court of Auditors and, before that, at the Academy of European Law (ERA) in Trier, Germany. He is an Irish barrister and a graduate of the College of Europe (Bruges), the Honourable Society of King's Inns (Dublin) and the University of Limerick. He has lectured on EU law at various universities around Europe and has published on different aspects of EU institutional and budgetary law.

Ioanna Hadjiyianni is Assistant Professor of Public Law at the University of Cyprus. Previously, she was a Max Weber Postdoctoral Fellow at the European University Institute. She is an editor for the Review Articles section at the *Journal of Environmental Law*. Her research focuses on the extraterritorial reach of EU environmental and climate law, access to justice in environmental matters, the use of EU funding to achieve the objectives of the European Green Deal, ship recycling, and the interaction between EU and international law.

Claire Kilpatrick is Professor of Law and Co-director of the Academy of European Law at the European University Institute, where she has been a Co-director of the Academy of European Law since 2015. Before coming to the European University Institute in 2011, she worked at the London School of Economics and Cambridge University. Her interests lie mainly in the law and policy construction of Social Europe, especially the EU's roles.

Emilia Korkea-aho is Professor of European Law and Legislative Studies at the University of Eastern Finland. Her research interests relate to law and democracy in the EU and national contexts, including lobbying, revolving doors, and funds governance. Methodologically, her work is interdisciplinary and socio-legally orientated, with an emphasis on expert interviews. In addition to her monograph *Adjudicating New Governance* (Routledge, 2015), she is co-editor of *EU Soft Law in the Member States* (Hart Publishing, 2021), *Law, Legal Expertise and EU Policy-Making* (CUP, 2022), *The Research Handbook on Soft Law* (Edward Elgar, 2023), and *The Oxford Handbook on Lobbying and Its Regulation* (OUP, forthcoming 2026).

Johannes Lindner is Co-director of the Jacques Delors Centre at the Hertie School, where he has led the think tank since 2022. In 2022–2023, he was, in addition, the first Henrik Enderlein Fellow at the Hertie School. From 2012 to 2022, he was Head of the EU Institutions and Fora Division, coordinating the relations of the European

Central Bank (ECB) with EU institutions, in particular the Council and the European Parliament. Previously, he had worked in several policy areas of the ECB. He studied economics and politics with Master's degrees from the London School of Economics and the University of Cologne and a doctorate in politics from the University of Oxford focusing on EU budgetary decision-making. Johannes Lindner is an Honorary Professor at Aston University.

Thu Nguyen is Deputy Director of the Jacques Delors Centre at the Hertie School, where she leads the think tank on institutional questions of EU policy. Her expertise lies in the area of EU institutions, rule of law, budget, and economic governance. Before joining the Jacques Delors Centre, she was Assistant Professor of EU and Comparative Constitutional Law at the Faculty of Law at Maastricht University. She holds a PhD in EU Constitutional Law from Maastricht University and was a re:constitution fellow in 2019–2020. Thu studied European Law in Maastricht, Rennes, and the College of Europe in Bruges.

Joanne Scott is Professor of European Law and Co-director of the Academy of European Law at the European University Institute. She is an Honorary Professor at University College London, Faculty of Laws, where she taught from 2005 to 2017. Before that, she taught at the University of Cambridge, Queen Mary University of London, and the University of Kent. Her research interests lie in the areas of environmental law and climate change law, EU extraterritoriality, new modes of EU governance, and the relationships between different legal orders.

Viorica Viță is European Integration Officer at the European Commission. She holds a PhD from the European University Institute, Law Department, where she also held the position of research associate at the Robert Schuman Centre from 2014 to 2019. Her seminal research on the law of spending conditionality has informed and shaped the EU academic and institutional debates, with a particular focus on the origins, evolution, and impact of this governance tool on the future of EU integration. She investigates the different ways in which the legal objectives of conditionality can materialize in practice, drawing on the use of conditionality in international relations and federalist systems, and critically analyses the limitations of the tool in achieving compliance.

1

New Frontiers of European Union Funding

*Claire Kilpatrick and Joanne Scott**

1. Introduction

Legal scholars are latecomers to European Union (EU) funding and the EU budget. Although EU spending has always been thoroughly encased by law, save when something out of the ordinary happened raising institutional or competence questions,[1] spending was seen as mainly of interest for EU studies rather than EU law. It was viewed as being about the power of the purse rather than rule by law. That began to change from 2010 onwards for two key reasons. First, the sovereign debt crisis brought considerably more attention to the EU's funding capacities although, owing to design constraints that we shall explore, the focus was more on extra-EU mechanisms than on the use of the EU budget itself. Second, the EU budget came into focus as part of discussions on how to address several issues affecting the EU, including the rule of law crisis in some EU Member States. However, it was 2020 that constituted a genuine turning point in terms of the level of interest in the legal aspects of EU funding. The emergence of the COVID-19 pandemic coincided with the new budget negotiations for 2021–2027 and led to a series of significant innovations informed by the sovereign debt and rule of law crises. These innovations were such that the ensuing complex legal issues were hard to ignore, and legal scholars joined other political and social scientists in seeking to make sense of these innovations.

In this analysis, we make the case that these innovations,[2] and the accompanying wave of new scholarly attention, can be fruitfully understood by

* Text based on the state of the law as at 1 August 2023.

[1] A good example is the Bangladesh case from 1993 in which the 'Member States meeting in Council' chose to use the budget key to give humanitarian assistance to Bangladesh. This was challenged by the Parliament as being essentially a Community act. The then European Court of Justice (ECJ) found that it was not an EU agreement but simply an agreement between Member States, and therefore the money was outside the budget: Joined Cases C-181/91 and C-248/91, *European Parliament v Council and Commission (Emergency aid to Bangladesh)* (EU:C:1993:271).

[2] In this volume, we do not look at the role of the European Central Bank (ECB), which was also transformed in the euro-crisis and the pandemic.

Claire Kilpatrick and Joanne Scott, *New Frontiers of European Union Funding*. In: *New Frontiers of EU Funding*.
Edited by: Claire Kilpatrick and Joanne Scott, Oxford University Press.
DOI: 10.1093/oso/9780198940319.003.0001

considering frontiers. A focus on frontiers shines a light on the process by which the EU and its institutions crossed into previously uncharted territory. Frontier-crossing raises important questions about the legal and institutional adjustments that may be necessary to ensure that EU funding is given appropriate boundaries and is democratically accountable. It also encourages us to be attentive to disciplinary boundaries and boundary-crossings within and between disciplines in relation to the same object of inquiry, here EU funding. Hence, frontiers are a way of calibrating EU developments as well as the scholarly responses they provoke.

To consider frontiers, a baseline for evaluation is required. The core of that baseline is that the EU, in budget terms as in so many others, resembles neither a state nor an international organization. This translates into a distinctively interesting budget and gives rise to funding questions that the national–international spectrum helps us to make sense of, especially when change occurs. Scholars have considered it particularly important to assess whether a given funding innovation is a game-changer in terms of the EU's potential fiscal capacity,[3] and whether it may thereby serve to recalibrate the relationship between the EU and the Member States.

In our analysis, we focus upon three new frontiers in EU funding, each of which provides inputs and insights into this foundational issue concerning the relationship between the national and the international. The concept of the international includes not only the EU but also more amorphous forms of governance by Member States through *inter se* international agreements, which will be discussed later.

The first of the three frontiers to be examined here concerns the drivers and channels, the why and how, of innovations in EU funding. The EU has been increasingly driven 'off-budget' (that is to say, using funding streams that are not formally part of the EU budget) and outside of the EU framework in relation to EU-relevant funding activities. When evaluating these developments, it is important to consider why this has occurred. Answers sometimes relate to differentiation between EU Member States. For example, non-Eurozone members do not wish to contribute to resolving Euro-area problems.

[3] The EU's small spending capacity, relative to states and the size of the EU economy, and its lack of freedom to autonomously raise and spend revenue is why it is not seen as having a fiscal capacity. In the wake of Next Generation EU, many argue it should be built on to provide macroeconomic stabilization and European public goods, especially in the light of green and security concerns. This comes up against the significant obstacle that its legal basis and legal agreement are premised on its temporary nature. Moreover, proposals vary significantly in terms of ambition and detail: See e.g. N. G. Arnold et al., 'Reforming the EU Fiscal Framework: Strengthening the Fiscal Rules and Institutions', IMF Departmental Paper 2022/14 (September 2022); Georgiou, 'Federal Fiscal Capacity and the Challenge of the Green Transition in the EU', 45 *Journal of European Integration* (2023) 871.

Furthermore, budgetary rule-making based on unanimity has led to extreme budgetary restraint and insufficient space for innovation. Both Richard Crowe (Chapter 2 in this volume) and Johannes Lindner and Thu Nguyen (Chapter 3 in this volume) point to a significant and enduring budgetary constraint that has forced the EU to look at funding opportunities outside of its budget, namely the Member States' commitment to capping the budget at around 1 per cent of gross national income (GNI). An understanding of the reasons for EU innovation in funding also requires awareness of the way events have galvanized political attention and opened new opportunities. Sovereign debt, migration, and the COVID-19 pandemic were important spurs. Considering how funding innovations occurred, the sovereign debt crisis, both legally and politically speaking, started the EU on the road to thinking creatively about funding. Nonetheless, this generated significant legacy issues, making certain kinds of funding unacceptable to states because of their association with the sovereign debt crisis. This was seen most clearly in relation to the blanket rejection of the pandemic funding offered by the European Stability Mechanism. Scholarly attention has also turned to how domestic politics shapes features of new agreements on funding. This helps to explain the creation of the Next Generation EU (NGEU)[4] and also the puzzle of why states with rule of law problems agreed to the introduction of a rule of law conditionality mechanism in funding.[5] The implications of this new world of EU funding, which is characterized by considerably more variety and a greatly enhanced scale, have also been analysed as issues of fragmentation, complexity, opacity, and oversight came to the fore. Attention has also focused on how these frontier-crossing developments within or at the boundaries of the EU have, or could be, given a firm grounding within EU law and within its institutional and democratic structures. While these discussions have mainly been the domain of political scientists, they intersect with legal scholarship in important ways.

[4] Armingeon et al., 'Voices from the Past: Economic and Political Vulnerabilities in the Making of Next Generation EU', 20 *Comparative European Politics* (2022) 144–165.

[5] See e.g. Editorial Comments, 'Compromising (on) the General Conditionality Mechanism and the Rule of Law', 58 *Common Market Law Review* (*CMLR*) (2021) 267–284. This recounts the 2020 campaign, which it terms 'blackmail', by Hungary and Poland to water down or hold up such rule of law conditionality. This led other Member States to consider proceeding by international agreement and was ultimately resolved by European Council conclusions of December 2020 'softening' and delaying activation of the Conditionality Regulation, including by requiring Commission guidelines for its operation. The latter would not be finalized until after a Court of Justice of the European Union (CJEU) judgment on the legality of the Regulation itself should Poland and Hungary exercise their right to take an annulment action. The annulment action was brought before the CJEU and resulted in rulings upholding the legality of the Regulation: Case C-156/21, *Hungary v. Parliament and Council* (EU:C:2022:97) and C-157/21, *Poland v. Parliament and Council* (EU:C:2021:978). See Viorica Viţă's chapter (Chapter 4 in this volume) for a critical assessment of the Court's judgments drawing on a broader analysis of conditionality.

The second frontier has mainly centred around the issue of the rule of law, raising two distinct concerns. The first, analysed by legal scholars in the main, is whether the EU has overstepped a normative frontier, acting inappropriately or even illegally, or whether it should rather be viewed as having made astute and imaginative use of available legal pathways in creating new EU funding streams. An increasingly central issue in this strand of legal scholarship is how acting off-budget, or exiting the EU framework, serves to evade various legal, representative, funding, and judicial protection controls.[6] The second distinctive concern arising here involves the harnessing of EU funding to address rule of law violations in states failing to respect rule of law values. On this issue, a distinct grouping of scholar activists from law and political science has examined the adequacy of EU and Council of Europe responses, especially regarding Poland and Hungary. Conditionality, and the effective withholding of EU funding, as well as fines for failing to comply with CJEU judgments, are the main EU funding mechanisms to address rule of law backsliding in EU Member States. The contributions to this volume reinforce the importance of embedding these discussions within the broader context of EU funding, including within the framework of its governing principles. Such principles include, most significantly, the partnership principle in relation to funds under shared management and the spread and practices of conditionality as an important feature of EU–Member State interactions in the shared management of funding. Emilia Korkea-aho (Chapter 6 in this volume) makes the case that the partnership principle serves to enhance accountability in EU funding, while Viorica Viţă (Chapter 4 in this volume) explores the asymmetric relations that conditionality and differential Member State reliance on EU funding creates.

The third frontier considers whether, and how, new EU funding has entered and fundamentally reshaped the terrain of substantive EU law and policy and the manner of their governance. Here, more recent work, which is also developed extensively in this volume, considers how new EU resources reshape substantive areas of EU law and policy, especially climate and the environment and, to a lesser extent, social policy and migration or alter the EU's governance

[6] A focus on such issues inside sovereign debt sources has been succeeded by a focus on NGEU: see De Witte, 'The European Union's COVID-19 Recovery Plan: The Legal Engineering of an Economic Policy Shift' 58 *CMLR* (2021) 635 (creative legal engineering); Leino-Sandberg and Ruffert, 'Next Generation EU and Its Constitutional Ramifications: A Critical Assessment' 59 *CMLR* (2022) 433 (troubling disregard of key Treaty principles). The political compromise in December 2020 delaying the introduction of the Conditionality Regulation was also depicted either as sensible agreement or as an EU rule of law departure. For a broader analysis in several areas of EU law and policy, see C. Kilpatrick and J. Scott (eds), *Contemporary Challenges to EU Legality* (2021).

architecture or toolkit. Such work has focused on the modalities of expenditure and the distributive (justice) issues to which these give rise. Distributive concerns form the focus of Ioanna Hadjiyianni's substantial contribution by to this volume (Chapter 5).

In what follows, this chapter delves deeper into the baseline EU funding model and the three funding frontiers of new drivers and channels, new rule of law dimensions, and the reshaping of substantive EU law and governance. It should already be clear from this brief overview that new EU funding opens a substantial and far-ranging agenda for the study of EU law, politics, and policy. It is relevant for distinct, albeit occasionally overlapping, groups going much further than the EU studies on 'budget' and 'structural funds' carried out by specialists of yesteryear. This volume brings together some of the most interesting new angles on EU funding and provides broader frameworks within which to locate recent developments and to encourage further work, especially by legal scholars, in this under-studied and exciting area. Above all, it makes the case for legal scholars to pay increasing attention to the EU budget rather than focusing primarily on non-budget funding or picking up on one specific angle—such as rule of law conditionality—without embedding the analysis in the broader context of EU budget and funding law and practice.

2. The Baseline for Evaluating and Understanding New Frontiers: The Classic Model of EU Funding via the Budget

The EU's High-Level Group on Own Resources, chaired by Mario Monti, reporting in 2017, captured the distinctive features of the EU budget well.[7] It is primarily an investment budget with some redistribution between Member States and is too small for real anti-cyclical economic stabilization. The amount of the budget has remained strikingly stable for decades at around 1 per cent of EU GNI. The EU has arguably no competence to levy taxes and is funded through a system of own resources.[8] It is further constrained by the Treaty requirements for the budget to be balanced annually[9] within a Multiannual

[7] The interinstitutional Monti Group was established to assess the functioning of the Union's financing system and present recommendations for reform. The Group's final report, entitled 'Future Financing of the EU' (2017) is available online at https://op.europa.eu/en/publication-detail/-/publication/4d14393d-1db0-11e7-aeb3-01aa75ed71a1 (last visited 6 February 2024).

[8] See Arts 311 and 310(4) of the Treaty on the Functioning of the European Union (TFEU). Title II of Part 6 (Institutional and Financial Provisions) of the TFEU concerns what De Witte (n. 6) calls 'EU public finance law' and is contained in Arts 310–325.

[9] Arts 313–316 TFEU concern the annual budget.

Financial Framework (MFF)[10] and underpinned by principles such as 'sound financial management'.[11] Further safeguards are provided by placing stepped ceilings above budgetary commitments[12] and by also requiring maximum limits for specified major policy areas (headings) to prevent moving money around. Hence, actual spending as well as spending commitments are lower than the ceilings in the MFF, while the own resources ceiling is always significantly higher than the MFF ceiling; this ensures that the EU can always cover all its obligations and liabilities, even in case of negative economic developments.[13] This means that the EU cannot, in the way states can, take the pandemic advice offered by Carmen Reinhart, the then Chief Economist of the World Bank: 'While the disease is raging, what else are you going to do? First you worry about fighting the war, then you figure out how to pay for it.'[14] Yet, having a system of own resources also distinguishes the EU from international organizations. Rather than the vagaries of contributions determined annually by states upon which international organizations typically depend, the EU has a legal claim to its 'money' once the Own Resources Decision becomes law. Late payers face steep interest payments.[15] The legal certainty, ceilings, and principle of sound financial management underpinning the EU budget provide autonomy in relation to the supranational budget and ensure that the EU continues to enjoy the top credit rating (AAA) from the main rating agencies.

The bulk of the budget (three-quarters) is spent via shared management of the Commission and Member States, encompassing the Common Agricultural

[10] See Art. 312 TFEU. Art. 312(2) TFEU establishes a hierarchy between the MFF and the annual budget, with the latter subject to the former.

[11] Art. 310 TFEU also requiring budgetary discipline, legally binding act authorizing expenditure, and balanced budgeting.

[12] Hence, e.g. the budget for the 2014–2020 period could not exceed the own resources ceiling (set at 1.2 per cent GNI), the overall payment ceiling for the period (just over EUR 1 trillion), and the annual maximum limit (e.g. EUR 145 billion in 2016).

[13] See Art. 310(4) TFEU providing inter alia that, 'the Union shall not adopt any act which is likely to have appreciable implications for the budget without providing an assurance that the expenditure arising from such an act is capable of being financed within the limit of the Union's own resources'.

[14] C. Reinhart, 'Borrow to Fight Economic Impact of Pandemic, says World Bank's Chief Economist', *Financial Times* (8 October 2020), https://www.ft.com/content/0582e495-765a-46a1-98f9-ac48e80a139c (last visited 22 November 2023). This was particularly resonant given that her work with Kenneth Rogoff is associated with the position that public debt must be strictly policed to avoid negative impacts on growth: Reinhart and Rogoff, 'Growth in a Time of Debt', 100(2) *American Economic Review* (2010) 573–578.

[15] Originally, the European Economic Community (EEC) was more international organization (IO)-like, reliant on a system of national contributions, with the shift to a system of own resources in 1970. However, the traditional own resources (customs duties, sugar levies, a part of value-added tax (VAT)) have, over time, been outstripped by greater EU spending, leading to the introduction in 1988 of a residual GNI resource to make up shortfalls. The 'residual' GNI now makes up 70 per cent of the EU budget, bringing the EU closer again to an IO-style funding system. Brexit removed the notorious rebate and accompanying 'rebates on the rebate', which had been part of budgetary politics and calculations from 1985.

Policy and the structural funds or European Structural and Investment Funds (ESI). Just under one-fifth of the EU budget is directly managed by the EU and close to one-tenth is managed by non-EU actors including international organizations and non-EU states. The ESI funds spent via shared management have a further layer of regulation laying down common provisions for that spending (the Common Provisions Regulation) as well as specific rules for each fund. The Financial Regulation is a further central legal source which, while of great importance in the law[16] and practice of EU spending, has been subject to almost no analysis. Yet, Richard Crowe shows (in Chapter 2 of this volume) how unremarked provisions, in the Financial Regulation and elsewhere, greatly facilitate funding flexibility when it is required. A further crucial source for understanding the budget is the interinstitutional agreement accompanying each MFF.[17]

The EU budget is, by design, conditional in the sense that money is only allocated for legally predefined objectives. As Heinemann states, 'By design, all major EU spending programmes are conditional in the sense that they have specified objectives, a well-defined programming procedure and a comprehensive control system.'[18] However, 'conditionality', in the sense of other conditions separate from what the funds are to be spent on, is a twenty-first-century feature of EU spending that has grown in importance over time. Hence, the budget is developed through a bewildering array of legal sources, both in its genesis and in its implementation. Yet, its implementation is a classic case of managerial and bureaucratic interactions blurring the budget law-on-the-books and spending in practice. Regarding shared management, this creates a long-term relationship between the ultimate repeat players, the EU Commission and each Member State, negotiated and played out within each spending period's priorities and legal framework. While the budget law-on-the-books is far from irrelevant, it is best viewed as a guide to how that repeat relationship will be governed rather than as a set of clear-cut legal obligations to be routinely enforced. While

[16] The TFEU Title on public finances makes clear the centrality of the Financial Regulation, which has its legal basis in Art. 322 TFEU. The Title is replete with links making other public finance matters subject to the provisions of the Financial Regulation. Hence, it underpins authorization of expenditure (Art. 310(2)), implementation of expenditure (Art. 310(3)), the budget headings (Art. 316), budget implementation (Art. 317), and contingency budgetary arrangements in the absence of an agreement on the annual budget (Art. 315).

[17] The current agreement encompasses the special COVID-19 funding deal: Interinstitutional Agreement of 16 December 2020 between the European Parliament, the Council of the European Union and the European Commission on budgetary discipline, on cooperation in budgetary matters and on sound financial management, as well as on new own resources, including a roadmap towards the introduction of new own resources, OJ 2020 L 433 I/28.

[18] Heinemann, 'Going for the Wallet? Rule-of-Law Conditionality in the Next EU Multiannual Financial Framework', 53 *Intereconomics* (2018) 297.

the Commission could enforce obligations, it rarely does so as this could disrupt long-term repeat-player relations between the Commission and the Member States. This central feature is brought out in the analyses of Emilia Korkea-aho (Chapter 6) and Viorica Viţă (Chapter 4) in this volume.

The budget is also an important site for considering EU democratic representation via direct representation and Member State control. The ordinary legislative procedure never applies to the central foundations of the EU budget, it being governed instead by distinctive special legislative procedures. Member States maintain careful control of the Own Resources Decision, acting unanimously in Council to adopt the decision and requiring Member State approval in accordance with each state's constitutional requirements before the decision enters into force. Unanimity is also required for the MFF. The European Parliament has distinct roles at different stages; it is merely consulted on the Own Resources Decision but must give its consent to the MFF. It co-decides the annual EU budget. Hence, the EU budget is carefully designed and circumscribed by EU law. In fact, it is more dramatically underpinned by law than many national budgets. Moreover, each piece of spending requires a dual authorization, via the budget and via legislation. For instance, Articles 162–164 TFEU establish the European Social Fund to render the employment of workers easier, increase mobility, and facilitate adaptation to changes in work. The detailed legislative rules are adopted via the ordinary legislative procedure, which includes the financial envelope required, and this in turn provides the reference for budgetary authorizations through commitment and spending appropriations within the budgetary procedure.

To sum up, in the classical model, the EU, as compared to states, has a small budget to provide money for specific purposes. This is embedded in a dense legal framework. Although there have always been significant exceptions, EU funding mainly takes place through the budget, and this remains a clear aspiration for the EU.[19] Compared to international organizations, the EU's budget is much more legally secure. However, borrowing and lending to leverage the EU's good credit rating, which is enhanced by this legal security, has not historically been a central feature of the budget, especially for EU internal spending.[20]

[19] See Art. 310 TFEU, providing that all items of revenue and expenditure should be shown in the budget, and Art. 311 TFEU: 'without prejudice to other revenue, the budget shall be financed wholly from own resources'.

[20] There was, however, some provision for borrowing and lending for balance of payments assistance for EU states in the Treaties from the outset: in 2002, this was restricted to non-euro area states and scaled back (shortly before the financial crisis, when it was reactivated) to EUR 12 billion: Art. 143 TFEU and Council Regulation (EC) 332/2002 of 18 February 2002 establishing a facility providing medium-term financial assistance for Member States' balances of payments, OJ L 53 (23 February 2002) 1–3, Art. 1 of which provides that 'the Commission shall be empowered on behalf of the European Community

The EU budget is underpinned by detailed legal rules. While it has carefully differentiated roles for the Council and the European Parliament, with annual spending decided between them equally, states take the lead role in relation to own resources. Taking this as our baseline, we consider how, and how much, this classical model of EU funding has changed by charting and evaluating its developments against the new frontiers we have identified.

3. The First Funding Frontier: Drivers and Channels

The statement 'events, my dear boy, events' has been attributed to Harold Macmillan, UK prime minister 1957–1963, as his response to the most troubling challenges of his time as prime minister. Events can be politically galvanizing, and this has certainly been true for the EU in the twenty-first century. Unexpected political, economic, and societal events have been an important driver for pushing at the frontiers of EU funding. Linked to these events has been a broader realization that the world has changed in ways that demand more and different actions from the EU. Johannes Lindner and Thu Nguyen develop a useful model for calibrating how this does, and should, reshape the budget Chapter 3 of this book.

A. Significant Adjustments to EU Funding Pre-COVID

The pre-COVID decade added several new layers and extensions to the classical model of EU spending. The sovereign debt crisis and the migration 'crisis' were two important drivers. The sovereign debt crisis first led to an expansion by using the flexibility available in the existing budgetary system to conjure up some resources for financial assistance at short notice. Article 122(2) TFEU[21]

to contract borrowings on the capital markets or with financial institutions'. The legal basis for the borrowing is the flexibility clause (now Art. 352 TFEU). Borrowing and lending is also long established to provide EU financial support (macro-financial assistance or MFA) to third countries: for further details, see European Commission, *Macro-Financial Assistance*, https://economy-finance.ec.europa.eu/eu-financial-assistance/macro-financial-assistance-mfa_en (last visited 6 February 2024).

[21] See Art. 122(2) TFEU:

> Where a Member State is in difficulties or is seriously threatened with severe difficulties caused by natural disasters or exceptional occurrences beyond its control, the Council, on a proposal from the Commission, may grant, under certain conditions, Union financial assistance to the Member State concerned. The President of the Council shall inform the European Parliament of the decision taken.

is the legal basis for Council Regulation 407/2010 of 11 May 2010 establishing a European Financial Stability Mechanism (EFSM), which was used to authorize sovereign debt funding to eurozone states. The money was 'found' by the Commission using the margin available between the MFF and own resources ceilings for borrowing and lending. This allowed the Commission to borrow EUR 60 billion for the EFSM[22] and a smaller amount for balance of payments assistance.[23] The own resources margin provided a guarantee that the Union was able to repay the amounts concerned as it could require states to provide the money to the Union budget even in the event of a sovereign debt state defaulting on the loan. This drew attention to two interesting possibilities: first, the way the difference between the own resources and MFF ceilings could be productively exploited rather than strictly respected as a safety buffer, and second, the use of the EU budget as a basis for borrowing and lending (rather than simply disbursement). However, this EU mechanism was suitable only for emergencies on a much smaller financial scale than the eurozone crisis. The loan amount available for the EFSM was limited by the EU budget to EUR 60 billion, while shortly before the crisis, balance of payments assistance had been scaled back to EUR 12 billion (with the maximum total amount loaned being set by the limit between the MFF ceiling and the own resources ceiling). Indeed, the difficulties of increasing the EU's budget pushed all remaining foundational financial assistance instruments outside the EU Treaty framework. This led to the second important development driven by the sovereign debt crisis: the creation of massive additional funding for eurozone states so that the EU institutions disbursed approximately EUR 500 billion in sovereign debt programmes in addition to the budget. Although disbursed and managed by EU institutions, the big money to provide sovereign debt loans came from exiting the EU Treaties to create funding mechanisms via various kinds of international agreements between the euro area states. Various temporary arrangements from 2010[24] were replaced by the European Stability Mechanism (ESM) in 2012, with capital of over EUR 700 billion. The last of the ten sovereign debt programmes ended with the exit of Greece from its third programme in August 2018. The management of the migration 'crisis' from 2015 also led to some funding innovations. Hence, the infamous EU–Turkey agreement of 2016 was accompanied by a Facility for Refugees in Turkey comprised of EUR

[22] See Art. 2(2) EFSM, limiting the financial assistance to 'the margin available under the own resources ceiling for payment appropriations'.

[23] See n. 20. Loan assistance was provided to Hungary, Latvia, and Romania in the first wave of what became the decade of euro-crisis and financial loan programmes.

[24] The so-called Greek Loan Facility and the European Financial Stability Facility (EFSF).

1 billion from the EU budget and EUR 2 billion from the EU states[25] as external assigned revenue (i.e. outside the budget procedure).[26]

B. The New Frontiers of EU Funding from 2020

COVID-19 took centre stage from March 2020 and played a key role in the law and politics of the mega-financial package agreed in July and December of that year. This introduced a new EUR 750 billion fund of grants and loans in NGEU, in addition to the EU budget, both of which were linked to a new Own Resources Decision and a general conditionality mechanism driven by rule of law concerns.[27] Intriguingly though, often COVID-19 provided opportunities not to deal with it directly but rather to deal with urgent existing challenges that were already on the EU agenda: political and economic legacies of the sovereign debt crisis, the worsening rule of law crisis in several Member States, the need for new own resources, and the climate and digital transitions. In other words, the drivers and the channels of new frontiers are distinct in interesting ways.

The politics of agreeing new funding were fraught with difficulty. The COVID-19 mega-financial agreement was thrashed out at the European Council's extraordinary meeting of 17–21 July 2020—one of the longest in the history of the institution. The 11–12 December 2020 meeting required agreement mainly on the very delicate question of rule of law conditionality, leading to an unorthodox solution effectively suspending its application until the Court of Justice had had an opportunity to rule on its legality.[28]

Table 1.1 summarizes what was agreed in 2020 in the COVID-19 turbo-charged negotiations. It spans a range of EU funding options: the 2014–2020

[25] The legal basis was Art. 210(2) TFEU on coordination for development cooperation and Art. 214(6) TFEU on coordination for humanitarian aid. See Commission Decision C(2015) 9500 of 24 November 2015 on the coordination of the actions of the Union and of the Member States through a coordination mechanism—the Refugee Facility for Turkey, OJ 2015 C 407/8, as amended by Commission Decision of 10 February 2016 on the Facility for Refugees in Turkey amending Commission Decision C(2015) 9500 of 24 November 2015, OJ 2016 C 60/3.

[26] External assigned revenues are not processed through the budgetary procedure laid down in Art. 314 TFEU but are contributed directly to the Union budget by the Member State or other contributor for a specified purpose.

[27] Expressed in 2018 prices. Council Regulation (EU, Euratom) 2020/2093 of 17 December 2020 laying down the multiannual financial framework for the years 2021 to 2027, OJ 2020 L 433 I/11–22; Council Decision (EU, Euratom) 2020/2053 of 14 December 2020 on the system of own resources of the European Union and repealing Decision 2014/335/EU, Euratom, OJ 2020 L 424; Regulation (EU, Euratom) 2020/2092 of the European Parliament and of the Council of 16 December 2020 on a general regime of conditionality for the protection of the Union budget, OJ 2020 L 433 I/1–10.

[28] See n. 5.

Table 1.1 Key features of new frontiers of EU funding agreed in 2020

EU budget 2014–2020	ESM	NGEU	EU budget 2021–2027
		General Conditionality Regulation linked to Rule of Law 2020/2092	
March 2020 Coronavirus Response Investment Initiatives* EUR 37 billion Arts 177–178 TFEU *May 2020* SURE Regulation EUR 100 billion Art. 122 TFEU	*April 2020* ESM Pandemic Fund *Unused*	EUR 750 billion off-budget (in 2018 prices). Art. 122 TFEU.** Revenue raised by temporarily raising the EU own resources ceiling and the EU using its strong credit rating to borrow against this.*** Off-budget (external assigned revenue: assigned by the EU Recovery Instrument to the Union programmes adopted). Repayment of the principal (EUR 750 billion in 2018 prices) via *new own resources* (for grants) and repayment by states (of loans). Repayment period mainly 2028–2058. Consequent agreement**** on creation of new own resources e.g. Carbon Border Adjustment Mechanism, Emission Trading System, non-recycled plastics, digital tax.	EUR 1,074 trillion (in 2018 prices) Greater authorized 'agility' between budget headings than previously. Expanded and refined budget conditionality.

Notes: * Regulation 2020/460 of the European Parliament and the Council of 30 March 2020, OJ 2020 L 99/5 and Regulation 2020/558 of the European Parliament and the Council of 23 April 2020, OJ 2020 L 130/1.

** Council Regulation (EU) 2020/2094 of 14 December 2020 establishing a European Union Recovery Instrument to support the recovery in the aftermath of the COVID-19 crisis, OJ L 433I (22 December 2020) 23.

*** Council Decision 2020/2053 of 14 December 2020 on the system of own resources of the European Union and repealing Decision 2014/335/EU, Euratom, OJ 2020 L 424/1.

**** Note that pre-COVID, the Commission had already proposed new own resources. Hence, this is further evidence that COVID-19 provided a new driver and adapted channel for existing proposals: European Commission, Proposal for a Council Decision on the system of Own Resources of the European Union (2 May 2018), COM(2018) 325.

budget, the intergovernmental ESM, the new budget for 2021–2027, the special NGEU pot linked to an agreement on new own resources and a new rule of law conditionality mechanism. Looking at the legal basis and construction of these new pots of funding shows us how the sovereign debt crisis laid down markers and showed new paths that were dramatically and rapidly expanded from 2020 onwards. Most importantly, the creation of the EFSM in 2010 trialled the technique of using the margin between budget ceilings to borrow and the use of Article 122(2) TFEU as a legal basis for providing EU funding. This was built on in the initial response to the COVID-19 pandemic in creating the Support to mitigate Unemployment Risks in an Emergency (SURE) programme.[29] Using Article 122 TFEU as its legal basis,[30] it provided EUR 100 billion,[31] mainly to fund employment support schemes in what Eurogroup President Mario Centeno called 'European solidarity, in the form of cheap loans'.[32] In turn, this was a stepping stone to NGEU, which combines Article 122 TFEU as its legal basis with the technique of borrowing and lending. Apart from the sheer scale of the borrowing, itself of enormous significance, the key novel elements added by NGEU are an extensive use of grants rather than loans; the raising of the own resources ceiling to allow for the scale of the borrowing;[33] the consequent agreement to create new own resources to repay the EU loans over a multi-generational time horizon; and the fact that the funds generated, being external assigned revenue, are therefore outside the normal budgetary approval procedures.

What is the money spent on? Table 1.2 shows that the two big-ticket items are (and remain) regional and cohesion policy (called Cohesion, Resilience and Values) which is the lion's share of both the budget and NGEU in the current

[29] Council Regulation 2020/672 of 19 May 2020 on the establishment of a European instrument for temporary support to mitigate unemployment risks in an emergency (SURE) following the COVID-19 outbreak, OJ 2020 L 159/1.

[30] Unlike the EFSM, SURE uses both limbs of Art. 122 TFEU. Although it does not explicitly state this, as De Witte (n. 6) notes, Art. 122(1) is used to provide a legal basis for the collective guarantee that the EU is able to repay the money and Art. 122(2) as a legal basis to provide the financial assistance. Art. 122(1) provides that the EU 'may decide, in a spirit of solidarity between Member States, upon the measures appropriate to the economic situation, in particular if severe difficulties arise in the supply of certain products, notably in the area of energy'.

[31] Given the limited amount available between the MFF and the Own Resources Decision (ORD) ceilings, to guarantee the entire EUR 100 billion fund, further 'irrevocable, unconditional and on-demand guarantees' by Member States were added to SURE to make up the difference (Art. 11). Although voluntary, the instrument could only enter into effect once sufficient guarantees were received (Art. 12).

[32] See European Council, 'Remarks by Mário Centeno Following the Europgroup Videoconference of 15 May 2020', https://www.consilium.europa.eu/en/press/press-releases/2020/05/15/remarks-by-mario-centeno-following-the-eurogroup-videoconference-of-15-may-2020 (last visited 6 February 2024).

[33] The normal ORD ceiling is set at 1.4 per cent GNI (Art. 3(1) ORD), while the temporary lift for NGEU sets it at 2 per cent GNI (Art. 6 ORD): Decision 2020/2053 (n. 27).

Table 1.2 Allocations per heading (all amounts in EUR billion)

	MFF	NGEU	TOTAL
1. Single Market, Innovation and Digital	149.5	11.5	161.0
2. Cohesion, Resilience and Values	426.7	776.5	1,203.2
3. Natural Resources and Environment	401.0	18.9	419.9
4. Migration and Border Management	25.7	–	25.7
5. Security and Defence	14.9	–	14.9
6. Neighbourhood and the World	110.6	–	110.6
7. European Public Administration	82.5	–	82.5
TOTAL	**1,210.9**	**806.9**	**2,017.8**
TOTAL expressed in 2018 prices	**1,074.3**	**750.0**	**1,824.3**

funding period (2021–2027) and natural resources and environment (mainly the Common Agricultural Policy (CAP)). The money is not equally distributed across or within Member States: indeed, one of the *raisons d'être* of cohesion policy is to give more to less-developed regions.[34] However, other spending headings are far from negligible, and this is certainly an area where the detail within each heading is also extremely important. Although this volume does not investigate this in detail, it does indicate, through its focus on new environmental own resources in Ioanna Hadjiyianni's analysis (Chapter 5 of this volume) and this simple presentation of spending headings in the budget and NGEU, that the time is ripe for further work to test afresh Giandomenico Majone's early 1990s withering assessment that EU spending was too little to be consequential and that where it was consequential (the CAP and regional policy), it was perverse in its distributive goals by further enriching wealthy farm owners and affluent people in poor EU regions.[35]

The chapters in this volume all serve, in different ways, to increase our understanding of the nature of the transition from the classical model of EU funding to the new frontiers of EU funding and shed light on the challenges that frontier-crossing in this context raises.

[34] See, for the current 2021–2027 MFF budget distribution: Spending and revenue, http://europa.eu (last visited 4 July 2024). See also the distribution of Recovery and Resilience Facility (RRF) per member state here: Recovery and Resilience Scoreboard, http:europa.eu (last visited 4 July 2024). The RRF allocations as share of gross domestic product (GDP) are Greece (16 per cent), Romania (12 per cent), Croatia (11 per cent), Italy (10 per cent), Bulgaria (9 per cent), Portugal (8 per cent); as opposed to Luxembourg (0.1 per cent), Ireland (0.2 per cent), Denmark (0.4 per cent), the Netherlands (0.5 per cent), Sweden (0.6 per cent), or Germany (0.7 per cent). Of special interest in relation to the rule of law are Poland (6.16 per cent) and Hungary (3.77 per cent).

[35] Majone, 'The European Community between Social Regulation and Social Policy', 31 *Journal of Common Market Studies* (1993) 153.

Richard Crowe is already well known as one of the notable pioneers in developing compelling legal analyses of EU spending, spanning the EU budget and extra-budgetary expenditure. In his contribution to this volume (Chapter 2, 'The European Union's Public Finances in Times of Crisis: Fragmentation, Innovation, and Consolidation'), an indispensable tour de force, he examines what he terms the new flux for EU spending post-Lisbon. Combining nimble and insightful legal, EU institutional, and policy analysis, his examination provides both a precious guide to the legal construction of EU spending and its recent evolution and makes the case for allowing the legislative and budgetary lungs of the EU to breathe more easily to allow the EU to meet the demands made on it today.

He first carefully demonstrates the deep and complex intertwining of EU legal and budgetary sources, starting with the status of the budget itself which, although adopted through a special legislative procedure, is not a legislative act. The legal underpinnings of EU budgetary law—relating, for instance, to the MFF and the ORD—are considered. The need for spending to have a dual authorization—in legislation and the budget—as now codified in Article 310(3) TFEU, is emphasized, as well as the constitutional importance of master regulations such as the Financial Regulation and the Common Provisions Regulation for the Structural Funds.

He then examines how that framework fits the post-Lisbon Treaty world, noting that the seven-year MFF framework, while well suited to a Europe of Rules and orderly planned spending, struggles to deal with a Europe of Events. He demonstrates how almost unnoticed technical provisions and previous spending paths for modest amounts were used to provide most notably NGEU, by borrowing and lending on a vast scale to provide a new source of external assigned revenue. These new resources, although administered through the budget, are not counted within MFF ceilings and not authorized through the budgetary procedure. Their flexibility, speed, and (in the case of NGEU) scale, need to be considered against their diminishment of the EU budgetary procedure. Although the financial responses to the COVID-19 pandemic, and subsequently Russia's war on Ukraine, were bold and innovative, nonetheless routines and options first explored during the sovereign debt and migration crises allowed each successive 'event' response to be more planned and coordinated. Indeed, using the examples of defence and health, he makes the powerful point that spending lines today provide a more reliable guide to developing centres of EU activity than legislative competences. Looking ahead, Crowe makes the case for EU borrowing becoming a more central feature of EU funding, examining the options and constraints on so doing while making the case for external assigned revenue being limited to maintain the integrity of the EU budget and the democratic processes underpinning it. He considers that the changes needed to better match the EU budget to new EU roles, while constitutionally significant and in the long run requiring Treaty revision to consolidate EU borrowing, can in many ways already be achieved via legislative processes and adjustment to the new funding needs of the EU.

In a shorter and complementary contribution to the volume, Johannes Lindner and Thu Nguyen consider 'The Politics of EU Funding: Time for Treaty Change?' (Chapter 3). Their chapter has an interesting focus on budgetary law while setting that within illuminating political science analyses on the relationship between the budget and particular phases of EU integration. The fulcrum of the analysis helps sharpen the contrast with earlier but still very recent history. They note that in 2005, an important assessment by Henrik Enderlein and colleagues concluded that Treaty change in relation to the budget was undesirable, and their analysis goes on to consider why the conditions under which that position was adopted have changed. Essentially, the changing conditions they present in their analysis are that political integration has dramatically increased, and NGEU, as a special example of that, shows that various funding taboos, especially large-scale EU debt issuance, are being breached. However, they consider that budget law, especially since the Lisbon Treaty came into force, and in ways perhaps underestimated by Enderlein and colleagues in 2005, has not matched these developments and requires adjustment to do so, with a special focus on Treaty change in line with their title. While noting when Treaty change would be necessary, they also discuss the many ways in which positive changes could be introduced without Treaty change.

Taken together, such analyses mean that the volume provides vital scrutiny and matters to be considered in further debates on what change is needed—in particular, whether Treaty change is actually required or whether simple tweaks to existing secondary sources and institutional arrangements will suffice—as well as the legal and political workarounds that political resistance to increasing the budget have compelled and what the prospects of that changing are. All agree that unless and until the political will is found to increase the budget beyond the 1 per cent GNI it has been stuck at since the budgetary reforms of 1988, building 'outside' the house of the EU budget will continue to occur, with such extensions continuing to raise legal and political objections.

4. The Second Frontier: The Two Dimensions of the Rule of Law in European Union Funding

The first dimension of the rule of law assesses compliance by the EU itself. To put this another way, it asks: are the new frontiers ingenious or unacceptable in legal terms? The second focuses on the EU as a protector and defender of the rule of law in the Member States. It evaluates how the EU uses the various legal and funding levers at its disposal to sanction states that fall short of respecting the rule of law.

This volume expressly engages with the rule of law frontier and does so in ways that place these two dimensions in a broader context. With regard to the first, in his chapter, Richard Crowe uses comparative examples from national constitutional budgetary laws to add nuance to existing understandings. For example, he views the requirement of a balanced budget in an accounting sense rather than as prohibiting borrowing. Viorica Viţă's chapter (Chapter 4, '(Un) Constitutional Conditions: A European Perspective') develops and applies an important constitutional framework for analysing EU spending conditionality. Looking at issues of constitutional ends and constitutional limits, and drawing on suitable US constitutional comparisons, she considers whether spending conditionality can unacceptably enlarge EU competence by bypassing legislative routes or enforcing soft law, whether it respects the principle of equality between Member States, and whether conditionalities affecting individual rights can be challenged. The application of well-known EU constitutional standards and questions to the largely uncharted and extensive terrain of EU spending conditionality is fruitful for both EU constitutional law and the law of conditionality. The constitutional framework of ends and limits is applied to offer a nuanced assessment of rule of law conditionality, asking whether it is a suitable cure for rule of law 'disease' or whether it risks exacerbating the decline in EU values in backsliding Member States. Ioanna Hadjiyianni's contribution (Chapter 5) further enriches the discussion of conditionality by considering environmental conditionalities in EU funding.

5. The Third Frontier: How EU Funding Reshapes EU Tasks and Governance

There are several highly productive locations and sources for considering how EU funding reshapes EU tasks and governance. Building on Table 1.2, which outlined what spending is allocated to, we take the example of NGEU to briefly indicate how such a reshaping of EU tasks and governance can occur. NGEU comprises seven distinct sub-programmes: the Recovery and Resilience Fund (RRF), ReactEU, the Just Transition Fund, the European Agricultural Fund for Rural Development, rescEU, Horizon Europe, and InvestEU.[36] The RRF is by far the largest, amounting to EUR 672.5 billion (EUR 360 billion in loans and EUR 312.4 billion in grants) out of the overall package of EUR 750 billion (although not all loans may be requested, making the overall sum smaller). Each of these programmes can then be looked at more closely. The RRF has six pillars:[37] (a) green transition; (b) digital transformation; (c) smart, sustainable, and inclusive growth, including economic cohesion, jobs, productivity, competitiveness, research, development, and innovation, and a well-functioning internal market with strong small and medium-sized enterprises (SMEs); (d) social and territorial cohesion; (e) health, and economic, social and institutional resilience, with the aim of, inter alia, increasing crisis preparedness and crisis response capacity; and (f) policies for the next generation, children and young people, such as education and skills. However, these are not equally weighted as states are required to allocate a minimum of 37 per cent to green transition and 20 per cent to the digital transition.

RRF governance can also be compared with MFF governance, in particular policy domains. For instance, Annex VI of the RRF contains climate-tracking and environmental methodologies. All fields of intervention by the facility are individually identified, with each given separate climate and environmental coefficients. For instance, one such field is renewable solar energy, which is given a climate coefficient of 100 per cent and an environmental coefficient of 40 per cent. Yet, in contrast to the budget, the RRF does not carve out special funding allocations or spending methodologies for biodiversity.[38] In turn, these coefficients link to non-EU markers and indicators such as the Organisation for Economic Co-operation and Development Rio Markers. These few examples serve to illustrate that research tracing EU governance via EU funding is a rich terrain.

[36] De Witte (n. 6) explores the key role of Art. 175(3) TFEU, allowing EU actions relating to economic, territorial, and social cohesion 'outside the Funds' as a significant legal basis for several of these NGEU funds (the RRF itself, the Just Transition Fund) and significant predecessors, including the 2006 European Globalisation Adjustment Fund and the 2014 European Fund to Aid the Most Deprived (although the latter has now been included in the European Social Fund in the 2021–2027 MFF).

[37] See Art. 3 of Regulation (EU) 2021/241.

[38] While there is no spending target for biodiversity for NGEU, 7.5 per cent of MFF funds must be allocated to enhancing biodiversity in 2024, and 10 per cent in 2026 and 2027. On climate and biodiversity in EU funding, see the report prepared for the Budgetary Committee of the European Parliament: F. Levarlet et al., *Climate Mainstreaming in the EU Budget: A 2022 Update* (April 2022, 78 pages).

Ioanna Hadjiyianni's ground-breaking chapter (Chapter 5, 'The Emergence of New Own Resources to Strengthen the European Union Budget and Achieve Green Policy Objectives: A Win–Win or a Difficult Fit?') explores 'green' sources of EU funding, which have emerged to facilitate realization of the Green Deal's objectives and the repayment of borrowing to fund the COVID-related NGEU. It explores the creation of new EU own resources for the first time since 1988 and the shift this implies towards greater EU budgetary autonomy. These new own resources include the revenue generated from the EU's non-recyclable plastic charge, its greenhouse gas emissions trading scheme, and its carbon border adjustment mechanism (CBAM). This wide-ranging chapter also explores environmental conditionality in relation to EU spending streams and the establishment of free-standing funds such as the Social Climate Fund.

Drawing on existing academic literature and agreement at the EU level, the chapter uses the criteria of 'genuine', 'suitable', and 'fair' to assess the legitimacy of the EU's new green own resources. Taking these interrelated and clearly defined criteria, Hadjiyianni argues that legitimacy depends on the design of the instruments establishing the new resources, the broader regulatory framework, and mechanisms to integrate EU funding with EU policy priorities. She rigorously analyses the plastic tax, Emissions Trading System (ETS), and CBAM from the perspective of each of these three criteria and sums up her 'scoring' in concluding tables. As a result, her findings are extremely accessible. Among Hadjiyianni's many interesting observations is her insight that two of these instruments present distinct fairness challenges internationally, given that a large amount of the revenue will be raised by 'taxing foreigners'. In relation to ETS, she concludes that international distributive justice concerns are not sufficiently addressed and that such concerns are acute in relation to CBAM.

Emilia Korkea-aho's chapter (Chapter 6, 'Accountable National Governance of European Union Funds') explores the concept of accountability in the management of EU funds. Arguing against the mainstream view that the sharing of responsibility for the management of these funds between the Commission and the Member States creates an accountability gap, she finds that in a context of shared governance, accountability is not hollowed out but rather changed. Looking to the practices, relationships, and structures that underpin the European Regional Development Fund (ERDF) as an example, she identifies a form of 'bottom-up accountability' that is (imperfectly) deliberative, inclusive, and adaptive. Her conclusions are based both on a careful analysis of relevant texts and interviews with relevant officials and other stakeholders.

Korkea-aho carefully describes the different stages of the ERDF decision-making process, paying particular attention to the role of law, institutional forms, and the balance of power between the Commission, Member States and sub-state authorities. She describes a dense and evolving governance landscape, which is shaped by 'routinized processes' that more often than not have their origins in law. The story she tells belies simple characterization. On the one hand, the 'partnership principle' looms large in the governance of the ERDF. On the other hand, there is evidence of a trend (not always welcome) towards a centralization of management in the hands of the Commission. In pursuit of European-level objectives, the Commission's role is becoming increasingly 'muscular'. Nonetheless, Korkea-aho finds that there is still space for the emergence of accountability-enhancing administrative practices within the Member States.

Korkea-aho's chapter concludes by exploring 'the fight against fraud' in the context of EU cohesion funding. With the establishment of the European Public Prosecutor's Office (EPPO), criminal law instruments have come to the fore. While not denying the importance of the anti-corruption agenda, Korkea-aho explains why a 'penal rationality' is incompatible with the processes inculcating bottom-up accountability she has described. She carefully unpacks the tensions between the emerging penal rationality and key features of the funding governance landscape, arguing bluntly that '[t]he penal rationality risks overriding and weakening the accountability tools that are built into the national governance model'. She sets up an interesting research agenda around the role of law firms in mobilizing for the introduction of criminal law instruments in this area. The story that she tells in this chapter is thus one of hope and caution. There is something worth fighting to preserve in the shared management of cohesion funds.

6. Conclusion

This introduction looked to the concept of frontiers to capture the many salient innovations that have occurred in EU funding over recent years. This included the foundational issue pertaining to the relationship between the national and the international as the EU has greatly increased its spending capacity and altered the modalities of EU funding. The EU has crossed frontiers, each of which speaks to this foundational issue in important ways. Against the backdrop of varied drivers, the EU has exploited new channels for EU funding by, on the one hand going 'off-budget' and, on the other, by exiting the EU legal framework in order to reach accord through *inter se* agreements between Member States. The funding domain has witnessed the EU's increasing efforts to tackle rule of law violations in certain Member States and has also highlighted the risk that funding innovations may cross the line between the lawful and unlawful and facilitate evasion of constraints on legal, democratic, and judicial protection. We see that there is an overlap between these different frontiers as the EU's tendency to go 'off-budget' and to exit the EU legal order raises complex issues of EU legality. It is also clear from our analysis of frontier-crossing that EU funding is becoming an ever more important part of substantive EU law and governance and that key policy domains such as the environment, climate, social policy, and migration can no longer be researched without having the funding dimension clearly in mind.

Using the baseline of the classical model of EU funding as captured by the EU's High-Level Group on Own Resources, which reported in 2017, we suggest that, for a range of reasons fleshed out in this volume, the twenty-first century has moved EU funding from a small, planned, and legally constrained budget to a larger and more flexible EU funding model in which the budget plays various roles. Understanding this process of change is not straightforward as a high level of technical understanding is required. Moreover, while these transformations were driven by events such as the sovereign debt crisis, the migration 'crisis', and above all, the COVID-19 pandemic, they were also seized upon to tackle existing challenges already on the EU agenda, including the climate emergency. It seems likely that EU funding has escaped its small and constrained box and will not readily be put back into it. It has also become much more politically and legally salient in several ways. The amount of EU funding required is a live question. While increasing the budget remains subject to significant opposition from several Member States, failure to increase it has led to workarounds that have other costs, including a marginalization of the budgetary system and of democratic and judicial control.

Above all, this volume makes the case for legal scholars to pay increasing attention to the EU budget rather than focusing primarily on non-budget funding or picking up on one specific angle—such as rule of law conditionality—without embedding the analysis in the broader context of the EU budget and funding law and practice. To this end, the chapters in this volume provide a rich and varied resource.

2

The European Union's Public Finances in Times of Crisis

Fragmentation, Innovation, and Consolidation

*Richard Crowe**

1. Introduction

The relationship between the European Union's values and objectives, on the one hand, and the budgetary resources needed to promote and defend them, on the other hand, has come sharply into focus in the years since the entry into force of the Treaty of Lisbon.[1] The Court of Justice of the EU has long asserted that the Union has an autonomous legal order,[2] and it enjoys extensive law-making competences across a wide range of policy areas. However, as the Union's responses to the COVID-19 pandemic and Russia's invasion of Ukraine illustrate, the pursuit of the Union's aim under Article 3(1) Treaty on European Union (TEU) 'to promote peace, its values and the well-being of its peoples' increasingly also requires the mobilization of massive amounts of budgetary resources at European level. The exercise of the Union's legal competences has been the subject of much scholarly attention in the post-Lisbon era.[3] However, up until recently, rather less attention has been paid to the exercise of its budgetary competences.[4]

* All views expressed are personal to the author. Text based on the state of the law as at 1 August 2023.

[1] The Treaty of Lisbon amending the Treaty on European Union and the Treaty establishing the European Community (OJ C 306 (17 December 2007)) entered into force on 1 December 2009.

[2] See e.g. Opinion 1/17, *Comprehensive Economic and Trade Agreement with Canada (CETA)* (EU:C:2019:341), paras 109–110; Da Silva Passos, 'The Scope of the Principle of the Autonomy of the European Union Legal Order: Recent Developments', in K. Lenaerts et al. (eds), *Building the European Union: The Jurist's View of the Union's Evolution* (2021) 19.

[3] See e.g. L. Azoulai, *The Question of Competence in the European Union* (2014); S. Garben and I. Govaere (eds), *The Division of Competences between the EU and the Member States: Reflections on the Past, the Present and the Future* (2020).

[4] For an in-depth analysis of the Union's revenue and expenditure competences in the pre-Lisbon context, see A. Potteau, *Recherches sur l'autonomie financière de l'Union européenne* (2004).

Richard Crowe, *The European Union's Public Finances in Times of Crisis*. In: *New Frontiers of EU Funding*.
Edited by: Claire Kilpatrick and Joanne Scott, Oxford University Press. © Richard Crowe 2024.
DOI: 10.1093/oso/9780198940319.003.0002

In particular, the legal and budgetary dualism that runs through the Union Treaties and the implications of that dualism for the functioning of the Union have been little explored. Article 1 TEU provides that the Member States confer competences on the Union 'to attain objectives they have in common'. According to Article 3(6) TEU, the common objectives are to be pursued 'by appropriate means' commensurate with those competences. The principal legal acts of the Union are set out in Article 288 Treaty on the Functioning of the European Union (TFEU), which states that '[t]o exercise the Union's competences, the institutions shall adopt regulations, directives, decisions, recommendations and opinions'.[5] However, when funding from the Union budget is involved, the mere adoption of legal acts is not sufficient. Legal acts cannot, in themselves, make available the corresponding appropriations from the Union budget needed to support their implementation.

Instead, Article 314 TFEU lays down a separate procedure for the establishment of the budget. The budget is not a legislative act, even though it is established in accordance with a special legislative procedure.[6] In order to implement the expenditure shown in the budget, Article 310(3) TFEU requires 'the prior adoption of a legally binding Union act providing a legal basis for its action and for the implementation of the corresponding expenditure'.[7] When funding is involved, the pursuit of Union policy objectives entails both the adoption and implementation of a basic act (usually an act of legislation), which provides a legal basis for the expenditure, and the implementation of budgetary appropriations, which are made available on a corresponding line of the budget through the budgetary procedure. The legislative and the budgetary must function in parallel, like two lungs breathing in sync.

However, the budget itself is also constrained by a body of legal principles and rules laid down in the Treaties and in the financial legislation provided for in Title II of Part Six TFEU (Articles 310–324 TFEU) on 'Financial Provisions'. Under that Title, the institutions enjoy broad discretion in the design of the Union's budgetary system, particularly with regard to the sources of revenue, the categories of expenditure for which ceilings should be fixed, and the rules on implementation of the budget. In practice, however, the seven-year Multiannual Financial Framework (MFF) programming model that has been

[5] On legal acts, see M. Cremona and C. Kilpatrick (eds), *EU Legal Acts: Challenges and Transformations* (2018).

[6] Case C-77/11, *Council v. European Parliament* (EU:C:2013:559), paras 57–60.

[7] This paragraph enshrines what Advocate General Mancini referred to in the 1980s as the 'principle of "dual implementation" (that is to say, budgetary, on the one hand, and legislative or administrative, on the other)'. See Opinion of Mancini AG in Case 85/86, *Commission v. Board of Governors of the EIB* (EU:C:1987:504), para. 6.

applied over the past three decades imposes rigid constraints on the budget. Union expenditure is capped at around 1 per cent of total EU gross national income (GNI), revenue is drawn mainly from de facto national contributions, and the bulk of Union funding is pre-allocated for each seven-year programming period.

Over the past decade, a series of crises has exposed the limitations of this model.[8] The Union's policy responses to the sovereign debt crisis in the euro area, the migration crisis, the climate crisis, the COVID-19 health pandemic, the Russian war on Ukraine, and the recent energy crisis all entailed recourse to financing drawn from outside the own resources system, such as off-budget borrowing or external assigned revenue. At times, Member States exercised their budgetary competences collectively to compensate for shortcomings in the Union's own capacities. The corresponding emergence of a 'galaxy' of European-level funds and instruments around the Union budget, with variable participation of Member States and diverse governance arrangements, has been criticized as undermining transparency and accountability in the Union's public finances.[9]

Alongside fragmentation, however, the pressure to do 'more with less' in times of crisis has also prompted innovations in how the Union budget is used to pursue policy objectives. For example, budgetary guarantees are increasingly used to leverage private-sector investments aligned with Union policy objectives. Experimentation with new ways of delivering Union funding seeks to maximize its impact in times of crisis. Elements of consolidation are also apparent. For example, the formerly intergovernmental European Development Fund (EDF) has been incorporated into the Union budget.[10] Structural consolidation is apparent in the establishment of a Common Provisioning Fund to

[8] On the notion of crises in the Union context, see M. Riddervold, J. Trondal, and A. Newsome (eds), *The Palgrave Handbook of EU Crises* (2021); D. Dinan, N. Nugent, and W. E. Paterson (eds), *The European Union in Crisis* (2017). See also De Witte, 'Guest Editorial—EU Emergency Law and Its Impact on the EU Legal Order', 59(1) *Common Market Law Review* (*CMLR*) (2022) 3; Editorial Comments, 'Union Membership in Times of Crisis', 51(1) *CMLR* (2014) 1.

[9] See Begg et al., 'The Next Revision of the Financial Regulation and the EU Budget Galaxy: How to Safeguard and Strengthen Budgetary Principles and Parliamentary Oversight', Study for Directorate-General for Internal Policies of the Union (DG IPOL), European Parliament (March 2022); Crowe, 'The European Budgetary Galaxy', 13(3) *European Constitutional Law Review* (*EuConst*) (2017) 428.

[10] For the MFF 2021–2027, the EDF is incorporated into the Neighbourhood, Development and International Cooperation Instrument (NDICI)–Global Europe programme. See Regulation (EU) 2021/947 of the EP [European Parliament] and of the Council of 9 June 2021 establishing the Neighbourhood, Development and International Cooperation Instrument—Global Europe, amending and repealing Decision 466/2014/EU of the EP and of the Council and repealing Regulation (EU) 2017/1601 of the EP and of the Council and Council Regulation (EC, Euratom) 480/2009, OJ 2021 L 209/1.

replace a previously fragmented range of guarantee funds[11] or in the adoption of rules allowing the Commission to issue single, EU-branded, bonds to the capital markets, instead of issuing separate bonds for each borrowing instrument.[12]

Under the pressures of multiple crises, the legal framework governing the Union's public finances appears to be in a state of flux, with elements of fragmentation, innovation, and consolidation apparent at the same time. Starting from the premise that the current flux in the Union's finances is symptomatic of a difficult transition from the rather archaic budgetary architecture of the 1980s to a more modern public finance system for the larger and more diverse 'geopolitical' Union of today, with its broader range of policy competences and more unpredictable financing needs, this contribution seeks to explore that flux, paying particular attention to the interplay between the legislative and the budgetary in times of crisis.

At the outset, the relationship between the legislative and budgetary functions in matters of funding is recalled (section 2). Attention then turns to the legal mechanisms and techniques that have been used to get around the constraints of the budgetary ceilings in times of crisis (section 3), with a particular focus on off-budget borrowing and external assigned revenue. The focus then shifts to consolidation (section 4), looking at how the ad hoc innovations of the crisis years could lead to more lasting structural evolutions in the Union's public finance architecture. The increasingly central role of funds in shaping and driving Union policy initiatives, the possible longer-term role of borrowing, and the evolving institutional balance in matters of funding are discussed. Some reflections on possible directions for future reform are presented in the conclusion (section 5).

2. The Relationship between the Legislative and Budgetary Functions in Union Funding

A. The Union Budget

The Union budget is established on an annual basis by the European Parliament and the Council, acting jointly, in accordance with the procedure

[11] See Art. 212 of Regulation (EU, Euratom) 2018/1046 of the EP and of the Council of 18 July 2018 on the financial rules applicable to the general budget of the Union, amending Regulations (EU) 1296/2013, (EU) 1301/2013, (EU) 1303/2013, (EU) 1304/2013, (EU) 1309/2013, (EU) 1316/2013, (EU) 223/2014, (EU) 283/2014, and Decision 541/2014/EU and repealing Regulation (EU, Euratom) 966/2012, OJ 2018 L 193/1 (hereinafter the 'Financial Regulation').

[12] See Regulation (EU, Euratom) 2022/2434 of the EP and of the Council of 6 December 2022 amending Regulation (EU, Euratom) 2018/1046 as regards the establishment of a diversified funding strategy as a general borrowing method, OJ 2022 L 319/1.

laid down in Article 314 TFEU. In the *Budget Signature* case,[13] the Court of Justice confirmed that, post-Lisbon, the budget is not a legislative act in the form of a regulation, directive, or decision.[14] The budget is essentially an accounting document, often running to several thousand pages, which 'forecasts and authorises all revenue and expenditure considered necessary for the Union'.[15] The budget is annexed to an act of definitive adoption signed by the President of Parliament alone on the basis of Article 314(9) TFEU.[16] It is this act that 'endows the budget with binding force vis-à-vis both the institutions and the Member States'.[17]

However, the European Parliament and the Council, acting as the Union's budgetary authority, do not have unfettered discretion with regard to the contents of the budget. In the first instance, Title II of Part Six TFEU lays down a number of fundamental budgetary principles that must be respected. These are further elaborated in the financial legislation adopted under that Title.[18] In particular, the principle of the unity of the budget derives from the first sentence of Article 310(1) TFEU, which requires that 'all revenue and expenditure of the Union ... shall be shown in the budget'. The principle of budgetary balance, or equilibrium, is set out in the third sentence of the same paragraph, which states that '[t]he revenue and expenditure shown in the budget shall be in balance'. The principle of annuality derives from Articles 310(2) and 313 TFEU, which provide for the authorization of expenditure for an annual budgetary period, running from 1 January to 31 December. Article 316 TFEU concerns the structure and nomenclature of the budget. The contents of the revenue side of the budget, meanwhile, are determined through the application of the own resources legislation.

The scope of the principle of budgetary balance, as laid down in Article 310(1) TFEU, has attracted much attention in the context of Union borrowing under the Next Generation EU (NGEU) COVID-19 recovery plan.[19] An

[13] Case C-77/11, *Council v. European Parliament* (n. 6), paras 57–60.

[14] However, under Art. III-404 of the Treaty establishing a Constitution for Europe, OJ 2004 C 310/1, the budget would have been established by European laws. Under Art. I-33, European laws would have produced the same legal effects as regulations under the current Treaties. See OJ 2004 C 310/1.

[15] See Art. 7(1) of the Financial Regulation (n. 11).

[16] For the adoption of the budget for 2023, see Definitive adoption (EU, Euratom) 2023/278 of the European Union's annual budget for the financial year 2023, OJ 2023 L 58/1.

[17] Case C-77/11, *Council v. European Parliament* (n. 6), para. 51.

[18] See Title II (Arts 6–38) on Budgetary Principles of the Financial Regulation (n. 11).

[19] On the NGEU recovery plan, see P. Dermine, *Le plan de relance "Next Generation EU" de l'Union européenne: Analyse constitutionnelle d'une initiative historique* (2023); Porras-Gómez, 'The EU Recovery Instrument and the Constitutional Implications of Its Expenditure', 19(1) *EuConst* (2023) 1; De Witte, 'The European Union's COVID-19 Recovery Plan: The Legal Engineering of an Economic Policy Shift', 58(3) *CMLR* (2021) 635; de Gregorio Merino, 'The Recovery Plan: Solidarity and the Living Constitution', 50 *EU Law Live* (6 March 2021).

excessively strict interpretation of this principle would render the budgetary system unworkable. In the first instance, it is clear from the wording and context of Article 310(1) TFEU that the 'budget' that must be in balance is the accounting document that is established annually in accordance with Article 314 TFEU. The budget is adopted in balance at the start of the year, but there will inevitably be a discrepancy between the outturn and the initial estimates for revenue and expenditure at the end of the year. At that point, balance is restored by carrying over the expected surplus to the following year's budget, as provided for in Article 8 of the Own Resources Decision.[20] Article 18 of the Financial Regulation further provides that the balance from each financial year shall be entered in the budget for the following year as revenue, in the event of a surplus, or as a payment appropriation, in the event of a deficit.[21]

A similar rule of budgetary balance can be found in certain national constitutions, such as the German *Grundgesetz* (GG). Article 110(1) GG states, in identical terms to Article 310(1) TFEU, that the revenue and expenditure shown in the budget shall be in balance. This implies that the budget must be in balance in an accounting sense.[22] It follows implicitly from Article 115(2) GG, which lays down limits to the amount of revenue that may be drawn from debt in order to keep the budget in balance, and Article 109(3) GG on the debt brake, that financing the budget through debt is possible, within strict limits.[23] Similarly, Article 310(1) TFEU does not, in itself, prohibit the Union from issuing debt.[24] Today, Article 4 of the Own Resources Decision provides that

[20] Council Decision (EU, Euratom) 2020/2053 of 14 December 2020 on the system of own resources of the European Union and repealing Decision 2014/335/EU, Euratom, OJ 2020 L 424/1. A surplus generally arises because it is not possible to exhaust every appropriation on every budget line. Also other revenue from sources such as competition fines and late interest payments is often budgeted at the end of the year. For the entry of the surplus from 2021 in the budget for 2022, see Definitive Adoption (EU, Euratom) 2022/1432 of amending budget No. 2 of the European Union for the financial year 2022, OJ 2022 L 230/1. See also Case C-284/90, *Council v. European Parliament (Budget Surplus)* (EU:C:1992:154) and the discussion of the topic in the Opinion of Advocate General Jacobs in that same case (EU:C:1991:396).

[21] A rare instance of a deficit being carried forward to the next financial year occurred at the end of 1983, owing to problems in the financing of the Common Agricultural Policy. See D. Strasser, *The Finances of Europe* (7th ed., 1991) 58–59.

[22] See e.g. H. Dreier (ed.), *Grundgesetz-Kommentar*, Band III: Artikel 110, C.II.3.(f) 'Ausgleich von Einnahmen und Ausgaben' (3rd ed., 2018); Beltrame, 'Allemagne', in G. Orsoni (ed.), *Les finances publiques en Europe* (2007) 1, at 13–14.

[23] On the evolution over time of these provisions, see Thiele, 'The "German Way" of Curbing Public Debt: The Constitutional Debt Brake and the Fiscal Compact—Why Germany Has to Work on Its Language Skills', 11(1) *EuConst* (2015) 30. On balanced budget rules and debt brakes more generally, see E. S. Tănăsescu and E. Oliva (eds), *Constitutional Law and the EU Balanced Budget Principle* (2022).

[24] In 2015, the Commission stated in reply to a parliamentary question that Art. 310(1) TFEU does not prohibit the Union from issuing debt, but it did interpret that provision as preventing the Union from using debt to balance its budget. See Answer given by Vice-President Georgieva on behalf of the Commission to Parliamentary Question E-005201/2015 (3 June 2015). On seemingly contradictory past statements by the institutions on this issue, see Leino-Sandberg, 'Who Is Ultra Vires Now? The

the Union shall not use funds borrowed on capital markets for the financing of operational expenditure. Article 5(1)(b) then creates a derogation for borrowing for operational expenditure under NGEU. The Financial Regulation also recognizes that the Union may raise loans, albeit not 'within the framework of the budget'.[25]

The Union budget is established in both commitment appropriations and payment appropriations, and there are MFF and own resources ceilings for both.[26] For the financial year 2023, for example, the budget was established at EUR 186.6 billion in commitment appropriations and EUR 168.6 billion in payment appropriations. This system of differentiated appropriations allows commitments for multiannual actions to be engaged in one year, with the corresponding payments only made in later years, as the funded projects reach different stages of completion. As a result, there are always outstanding budgetary commitments at the end of a financial year for which the corresponding payments have not yet been made.[27] The Commission estimates that the outstanding commitments at the start of 2024 will amount to EUR 490.5 billion.[28] The budget nevertheless remains balanced in any given financial year in both commitments and payments.

B. The Legislation Governing the Budget

Title II of Part Six TFEU provides for a number of legal acts that regulate the Union budget. In the case of *Poland v. Parliament & Council (Conditionality Regulation)*, the Court of Justice held that the adoption, on the legal basis of Article 322(1)(a) TFEU, of rules governing the implementation of the Union budget 'falls within the exercise of a competence of the European Union relating to its functioning, which, by its nature, can be exercised only by the

EU's Legal U-Turn in Interpreting Article 310 TFEU', *Verfassungsblog* (18 June 2020), https://verfassungsblog.de/who-is-ultra-vires-now-the-eus-legal-u-turn-in-interpreting-article-310-tfeu (last visited 4 July 2024).

25 See Art. 17(2) of the Financial Regulation (n. 11).

26 According to ibid. Art. 7, commitment appropriations cover the cost of the legal commitments that may be entered into during a financial year. Payment appropriations cover the payments needed to honour the legal commitments entered into in the financial year or preceding financial years.

27 These outstanding commitments are commonly referred to as the RAL, from the French *reste à liquider*.

28 See European Commission, Long-term forecast of future inflows and outflows of the EU budget (2024–2028), COM(2023) 390, 18. Of the EUR 490.5 billion, EUR 273.7 billion relates to outstanding commitments under the MFF and EUR 206.8 billion relates to NGEU.

Union itself. Therefore, the principle of subsidiarity cannot apply.'[29] The same logic would apply equally to the adoption of the other acts provided for in Title II of Part Six TFEU, including the Own Resources Decision, adopted on the basis of Article 311 TFEU, and the MFF Regulation, adopted on the basis of Article 312(2) TFEU.

The Own Resources Decision and the accompanying implementing legislation govern the Union's system of revenue. In accordance with Article 311 TFEU, the Union 'shall provide itself with the means necessary to attain its objectives and carry through its policies'. Without prejudice to other revenue, the budget 'shall be financed wholly from own resources'. The Own Resources Decision is adopted by the Council, acting by unanimity, after consulting the European Parliament. It only enters into force following approval by the Member States in accordance with their national constitutional requirements.

The term 'own resources' of the Union, as employed in Article 311 TFEU, is not defined in the Treaties or in Union legislation. However, the historical origins of the term in Article 201 of the EEC Treaty suggest that it should be contrasted with the notion of national contributions.[30] Today, 'genuine' own resources, such as customs duties, account for only a small share of Union revenue. About 80 per cent of revenue is drawn from de facto national contributions, mainly in the form of GNI-based and VAT-based statistical resources. The deficiencies of the current own resources system have been well documented, notably in the Commission's Budget Review of 2010[31] and the Final Report of the Monti High-Level Group on Own Resources of 2016.[32]

With regard to expenditure, the purpose of the MFF, according to Article 312(1) TFEU, is to 'ensure that Union expenditure develops in an orderly manner and within the limits of its own resources'. According to Article 312(3) TFEU, the MFF 'shall determine the amounts of the annual ceilings

[29] Case C-157/21, *Republic of Poland v. European Parliament and Council (Conditionality Regulation)* (EU:C:2022:98), para. 241.

[30] Art. 201 EEC stated that the Commission 'shall study the conditions under which the financial contributions of Member States provided for in Article 200 may be replaced by other resources of the Community itself'. The first Own Resources Decision bore the title Council Decision 70/234 *on the replacement of financial contributions from Member States by the Communities own resources*, OJ L 1970 94/19 (emphasis added). See Ehlermann, 'The Financing of the Community: The Distinction between Financial Contributions and Own Resources', 19(4) *CMLR* (1982) 571.

[31] Commission Staff Working Paper, 'Financing the EU Budget: Report on the Operation of the Own Resources System', SEC(2011) 876.

[32] 'Future Financing of the EU: Final Report and Recommendations of the High Level Group on Own Resources' (December 2016) (hereinafter the 'Monti Report').

on commitment appropriations by category of expenditure and of the annual ceiling on payment appropriations'. The MFF Regulation is adopted by the Council, acting by unanimity, after obtaining the consent of the European Parliament.[33] The ceilings are set out in a one-page table that is annexed to the regulation.[34] Article 312(1) TFEU requires that the MFF is established for a period of at least five years. In practice, it has been established for seven-year periods since 1993. The MFF ceilings for the period 2021–2027 amount to EUR 1,074 billion in commitment appropriations and EUR 1,061 billion in payment appropriations, in 2018 prices.[35] These fixed amounts are subject to an annual deflator of 2 per cent per year.[36] In 2023, the MFF ceilings amounted to 1.12 per cent of EU GNI in commitments and 1.03 per cent of EU GNI in payments.[37]

In addition to the ceilings, the MFF Regulation also provides for a limited number of thematic and general 'special instruments', which, within strict limits, may be mobilized by the budgetary authority above the MFF ceilings for unpredictable items of expenditure, such as emergency aid in response to natural disasters.[38] These elements of flexibility within the MFF are based on the second sentence of Article 312(3) TFEU, which states that the MFF may also lay down 'any other provisions required for the annual budgetary procedure to run smoothly'. However, the amounts involved are relatively small (the Court of Auditors estimates they amount to about EUR 21 billion for the current MFF period),[39] and experience shows that they are quickly exhausted in times of crisis.

The MFF expenditure ceilings are the only budgetary ceilings explicitly mentioned in the Treaties. Nevertheless, Article 3 of the Own Resources Decision

[33] Council Regulation (EU, Euratom) 2020/2093 of 17 December 2020 laying down the multiannual financial framework for the years 2021 to 2027, OJ 2020 L 433I/11 (hereinafter the 'MFF Regulation').

[34] See ibid. Annex I.

[35] See European Commission, *The EU's 2021–2027 Long-Term Budget and Next Generation EU: Facts and Figures* (2021).

[36] See Art. 4(2) of the MFF Regulation (n. 33).

[37] See European Commission, Commission Communication on the Technical adjustment of the multiannual financial framework for 2024 in accordance with Article 4 of Council Regulation (EU, Euratom) 2020/2093 laying down the multiannual financial framework for the years 2021 to 2027, COM(2023) 320.

[38] The thematic special instruments provided for in the MFF Regulation (n. 33) are the European Globalisation Adjustment Fund (Art. 8), the Solidarity and Emergency Aid Reserve (Art. 9), and the Brexit Adjustment Reserve (Art. 10). The non-thematic special instruments are the Single Margin Instrument (Art. 11) and the Flexibility Instrument (Art. 12). On special instruments in the current MFF, see Potteau, 'La simplification en trompe-l'oeil des "instruments spéciaux" concourant à la flexibilité du cadre financier 2021–2027', *Revue trimestrielle de droit européen* (*RTDE*) (2021) 739.

[39] European Court of Auditors, *The EU's Financial Landscape: A Patchwork Construction Requiring Further Simplification and Accountability*, Special Report 5/2023, at 34.

also lays down own resources revenue ceilings in both commitments and payments. To the extent that these own resources ceilings might also function as de facto expenditure ceilings, one could query whether they are adopted on the correct legal basis. However, Articles 310(4) and 312(1) TFEU do mention the need to respect 'the limit of the Union's own resources', which implies that there is a limit. Since the GNI-based own resource functions as a balancing resource, which automatically covers any shortfall, after all other revenue has been taken into account, the 'limit' on maximum possible GNI-based revenue is fixed through the own resources ceilings.[40]

In practice, the own resources ceilings, which are fixed as a percentage of EU GNI, are calculated to remain well above the level of the fixed MFF ceilings. For the programming period 2021–2027, Article 3(1) of the Own Resources Decision states that the total annual amount of payment appropriations entered in the Union budget shall not exceed 1.40 per cent of EU GNI. Article 3(2) of the same Decision fixes the own resources commitments ceiling at 1.46 per cent of EU GNI. Article 6 of the Decision adds that these ceilings shall each be increased by 0.60 per cent of EU GNI for the sole purpose of covering liabilities under NGEU up to the year 2058.

Finally, the Financial Regulation, adopted under the ordinary legislative procedure on the legal basis of Article 322(1)(a) TFEU, lays down the financial rules concerning the establishment and implementation of the budget. When a new Financial Regulation was adopted in 2002, Paul Craig described it as a 'constitutional framework for Community administration of the kind that has not existed hitherto'.[41] The Financial Regulation applies horizontally across all Union funds. Its Article 3 stipulates that other legislation must comply with its Title II on budgetary principles, thereby purporting to give those provisions the status of higher norms in matters of budget implementation. The Common Provisions Regulation (CPR), which covers all the structural funds, is another important source of horizontal financial rules.[42]

[40] However, it might still be queried why it is necessary to have a commitments ceiling for own resources.

[41] P. Craig, *EU Administrative Law* (2006) 26.

[42] Regulation (EU) 2021/1060 of the EP and of the Council of 24 June 2021 laying down common provisions on the European Regional Development Fund, the European Social Fund Plus, the Cohesion Fund, the Just Transition Fund and the European Maritime, Fisheries and Aquaculture Fund and financial rules for those and for the Asylum, Migration and Integration Fund, the Internal Security Fund and the Instrument for Financial Support for Border Management and Visa Policy, OJ 2021 L 231/159.

C. The Relationship between the Legislative Authority and the Budgetary Authority

Articles 14(1) and 16(1) TEU provide that the European Parliament and the Council shall jointly 'exercise legislative and budgetary functions'. The particular significance of the distinction between legislative and budgetary functions in Union law has historical origins. As Jean-Paul Jacqué has written post-Lisbon, one of the distinctive features of the Union remains the absence of parallelism between the exercise of the legislative power and the budgetary power, since laws and budgets are adopted in accordance with procedures that imply different majorities.[43] It might be added that they are not always adopted by the same institutions.

For many years, beginning in the 1970s, the European Parliament enjoyed budgetary decision-making powers, alongside the Council, but it did not yet have any real powers in legislative matters.[44] This resulted in an imbalance between the composition of the legislative authority, consisting of the Council alone, and the budgetary authority, consisting of the Parliament and the Council. Over the course of a series of institutional battles in the 1970s and 1980s, the Parliament essentially sought to legislate through the budget, while the Council tried to use its legislative powers to limit expenditure by fixing maximum financial amounts in legislation that it adopted alone.[45]

In time, the Court of Justice confirmed that it is not sufficient merely to create a new budget line and enter appropriations on it in order to launch new policy actions entailing significant expenditure from the budget.[46] According to the Court, 'the requirement that a basic act must be adopted before an appropriation is implemented derives directly from the scheme of the Treaty, in accordance with which the conditions governing the exercise of legislative powers and budgetary powers are not the same'.[47] The 'implementation

[43] J.-P. Jacqué, *Droit institutionnel de l'Union européenne* (8th ed., 2015) 486.

[44] Under the Treaty of Rome, the Parliament was only consulted on legislative matters. The Parliament's legislative powers were progressively strengthened over a series of Treaty revisions, beginning with the Single European Act.

[45] Jacqué (n. 43) 442.

[46] See, in particular, Joined Cases C-87/77, C-130/77, C-22/83, 9/84, and C-10/84, *Salerno and Others v. Commission and Council* (EU:C:1985:318), para. 56; Case C-294/83, *Les Verts v. Parliament* (EU:C:1986:166), para. 28; Case C-242/87, *Commission v. Council* (EU:C:1989:217), para. 18; Case C-16/88, *Commission v. Council* (EU:C:1989:397), paras 15–19; and Case C-106/96, *UK v. Parliament* (EU:C:1998:218), para. 28.

[47] Case C-106/96 (n. 46), para. 28.

of Community expenditure relating to any significant Community action presupposes not only the entry of the relevant appropriation in the budget of the Community, which is a matter for the budgetary authority, but in addition the prior adoption of a basic act authorising that expenditure, which is a matter for the legislative authority'.[48] This rule is now codified in Article 310(3) TFEU.

The relationship between financial amounts laid down in legislation and amounts in the budget was finally resolved by means of interinstitutional agreements (IIAs). In modern times, the budgetary IIA of December 2020[49] provides that each legislative act concerning a multiannual programme adopted in accordance with the ordinary legislative procedure 'shall contain a provision in which the legislator lays down the financial envelope for the programme'.[50] This amount 'shall constitute the prime reference amount for the European Parliament and for the Council during the annual budgetary procedure'.[51] Except in justified circumstances, the institutions undertake, in the budgetary procedure, 'not to depart by more than 15 per cent from that amount for the entire duration of the programme concerned'.[52] Should the Council wish to include a reference amount in other legal acts that it adopts alone, 'that amount shall be taken as illustrating the will of the legislator and shall not affect the budgetary powers of the European Parliament and of the Council as set out in the TFEU'.[53]

Following the Treaty of Lisbon, the vast majority of Union funding programmes are established by regulations adopted in accordance with the ordinary legislative procedure. In the policy areas concerned, the Parliament and the Council decide jointly, as budgetary authority, on the budgetary nomenclature and on the annual allocation of resources to the different funding programmes, within the limits of the MFF. They also decide jointly, as legislative authority, on the policy objectives pursued and on the eligibility conditions for beneficiaries to access funding under individual programmes. The symmetric composition of the Union's legislative and budgetary authorities allows the 'power of the purse' to be exercised in a consistent and coherent way, based on the dual scheme of democratic representation set out in Article 10(2) TEU.

[48] Ibid. para. 26.

[49] Interinstitutional Agreement of 16 December 2020 between the EP, the Council of the European Union and the European Commission on budgetary discipline, on cooperation in budgetary matters and on sound financial management, as well as on new own resources, including a roadmap towards the introduction of new own resources, OJ 2020 L 433I/28.

[50] Ibid. point 18.

[51] Ibid.

[52] Ibid.

[53] Ibid. point 19.

Legislative and budgetary implementation then run in parallel, subject to democratic oversight by the same two institutions.

Article 310(4) TFEU further imposes a rule of multiannual budgetary discipline, which requires that no legal act shall be adopted by the law-making authority without providing an assurance that the expenditure arising from such an act is capable of being financed within the limit of the Union's own resources and in compliance with the MFF. In this way, the MFF also acts as a constraint on the actions of the legislative authority.[54] In practice, the Commission annexes a 'legislative financial statement', drawn up in accordance with Article 35 of the Financial Regulation, to every legislative proposal that entails expenditure from the budget. The co-legislators use the financial statement to assess the budgetary implications of the proposed act. Article 310(4) TFEU does not prevent the Union from committing to initiatives whose financial consequences may run far beyond the period of a single MFF, such as the International Thermonuclear Experimental Reactor (ITER) fusion energy project. However, the Union's contributions do then come up for internal reassessment in the context of each round of seven-yearly MFF negotiations.[55]

D. The Coordination of Legislative and Budgetary Programming: The MFF Package

The benefits of closely coordinating the exercise of the legislative and budgetary functions were well understood in the 1980s by then Commission President Jacques Delors, who proposed the adoption of the first binding multiannual financial perspectives for a period corresponding to the implementation of the Single Market legislative programme over the years from 1988 to 1992.[56] Today, the term 'MFF' refers, in a strict sense, to the multiannual expenditure ceilings and the accompanying provisions that are laid down in the MFF Regulation. However, the term is also used in a broader sense to refer to the MFF programming 'package'. The MFF package comprises almost 50 legislative acts linked to

[54] Jacqué (n. 43) 489.

[55] In the case of ITER, the basic act providing a legal basis for the Union's contributions was adopted by the Council in 2007 and set out indicative financial contributions up to the year 2041. The Decision was amended in 2021 to update the figures for the MFF period 2021–2027. See Art. 4(3) and (4) of Council Decision 2007/198/Euratom of 27 March 2007 establishing the European Joint Undertaking for ITER and the Development of Fusion Energy and conferring advantages upon it, OJ 2007 L 90/58.

[56] Interinstitutional Agreement on budgetary discipline and improvement of the budgetary procedure, OJ 1988 L 185/33.

the budget that are, in practice, renewed on a seven-yearly basis. The package includes the core financial legislation, including the Own Resources Decision and its implementing legislation, the MFF Regulation, and sector-specific regulations establishing some 43 Union funding programmes across all major policy domains.

The Commission presents proposals for all the legal acts contained in the MFF package about two years before the end of the preceding MFF programming period.[57] The negotiations within and between the Union institutions are invariably long and arduous. In practice, a lengthy political deliberation at the level of the European Council always takes place before the Council finalizes its positions.[58] The Council's sole power to adopt the revenue and expenditure ceilings, subject to the Parliament's consent for the expenditure ceilings, grants it a dominant role in the interinstitutional negotiations on figures. For net-contributor Member States, the traditional expenditure limit of around 1 per cent of EU GNI remains sacrosanct. The rigidity of the MFF is exacerbated by the tendency to 'pre-allocate' amounts in the legislative financial envelopes. This latter tendency is apparent even in the Parliament, where sectoral committees seek to use their legislative powers over the envelopes to 'lock down', to the maximum extent possible, the amounts available for their sectoral programmes over the seven-year period.

In essence, the seven-year MFF model that has prevailed since the early 1990s is effective for what Luuk Van Middelaar would term the 'Europe of Rules'.[59] It is a framework suitable for the programming of structural investments in policy areas where expenditure can be expected to develop in an orderly manner over a number of years, in line with the applicable sectoral funding legislation. However, it is less suited to the 'Europe of Events'. When it is necessary to mobilize massive amounts of resources going beyond the traditional limit of 1 per cent of EU GNI in response to crises, the functioning of the Union's budgetary 'lung' is constrained by the ceilings. If a revision of those ceilings is not feasible, the legislative authority is forced to innovate to find alternative sources of financing or to use the budget in new ways to pursue Union policy objectives. Section 3 looks at some of the legal mechanisms and techniques employed in pursuit of those alternative solutions.

[57] Art. 21 of the MFF Regulation (n. 33) provides that a proposal for the post-2027 MFF should be presented by the Commission before 1 July 2025.

[58] On the role of the European Council in the adoption of NGEU and the most recent MFF package, see De Witte (n. 19) 667–674. See also Crowe, 'The European Council and the Multiannual Financial Framework', 18 *Cambridge Yearbook of European Legal Studies (CYELS)* (2016) 69.

[59] See L. van Middelaar, *Alarums and Excursions: Improvising Politics on the European Stage* (2019).

3. Fragmentation and Innovation in Times of Crisis

A. The Budgetary 'Galaxy'

In 2017, the European Parliament's Committee on Budgets hosted a workshop to assess what it termed the 'galaxy' of intergovernmental or quasi-intergovernmental funds and instruments that was emerging around the Union budget in a context of multiple crises.[60] Parliamentarians criticized the tendency to resort to complex, off-budget, financing solutions instead of increasing the size of the Union budget and reforming its structure. It was suggested that the resulting fragmentation of the Union's public finances undermines budgetary transparency, accountability, and democratic oversight of public funds. More recently, the European Court of Auditors expressed similar concerns about what it refers to more soberly as the complex 'patchwork construction' of the Union's 'financial landscape'.[61]

Whatever metaphor is used, the proliferation of funds and instruments around the Union budget shows few signs of abating. In certain domains, such as the Common Foreign and Security Policy (CFSP), the off-budget nature of the funds is simply a consequence of the legal basis used. For example, the European Peace Facility (EPF) was created in 2021 on the basis of the TEU for the financing of CFSP actions 'to preserve peace, prevent conflicts and strengthen international security'.[62] It has played a central role in the Union's response to the Russian war on Ukraine. In accordance with Article 41(2) TEU, operating expenditure 'arising from operations having military or defence implications' is charged to the Member States. In an illustration of flux in the budgetary galaxy, the EPF itself represents an amalgamation of two earlier off-budget instruments, the African Peace Facility[63] and the Athena mechanism.[64]

[60] Workshop, 'The Galaxy of Funds and Instruments around the EU Budget' (18 January 2017), https://www.europarl.europa.eu/committees/en/product/product-details/20170118WKS00261 (last visited 24 January 2024). For visual representations of the 'galaxy', see Annex IV to the Monti Report (n. 32), Figure 4 in Annex I to the Study of Begg et al. (n. 9); Figure 3 in European Court of Auditors, Special Report 5/2023 (n. 39) 15.

[61] European Court of Auditors, Special Report 5/2023 (n. 39).

[62] See Art. 1(1) of Council Decision (CFSP) 2021/509 of 22 March 2021 establishing a European Peace Facility, and repealing Decision (CFSP) 2015/528, OJ 2021 L 102/14.

[63] The African Peace Facility was established in 2003 on the basis of the African, Caribbean and Pacific Group of States (ACP)–EU Partnership Agreement. It was financed under the old EDF.

[64] Council Decision (CFSP) 2015/528 of 27 March 2015 establishing a mechanism to administer the financing of the common costs of European Union operations having military or defence implications (Athena) and repealing Decision 2011/871/CFSP, OJ 2015 L 84/39.

Although the EPF, as well as other CFSP actions, such as Permanent Structured Cooperation (PESCO) projects,[65] are financed outside the Union budget by the participating Member States, they are, nevertheless, established within the Union's institutional framework. In fact, the creation of wholly intergovernmental funds and instruments to pursue Union policy objectives in times of crises has remained the exception. The creation of the European Financial Stability Facility (EFSF)[66] and the European Stability Mechanism (ESM)[67] by the euro area Member States in the context of the sovereign debt crisis did not, as it transpired, open the floodgates to the establishment of a plethora of purely intergovernmental funds that might have permanently undermined the Community method. Indeed, the Court's case law on the obligations of the 'borrowed' Union institutions to respect Union law, also when acting in the framework of the ESM Treaty,[68] has the effect, in essence, of keeping that mechanism close to the Union's orbit. This may facilitate its integration into the Union's institutional framework at a later stage.[69]

Apart from the wholly intergovernmental mechanisms outside the Union framework and the CFSP funds within it, the fragmentation of the past decade results mainly from recourse to two sources of financing outside the system of own resources, namely off-budget borrowing and external assigned revenue. In the subsections that follow, the use of borrowing in response to the various post-Lisbon crises will first be examined (section B), before going on to look at the use of external assigned revenue (section C). A selection of ways in which the Union's legislative authority has sought to do 'more with less' using the budget in times of crisis will then be highlighted (section D).

[65] See Art. 8 of Council Decision (CFSP) 2017/2315 of 11 December 2017 establishing permanent structured cooperation (PESCO) and determining the list of participating Member States, OJ 2017 L 331/57.

[66] The EFSF was incorporated as a special-purpose vehicle financed by the euro area Member States in Luxembourg on 7 June 2010.

[67] Treaty establishing the ESM, Brussels, 1 February 2012.

[68] See, in particular, Joined Cases C-8/15–C-10/15, *Ledra Advertising and Others v. Commission & ECB* (EU:C:2016:70). For commentary, see Repasi, 'Court of Justice Judicial Protection against Austerity Measures in the Euro Area: Ledra and Mallis', 54(4) *CMLR* (2017) 1123; Poulou, 'The Liability of the EU in the ESM Framework', 24 *Maastricht Journal of European and Comparative Law* (2017) 126: Dermine, 'ESM and Protection of Fundamental Rights: Towards the End of Impunity?', *Verfassungsblog* (21 September 2016), https://verfassungsblog.de/esm-and-protection-of-fundamental-rights-towards-the-end-of-impunity (last visited 4 July 2024).

[69] In 2017, the Commission proposed to integrate the ESM into the Union framework on the basis of Art. 352 TFEU as a European monetary fund. See Proposal for a Council Regulation on the establishment of the European Monetary Fund, COM(2017) 827.

B. Union Borrowing

Borrowing and lending has been described by Brigid Laffan as the 'second financial arm' of the Union.[70] Beginning in the 1970s, Community legislation established borrowing and lending instruments, guaranteed by the budget, mainly to provide financial assistance to Member States enduring balance of payments difficulties, notably following the oil shock of 1973.[71] The legal bases used for the early instruments were Articles 235 of the European Economic Community (EEC) Treaty and 308 of the European Community (EC) Treaty, which correspond to today's Article 352 TFEU. The Commission was empowered to borrow on the financial markets with the benefit of the Community's triple-A credit rating, and it immediately passed on the loans to beneficiary Member States on the same terms, in what are called 'back-to-back' operations. The Member State was responsible for making repayments. The Community budget guarantee was only called upon if the Member State defaulted on its repayments.

The quantity, size, and nature of Union borrowing instruments have evolved significantly over the course of the various post-Lisbon crises. Today, a number of provisions of the Treaties expressly allow the Union to provide financial assistance, which is generally delivered in the form of loans, to stabilize the economies of Member States and third countries. The main permanent instruments of financial assistance are the Euratom loans, created by the Council on the basis of the Euratom Treaty for certain nuclear investments,[72] the Balance of Payments Facility for non-euro-area Member States,[73] established by the Council on the legal basis of Article 143 TFEU, and Macro Financial Assistance (MFA) to third countries, which is decided jointly by the European Parliament and Council on the legal basis of Article 212 TFEU.[74]

In addition, Article 122(2) TFEU allows for the provision of financial assistance to a Member State in a crisis situation. The Council acts alone, on a

[70] B. Laffan, *The Finances of the European Union* (1997) 217–244.

[71] On the history of borrowing and lending, see European Commission, *European Union Public Finance* (5th ed., 2014) 281–289; Potteau, 'L'Union européenne et l'emprunt', in V. Dussart (ed.), *Les finances communautaires à l'aube des perspectives 2007/2013* (2011) 195–232.

[72] See Council Decision 94/179/Euratom of 21 March 1994 amending Decision 77/270/Euratom to authorize the Commission to contract Euratom borrowings in order to contribute to the financing required for improving the degree of safety and efficiency of nuclear power stations in certain non-member countries, OJ 1994 L 84/41.

[73] Council Regulation (EC) 332/2002 of 18 February 2002 establishing a facility providing medium-term financial assistance for Member States' balances of payments, OJ 2002 L 53/1.

[74] See e.g. Decision (EU) 2020/701 of the EP and of the Council of 25 May 2020 on providing macro-financial assistance to enlargement and neighbourhood partners in the context of the COVID-19 pandemic, OJ 2020 L 165/31.

proposal from the Commission. In the context of the sovereign debt crisis in the euro area, this paragraph served as the legal basis for the EUR 60 billion European Financial Stabilisation Mechanism (EFSM).[75] More recently, Article 122 TFEU as a whole served as the legal basis for the regulation establishing the European instrument for temporary support to mitigate unemployment risks in an emergency (SURE), which provided up to EUR 100 billion in financial assistance to Member States to support short-time work schemes or similar measures in the context of the pandemic lockdowns.[76] Article 122 TFEU as a whole also served as the legal basis for the EU Recovery Instrument (EURI) Regulation, which is the centrepiece of the legal architecture of the NGEU recovery plan.[77]

The early borrowing and lending operations were conducted off-budget, in the sense that they were not shown in the budget and were not subject to authorization by the budgetary authority in the annual budgetary procedure. An issue that complicated the incorporation of borrowing and lending operations into the budget, and which remains relevant today, was how to categorize borrowed funds and loans in terms of revenue and expenditure, bearing in mind that the Treaties require revenue and expenditure to be in balance. The solution chosen was to conduct borrowing and lending operations off-budget. This remains the approach today.

Although the operations are off-budget, the current Financial Regulation contains various provisions concerning borrowing and lending. In particular, Article 220 of the Financial Regulation, which applies since 1 January 2021, now lays down certain horizontal rules applicable to all financial assistance.[78] According to Article 220(1), 'the Commission shall be empowered, in the relevant basic act, to borrow the necessary funds on behalf of the Union on the capital markets or from financial institutions'. The Commission must conclude an agreement with the beneficiary country containing specified provisions.[79] For the European Parliament, including such horizontally applicable requirements in the Financial Regulation is a way to gain influence over rules on the

[75] Council Regulation (EU) 407/2010 of 11 May 2010 establishing a European financial stabilisation mechanism, OJ 2010 L 118/1.

[76] Council Regulation (EU) 2020/672 of 19 May 2020 on the establishment of a European instrument for temporary support to mitigate unemployment risks in an emergency (SURE) following the COVID-19 outbreak, OJ 2020 L 159/1 (hereinafter the 'SURE Regulation').

[77] Council Regulation (EU) 2020/2094 of 14 December 2020 establishing a European Union Recovery Instrument to support the recovery in the aftermath of the COVID-19 crisis, OJ 2020 L 433I/23.

[78] A number of provisions of the 2018 Financial Regulation were stated to be applicable only as from the start of the post-2020 MFF. See Art. 282 of the Financial Regulation (n. 11).

[79] See ibid. Art. 220(5).

implementation of financial assistance that would otherwise, in many cases, be laid down in basic acts adopted by the Council alone.

The level of borrowing and lending that may be conducted under a given instrument is determined by the law-making authority in the relevant basic act. However, such basic acts are acts which are likely to have appreciable implications for the budget for the purposes of Article 310(4) TFEU. Therefore, it is also necessary to provide an assurance that the potential expenditure arising from borrowing and lending operations can be covered within the limit of the Union's own resources and in compliance with the MFF. In this way, the budgetary ceilings impose constraints on the extent to which the Union can engage in borrowing and lending.

Guarantee funds have long provided a means to ensure that the Union can, within the limits of the MFF, honour any calls on guarantees under financial assistance mechanisms for third countries. For example, MFA assistance to third countries was long backed by a Guarantee Fund for External Actions (GFEA).[80] As of 1 January 2021, the GFEA was subsumed, together with various other Union guarantee funds, into a single Common Provisioning Fund (CPF), established by Article 212 of the Financial Regulation.[81] The CPF is a pot of money, valued at around EUR 14.39 billion at the end of 2022,[82] which is permanently available to the Commission so that it can swiftly honour any calls on the guarantees for which the CPF provides coverage. The CPF is provisioned from the Union budget to a rate corresponding to a certain percentage of the corresponding contingent liabilities.[83] By adjusting provisioning rates when needed and managing risk exposures over time, it is possible to ensure that the resources needed from the Union budget remain within the amounts programmed for the CPF over the course of the MFF.

In view of the much larger risk exposures when financial assistance is provided to Member States under mechanisms like the EFSM or SURE, the CPF

[80] Council Regulation (EC, Euratom) 480/2009 of 25 May 2009 establishing a Guarantee Fund for external actions (Codified version), OJ 2009 L 145/10.

[81] Prior to this date, a number of different guarantee funds existed, including the Guarantee Fund for External Actions (ibid.) and the EFSI Guarantee Fund under Art. 12 of the Regulation (EU) 2015/1017 of the EP and of the Council of 25 June 2015 on the European Fund for Strategic Investments, the European Investment Advisory Hub and the European Investment Project Portal and amending Regulations (EU) 1291/2013 and (EU) 1316/2013—the European Fund for Strategic Investments, OJ 2015 L 169/1.

[82] See European Commission, Report from the Commission to the EP and the Council on the common provisioning fund in 2022, COM(2023) 288, at 2. See also 'Budgetary Guarantees, Common Provisioning Fund and Contingent Liabilities', Working Document Part XI accompanying the Draft Budget 2024, COM(2023) 300.

[83] For examples of recent guarantee calls and payment claims, see Report on the common provisioning fund (n. 82) 13–14. On the CPF in general, see Begg et al. (n. 9) 20–21.

is not used to support those mechanisms. Instead, Article 2(3) of the MFF Regulation provides that '[w]here it is necessary to mobilise a guarantee for financial assistance to Member States authorised in accordance with Article 220(1) of the Financial Regulation, the necessary amount shall be mobilised over and above the MFF ceilings'. If a Member State were to default on its repayments, the necessary amounts to cover the call on the Union budget guarantee would be raised through the own resources system. In practice, this would mean calling up additional GNI-based contributions from the Member States. Rather like the MFF special instruments, the expenditure would be counted outside the MFF ceilings. The limit on the amounts that could be called up as own resources is determined by the own resources payments ceiling. Therefore, the level of financial assistance that can be provided must be calculated in light of the margin available between the own resources and MFF payments ceilings, which is commonly known as the 'headroom'.

In December 2022, Article 2(3) of the MFF Regulation was amended to allow for the use of the headroom to guarantee financial assistance to Ukraine over the years 2023 and 2024.[84] This amendment accompanied the adoption of the EUR 18 billion Macro-Financial Assistance Plus (MFA+) decision for Ukraine.[85] In essence, the increased risk involved in providing large-scale MFA assistance to Ukraine in times of war necessitated the use of the headroom, instead of the more limited CPF, to back that borrowing. In June 2023, the Commission presented a proposal to create a Ukraine Facility to support the country on a longer-term basis.[86] The proposal was accompanied by a separate proposal to revise the MFF Regulation so as to enable the Union to make available up to EUR 50 billion in support to Ukraine, comprised of both grants and loans. The loans would continue to be backed by the headroom, while grants would be provided through a new MFF special instrument, to be known as the Ukraine Reserve.[87]

In cases where the available headroom is not sufficient to guarantee a proposed borrowing mechanism, the conclusion of additional bilateral guarantees with Member States provides a feasible, albeit complicated, way to increase

[84] Council Regulation (EU, Euratom) 2022/2496 of 15 December 2022 amending Regulation (EU, Euratom) 2020/2093 laying down the multiannual financial framework for the years 2021 to 2027, OJ 2022 L 325/11.

[85] Regulation (EU) 2022/2463 of the EP and of the Council of 14 December 2022 establishing an instrument for providing support to Ukraine for 2023 (macro-financial assistance +), OJ 2022 L 322/1 (hereinafter the 'MFA+ Regulation').

[86] Proposal for a Regulation of the EP and of the Council on establishing the Ukraine Facility, COM(2023) 338.

[87] Proposal for a Council Regulation amending Regulation (EU, Euratom) 2020/2093 laying down the multiannual financial framework for the years 2021 to 2027, COM(2023) 337.

the available guarantee coverage, beyond the limits of the own resources ceiling. This option was pursued in the case of SURE in 2020. Following the withdrawal of the United Kingdom from the Union in January 2020, the own resources ceiling, which is calculated as a percentage of total EU GNI, fell significantly. Pending the entry into force of a new Own Resources Decision for the period 2021–2027, with a higher own resources ceiling, there was insufficient headroom available in 2020 to guarantee the EUR 100 billion borrowing and lending under SURE. The solution was that the Commission concluded bilateral guarantee agreements with Member States to cover 25 per cent of the exposures.[88]

In December 2022, a similar approach was proposed as a possible solution to allow 26 Member States to circumvent a veto threat from Hungary, which would have blocked the urgent revision of the MFF Regulation to allow the headroom to be used to guarantee the MFA+ assistance to Ukraine. The co-legislators could adopt the MFA+ regulation by qualified majority, but the necessary revision of the MFF Regulation to enable the budgetary implementation of that assistance required a decision by unanimity. In the end, Hungary lifted its veto, and the option of a differentiated solution through 26 bilateral guarantees, which was provided for in Article 5 of the MFA+ Regulation, was not activated.

During the sovereign debt crisis in the euro area, a different solution was found to accommodate differentiation in matters of borrowing. The initial EFSM was backed by the own resources headroom, which meant that all Member States would have been liable to make additional GNI-based own resources contributions to cover any defaults under an instrument that benefited only the euro area Member States. At the insistence of the United Kingdom, which was then still a Member State, the EFSM Regulation was amended in 2015 to provide that the euro area Member States would compensate non-euro-area Member States through intergovernmental transfers in the event that their own resources contributions would ever have to be increased due to a call under the EFSM guarantee.[89]

The response to the sovereign debt crisis in the euro area from around 2009 represents perhaps the clearest example of the Member States being forced by the pressure of events to accept the need for a larger common public finance capacity at European level. Having designed the monetary union on

[88] See Art. 11 of the SURE Regulation (n. 76).

[89] See Art. 1 of Council Regulation (EU) 2015/1360 of 4 August 2015 amending Regulation (EU) 407/2010 establishing a European financial stabilisation mechanism, OJ 2015 L 210/1.

the presumption that rules would, in themselves, be sufficient to avoid sovereign debt problems, the Greek crisis and the spread of instability to other peripheral Member States prompted the establishment of financial assistance mechanisms allowing for the mobilization of hundreds of billions in European-level funds. The initial Greek Loan Facility, which was based on bilateral loans to Greece from the euro area Member States and was managed by the Commission,[90] was followed by the EUR 60 billion EFSM,[91] which was backed by the headroom. The euro area Member States subsequently established the intergovernmental EFSF, which was authorized to borrow up to EUR 440 billion, and the permanent ESM, which has a maximum lending capacity of EUR 500 billion.[92]

The Union's response to the COVID-19 health pandemic, in the form of NGEU, again entailed resorting to borrowing on the capital markets on a scale of hundreds of billions, but this time entirely within the Union's institutional framework.[93] Apart from the sheer scale of the borrowing, the core innovation of NGEU is that it allows the Union to borrow to finance operational expenditure.[94] Under NGEU, the Commission may borrow up to EUR 750 billion (in 2018 prices) and pass the proceeds through Union programmes to support the economic recovery in the Member States. Up to EUR 390 billion may be used for operational expenditure, and a further EUR 360 billion may be used for loans to Member States. All commitments had to be made before the end of 2023 and payments by the end of 2026. Borrowing is authorized by a clause in the Own Resources Decision, which also sets aside a compartment of 0.60 per cent in the own resources headroom up to the year 2058 to cover the liabilities

[90] See Eurogroup, 'Statement', Brussels (2 May 2010).

[91] On the origins and legal basis of the EFSM, see Borger, 'EU Financial Assistance', in F. Amtenbrink and C. Herrmann (eds), *The EU Law of Economic and Monetary Union* (2020) 963.

[92] On the different financial assistance mechanisms created during the sovereign debt crisis, see de Gregorio Merino, 'Legal Developments in the Economic and Monetary Union during the Debt Crisis: The Mechanisms of Financial Assistance', 49(5) *CMLR* (2012) 1613. See also Martucci, 'Non-EU Legal Instruments (EFSF, ESM, and Fiscal Compact)', in F. Amtenbrink and C. Herrmann (eds), *The EU Law of Economic and Monetary Union* (2020) 293 and Forsthoff and Aerts, 'Financial Assistance to Euro Area Members (EFSF and ESM)', in F. Amtenbrink and C. Herrmann (eds), *The EU Law of Economic and Monetary Union* (2020) 979.

[93] On the legal architecture of NGEU, see Dermine (n. 19); De Witte (n. 19); de Gregorio Merino (n. 19). See also F. Fabbrini, *EU Fiscal Capacity: Legal Integration after Covid-19 and the War in Ukraine* (2022) 69–77; Fabbrini, 'Next Generation EU: Legal Structure and Constitutional Consequences', 24 *CYELS* (2022) 45.

[94] See Lukowiak, 'Combating the COVID-19 Crisis within the European Union: A Critical Assessment of the "Next Generation EU" in the Context of the Budgetary Balance', 19(1) *Utrecht Law Review* (2023) 53; Martucci, 'La crise de la COVID-19 et le changement de paradigme financier induit par le plan de relance', in E. Dubout and F. Picod (eds), *Coronavirus et droit de l'Union européenne* (2021), 483–509; Potteau, 'Le budget de l'Union européenne à la croisée des chemins: Une crise sanitaire puis économique révélatrice et inspiratrice', *RTDE* (2020) 567.

from NGEU borrowing.[95] Borrowing must be repaid in full from the Union budget by that year.

The question of the Union's competence to borrow on the capital markets to finance operational expenditure was subject to much debate in the context of NGEU.[96] From the perspective of the Union's legislative institutions, the 0.60 per cent compartment in the own resources headroom is intended to serve as an 'asset' that counterbalances the liabilities incurred through borrowing. The irrevocable, definitive, and enforceable guarantee of payment through the own resources system provides the necessary assurance of multiannual budgetary discipline, as required by Article 310(4) TFEU.[97] Illustrating again the innovative potential of the Financial Regulation, the logic of a counterbalancing 'asset' was drawn from the precedent of Article 266(6) of the Financial Regulation, which was introduced in 2012 and provided that the Union institutions could borrow to finance the acquisition of buildings.[98] With regard to NGEU, a question remains whether it was legally necessary to include the authorization to borrow in the Own Resources Decision, or whether the authorization to borrow could be contained in the relevant basic act, as in the case of the financial assistance instruments.[99]

In practical terms, Article 4 of the Own Resources Decision anyway now states explicitly that '[t]he Union shall not use funds borrowed on capital markets for the financing of operational expenditure'. Therefore, the creation of any further 'borrowing for spending' instruments would require a revision of the Own Resources Decision to amend or derogate from this rule, just as Article 6 of the Decision creates a derogation for the '[e]xtraordinary and temporary additional means to address the consequences of the COVID-19 crisis'.

C. External Assigned Revenue

Alongside revenue from own resources, the Union budget has always received other revenue from sources such as taxes on the salaries of Union

[95] See Art. 5 of the Own Resources Decision 2020/2053 (n. 20).

[96] For critical comments, see Leino-Sandberg and Ruffert, 'Next Generation EU and Its Constitutional Ramifications: A Critical Assessment', 59(2) *CMLR* (2022) 433; Nettesheim, 'Legally Feasible, Constitutionally Dubious: Establishing "Next Generation Europe" on the Basis of EU Secondary Legislation', *Verfassungsblog* (4 December 2020), https://verfassungsblog.de/legally-feasible-constitutionally-dubious (last visited 4 July 2024).

[97] See Opinion of the Council Legal Service on the NGEU proposals, Document 9062/20 (24 June 2020), paras 38–45.

[98] See Art. 266(6) of the Financial Regulation (n. 11).

[99] See E. Blaya, 'The Future of Common Borrowing: A Legal Analysis', Notre Europe Jacques Delors Institute, Policy Paper 283 (October 2022), 27–29.

officials, contributions from third countries that participate in Union programmes, and fines imposed on companies that infringe Union competition law. Traditionally, this other revenue only accounted for about 1 per cent of total Union income.[100] However, its use has multiplied many times over recent years. The overall amount of assigned revenue in 2020, for example, was EUR 7.4 billion in commitments and EUR 9.7 billion in payments. In 2021, the amount jumped to EUR 154 billion in commitments and EUR 62.3 billion in payments, mainly made up of the proceeds of borrowing for operational expenditure under NGEU.[101]

In accordance with the principle of universality, as laid down in Article 7 of the Own Resources Decision and Article 21 of the Financial Regulation, all revenue should, as a general rule, be entered into a single pot and used without distinction to finance all expenditure entered in the budget. Exceptionally, Article 21 of the Financial Regulation allows certain categories of revenue to be assigned to finance specific items of expenditure. This may be 'internal' assigned revenue, which is generated by activities of the Union, such as revenue from the rental of buildings or equipment, or the provision of services by Union institutions or bodies, or 'external' assigned revenue, which is drawn from an external source. Most usually, external assigned revenue is contributed by an external donor, such as a Member State or a third country, for a specific item of expenditure.[102]

External assigned revenue is additional to the adopted budget. The corresponding expenditure is not counted within the MFF ceilings.[103] This makes external assigned revenue a quick and convenient way to mobilize additional funding, beyond the MFF ceilings, in response to crises. However, excessive reliance on external assigned revenue risks undermining the budgetary procedure laid down in Article 314 TFEU. The budgetary authority does not authorize and allocate external assigned revenue in the same way that it authorizes revenue drawn from own resources. Article 22(2) of the Financial Regulation provides that appropriations corresponding to external assigned revenue are made available automatically when the revenue is received,

[100] See Inghelram, 'Budget and Finances', in P. J. Kuijper et al. (eds), *The Law of the European Union* (5th ed., 2018) 115.

[101] Special Report 5/2023 (n. 39) 35.

[102] Recital 11 to the Financial Regulation of 2012 defined external assigned as 'revenue which is collected from and assigned by various donors to a specific programme or action'. See Regulation (EU, Euratom) 966/2012 of the EP and of the Council of 25 October 2012 on the financial rules applicable to the general budget of the Union and repealing Council Regulation (EC, Euratom) 1605/2002, OJ 2012 L 298/1.

[103] This is stated explicitly in recital 5 of the preamble to the MFF Regulation (n. 33).

without any decision of the budgetary authority. It is only at the end of the year, when the accounts are closed, that the amounts received are shown on the relevant budget lines. At that point, external assigned revenue is incorporated into the Commission's accounts and becomes subject to the Union's *ex post* audit and budgetary discharge procedures.

The main categories of external assigned revenue traditionally provided for in the Financial Regulation are additional Member State contributions to supplementary research programmes and certain external aid actions,[104] as well as financial contributions from third countries that participate in Union programmes, such as contributions from the European Free Trade Area (EFTA) states.[105] In addition, Article 21(5) of the Financial Regulation states that a basic act may assign the revenue for which it provides to specific items of expenditure. In such a case, the legislator may specify that the revenue should constitute external assigned revenue.

In the context of the various post-Lisbon crises, two categories of external assigned revenue have proven especially important, namely additional national contributions from the Member States and revenue provided for in a basic act that is assigned to specific purposes. These will be examined in turn.

1. Additional Member State Contributions

Article 200 of the Treaty of Rome of 1957 provided that the revenues of the Community budget would comprise 'financial contributions of Member States', fixed according to a scale set out in the same article. Article 201 of the same Treaty envisaged that the Commission would examine the possibilities to replace that system of national contributions with a system of own resources. The system of own resources was duly introduced pursuant to the first Own Resources Decision of 1970, with revenue initially drawn from own resources in the form of customs duties, agricultural levies, and a statistical VAT-based own resource.[106]

Writing in 1982, the then Director-General of the Commission's Legal Service, Claus-Dieter Ehlermann, expressed the view that, following the transition to own resources, a budget financed by national contributions would no longer satisfy the objective of budgetary autonomy that the own resources system was established to achieve.[107] In particular, he considered that, in legal

[104] See Art. 21(2)(a) of the Financial Regulation (n. 11).

[105] See ibid. Arts 21(2)(e) and 24.

[106] Council Decision (EEC, Euratom) 70/243/ECSC of 21 April 1970 on the replacement of financial contributions from Member States by the Communities' own resources, OJ 1979 L 94/19.

[107] Ehlermann (n. 30) 589.

terms, it would not be possible to categorize contributions from national budgets based on national gross national product (GNP) as own resources of the Union, since they are, in substance, national contributions.[108] Nevertheless, the GNP-based own resource (now the GNI-based own resource) was introduced in the third Own Resources Decision of 1988[109] and it now accounts for about 70 per cent of Union revenue.

Post-Lisbon, the distinction between own resources and national contributions may be considered to persist in the Treaties, insofar as certain articles still provide for expenditure to be charged to the Member States. For example, Article 332 TFEU provides that expenditure resulting from the implementation of enhanced cooperation shall, as a general rule, be borne by the participating states.[110] As mentioned previously, Article 41(2) TEU lays down special rules for CFSP operational expenditure arising from operations having military or defence implications, which shall be charged to the participating Member States.

In addition, the Financial Regulation has long allowed Member States to make additional national contributions, in the form of external assigned revenue, in two specific policy areas, namely research and external aid. This remains the case today under Article 21(2)(a) of the current Financial Regulation. In the domain of research, it has long been possible for Member States to make additional national contributions to supplementary research programmes established under what is now Article 182 TFEU.[111] In essence, this is a mechanism to facilitate differentiation in areas where individual Member States may wish to contribute additional amounts to Union actions that are of particular interest to them.

[108] Ibid. 583–589. In contrast, certain other experts of the same era, such as Professor Guy Isaac, took the pragmatic view that any categories of revenue that are definitively and automatically allocated to the Union may constitute own resources, including a GNP-based own resource. See Isaac, 'La notion de ressources propres', in G. Isaac (ed.), *Les ressources financières de la Communauté européenne* (1986). On the differing interpretations of Ehlermann and Isaac, see Potteau (n. 4) 74–79.

[109] See Art. 2(1)(d) of Council Decision (Euratom) 88/376/EEC of 24 June 1988 on the system of the Communities' own resources, OJ 1988 L 185/24. GNI replaced GNP as the basis for calculating the own resources as from the Sixth Own Resources Decision of 2007. See Art. 2(1)(c) of Council Decision (Euratom) 2007/436/EC of 7 June 2007 on the system of the European Communities' own resources, OJ L 2007 163/17.

[110] The same article provides that the expenditure can be charged to the Union budget if all members of the Council, acting unanimously after consulting the European Parliament, so decide. For an example of budgetary arrangements under enhanced cooperation, see Art. 91(7) of Council Regulation (EU) 2017/1939 of 12 October 2017 implementing enhanced cooperation on the establishment of the European Public Prosecutor's Office ('the EPPO'), OJ 2017 L 283/1.

[111] On the history of variable geometry in Community research programmes, see Tuytschaever, *Differentiation in European Union Law* (1999) 184–210.

In the domain of external aid, the possibility to make additional national contributions can be traced back to the *Bangladesh Aid* case of 1991.[112] In that case, the Court of Justice found that the Member States were not precluded, under the Treaty, from exercising their competence in the field of humanitarian aid in a collective manner to grant special aid to a third country. In that specific case, the representatives of the Member States agreed that the aid was to be administered by the Commission, the Member States' contributions were to be calculated in accordance with the standard budget contribution key, and the aid was to be incorporated into the framework of the Community's general action towards Bangladesh.[113] Nevertheless, in response to a challenge brought by the European Parliament, the Court ruled that the Member States' contributions were not items of Community revenue within the meaning of the Treaty. Moreover, the expenditure did not constitute expenditure of the Community, and so the appropriations did not fall to be authorized by the budgetary authority.[114]

Following the *Bangladesh Aid* case, the Financial Regulation was amended to introduce the express possibility for Member States to make additional contributions to external actions managed by the Commission. The contributions would take the form of what today is termed 'external assigned revenue'. Again, the contributions are not authorized by the budgetary authority in the budgetary procedure, but they are administered by the Commission as part of its implementation of the budget, in conformity with the relevant basic act and the Union's financial rules. The appropriations appear in the Commission's final accounts, whereupon they become subject to the Union's *ex post* audit and discharge procedures.

In the context of the migration crisis in the middle of the 2010s, new instruments were created that allowed for additional Member State contributions to external actions, without raising the MFF ceilings. In the first instance, an innovation of the Financial Regulation of 2012[115] was the introduction of a possibility for the Union to create trust funds for external actions, to which other donors, including Member States, could contribute. Union trust funds are situated in the title of the Financial Regulation entitled 'Other budget

[112] Joined Cases C-181/91 and C-248/91, *European Parliament v. Council and Commission* (EU:C:1993:271).

[113] See Council Press Release 6004/91, 1487th Council meeting. For an account of the factual background to the case, see Opinion of Advocate General Jacobs in Joined Cases C-181/91 and C-248/91, *European Parliament v. Council and Commission* (EU:C:1992:520), paras 2–6.

[114] Joined Cases C-181/91 and C-248/91 (n. 112), paras 30–31.

[115] See n. 102.

implementation instruments'. As budget implementation instruments, trust funds are established on the basis of a simple executive decision of the Commission. Depending on the nature of the trust fund (emergency or thematic), the budgetary authority must be consulted or give its prior approval for the establishment of the fund.[116] Third-party contributions to trust funds are managed by the Commission together with the Union contribution, although they are not, strictly speaking, treated as external assigned revenue. To date, four trust funds have been created, namely the Bêkou Trust Fund, the Madad Trust Fund, the Emergency Trust Fund for Africa, and the Trust Fund for Peace in Colombia.[117]

The Facility for Refugees in Turkey (known in institutional circles as the 'FRiT'), was established in 2015 as a coordination mechanism set up by a decision of the Commission on the legal bases, in particular, of Articles 210(2) and 214(6) TFEU.[118] These provisions allow the Commission to coordinate the actions of the Union and the Member States in the areas of development cooperation and humanitarian aid. In accordance with the initial decision establishing the FRiT, as subsequently amended, half of an overall contribution of EUR 6 billion was to be contributed by the Union budget, and the other half would be contributed by the Member States as external assigned revenue for the purposes of what is now Article 21(2)(a)(ii) of the Financial Regulation. By splitting the costs of the overall Union contribution between the Union and the Member States acting collectively, it was possible to avoid a contentious upwards revision of the MFF ceilings.

Unlike revenue raised through the own resources system, Member States cannot be compelled by the Commission to make additional external assigned revenue contributions, although the Member States may conclude an agreement among themselves on the repartition of their contributions.[119] For the programming period 2021–2027, many of the abovementioned instruments were incorporated into the NDICI–Global Europe programme,[120] which suggests that extensive recourse to additional national contributions during

[116] See Art. 234 of the Financial Regulation (n. 11).

[117] For an overview, see Lilyanova, 'Implementation of the EU Trust Funds and the Facility for Refugees in Turkey', European Parliament EPRS Briefing (March 2020).

[118] See Commission Decision C(2015) 9500 of 24 November 2015 on the coordination of the actions of the Union and of the Member States through a coordination mechanism—the Refugee Facility for Turkey, OJ 2015 C 407/8, as amended by Commission Decision of 10 February 2016 on the Facility for Refugees in Turkey amending Commission Decision C(2015) 9500 of 24 November 2015, OJ 2016 C 60/3.

[119] This was suggested, for example, in the failed Proposal for a Regulation of the EP and of the Council on the establishment of a European Investment Stabilisation Function, COM(2018) 387.

[120] See n. 10.

the migration crisis may have been a transitional phenomenon. On the other hand, the Commission recently proposed to amend the Financial Regulation to open up the possibility of receiving national contributions in the form of external assigned revenue in all policy domains, going beyond research and external development aid.[121]

2. External Assigned Revenue Provided for in a Basic Act

Article 21(5) of the Financial Regulation provides that '[a] basic act may assign the revenue for which it provides to specific items of expenditure'. Such revenue is stated to constitute internal assigned revenue unless the basic act provides otherwise. This revenue is not to be understood as a tax but as revenue generated in the implementation of a Union policy. A classical application of Article 21(5) in respect of internal assigned revenue, which is generated by the activities of the institutions, concerns the European Travel Information and Authorisation System (ETIAS). In accordance with Article 86 of the ETIAS Regulation,[122] revenue generated from the payment of travel authorization fees by users of the system is assigned, as internal assigned revenue, to cover the recurring operational and maintenance costs of the ETIAS system. In this way, the system becomes largely self-financing.

In a context of multiple crises, reliance on Article 21(5) of the Financial Regulation has increasingly come to be viewed as an efficient way to incorporate massive amounts in external assigned revenue into the Union's expenditure system, outside the MFF ceilings. In some instances, it is used to allow Member States to make top-up contributions to emergency funds, such as the Emergency Support Instrument (ESI), which was established on the legal basis of Article 122(1) TFEU and was used extensively during the COVID-19 pandemic, including for the purchase of vaccines.[123] Under the NGEU recovery plan, Article 3(1) of the EURI Regulation assigns up to EUR 390 billion from the proceeds of borrowing to different policy objectives as external assigned revenue for the purposes of Article 21(5) of the Financial Regulation. In the context of the COVID-19 pandemic, this short subparagraph, initially intended for relatively minor operations such as the assignment of ETIAS fees,

[121] See draft Art. 21(2) of the Proposal for a Regulation of the EP and of the Council on the financial rules applicable to the general budget of the Union (recast), COM(2022) 223.

[122] Regulation (EU) 2018/1240 of the EP and of the Council of 12 September 2018 establishing a European Travel Information and Authorisation System (ETIAS) and amending Regulations (EU) 1077/2011, (EU) 515/2014, (EU) 2016/399, (EU) 2016/1624 and (EU) 2017/2226, OJ 2018 L 236/1.

[123] See Art. 4(2) of Council Regulation (EU) 2016/369 of 15 March 2016 on the provision of emergency support within the Union, OJ 2016 L 70/1.

functions rather like the eye of a needle, through which hundreds of billions in external assigned revenue are squeezed into the Union's budgetary system.

Article 21(5) of the Financial Regulation is also playing an important role in the Union's response to the climate crisis. The proceeds from the sale of emissions allowances under the Emissions Trading System (ETS) established by Directive 2003/959 have long been considered a possible future own resource of the Union. In December 2022, alongside its Fit for 55 legislative package, the Commission presented a proposal to amend the Own Resources Decision to introduce new own resources based on a share of ETS revenue and on revenue from a new carbon border adjustment mechanism.[124] A share of the proceeds of ETS revenues are already used for climate transition objectives through the off-budget Modernisation Fund[125] and the Innovation Fund within the budget.[126] The creation of an ETS-based own resource is a logical next step.

As part of the Fit for 55 package, the Commission also proposed the creation of a Social Climate Fund (SCF), which would compensate those who lose out most due to the climate transition. The SCF was adopted in May 2023, with a massive financial envelope of EUR 65 billion for the period 2026–2032.[127] In addition to proposing the creation of an own resource based on a share of ETS revenue, the Commission also proposed an upwards revision of the MFF ceilings to incorporate the SCF into the MFF.[128] However, the necessary unanimity could not be obtained to adopt either proposal. Instead, the co-legislators agreed that, pending the future introduction of an ETS-based own resource, the revenue to finance the SCF will be provided by the Member States as external assigned revenue for the purposes of Article 21(5) of the Financial Regulation.[129] Article 27(4) of the SCF Regulation makes clear that the fund is 'temporarily and exceptionally financed by external assigned revenue generated from allowances of the emission trading system'. The Commission is

[124] Proposal for a Council Decision amending Decision (EU, Euratom) 2020/2053 on the system of own resources of the European Union, COM(2022) 570. The proposal was amended in June 2023 by the Amended proposal for a Council Decision amending Decision (EU, Euratom) 2020/2053 on the system of own resources of the European Union, COM(2023) 331.

[125] See Art. 10d of Directive 2003/87/EC of the EP and of the Council of 13 October 2003 establishing a scheme for greenhouse gas emission allowance trading within the Community and amending Council Directive 96/61/EC, OJ 2003 L 275/32.

[126] Ibid. Art. 10a(8).

[127] Regulation (EU) 2023/955 of the EP and of the Council of 10 May 2023 establishing a Social Climate Fund and amending Regulation (EU) 2021/1060, OJ 2023 L 130/1 (hereinafter the 'SCF Regulation').

[128] Proposal for a Council Regulation amending Regulation (EU, Euratom) 2020/2093 laying down the multiannual financial framework for the years 2021 to 2027, COM(2021) 569 (22 December 2021).

[129] See Art. 10(1) of the SCF Regulation (n. 127).

expected to present proposals to amend the regulation, should a new ETS-based own resource be introduced at a later stage.

In light of this increased reliance on external assigned revenue, the European Parliament's Committee on Budgets recently requested a group of external experts to examine its use in a comparative perspective.[130] In the first instance, the experts found it difficult to find anything similar to external assigned revenue in national budgetary systems. A somewhat analogous example they identified is the incorporation of structural funds into national budgetary systems under shared management, since these funds are also assigned from outside the jurisdiction to pursue specified policy objectives.[131] Furthermore, they issued a warning based on the experience of the United Nations (UN). Sometime in the 2000s, the amount of voluntary and earmarked contributions from member countries to UN programmes began to exceed the level of regular, assessed, contributions to the UN budget.[132] Since then, the trend has only intensified, with the result that some fear a shift in the balance of budgetary power away from the General Assembly to the benefit of the contributing countries.[133]

In the Union context, the increased use of external assigned revenue, including from additional national contributions, exacerbates a situation where the own resources system itself is already reliant on de facto national contributions. Even the Commission's latest proposals for new own resources bear some characteristics of national contributions. For example, revenue from the proposed ETS-based own resource would not accrue directly to the Union budget, but Member States would instead transfer to the Union budget an amount corresponding to a share of their national revenue from ETS emissions.[134] The Explanatory Memorandum accompanying the Commission's own resources proposal of December 2022 further states that 'a share of the revenues from the sale of carbon border adjustment mechanism (CBAM) certificates will be transferred to the EU budget as own resources in the form of a national contribution'.[135] For many in Claus-Dieter Ehlermann's generation, the notion of 'own resources in the form of a national contribution' would have been considered a contradiction in terms.[136]

[130] See Begg et al. (n. 9).
[131] Ibid. 64.
[132] Ibid. 12 and 63–64.
[133] Ibid. On the finances of the UN more generally, see M. Larhant, *Le financement de l'ONU, ou la crise permanente* (2016).
[134] See n. 124.
[135] Ibid.
[136] On the dilution of foundational concepts of Union law over time, see J. Baquero Cruz, *What's Left of the Law of Integration?: Decay and Resistance in European Union Law* (2018).

D. Doing 'More with Less'

Traditionally, the vast bulk of Union funding is delivered to beneficiaries in the form of grants, subsidies, and other forms of one-off, non-repayable, financial support.[137] Faced with tight budgetary ceilings in times of crisis, however, the Union's legislative authority has innovated with a view to maximizing the policy impact of the limited budget that is available, notably by using it to leverage additional private-sector investments. Over the course of the various post-Lisbon crises, the Union institutions have increasingly turned to modern and more complex public financing techniques, such as financial instruments and budgetary guarantees.

In particular, the flagship initiative of the Commission presidency of Jean-Claude Juncker, who entered office in late 2014, in the aftermath of the financial crisis, was to be an economic stimulus initiative in the form of a major strategic investment programme. However, the MFF for 2014–2020 had already been agreed at the end of 2013 and would cover the entire duration of his term of office, which ran from 2014 to 2019. Having been agreed in times of austerity, the MFF ceilings for that period were particularly tight. It might be expected that the creation of a major investment plan would inevitably require an upward revision of the MFF ceilings. However, government leaders made clear that a revision of the MFF was not an option. Essentially, the Juncker Commission was expected to submit a legislative proposal to create a major investment initiative, but without any fresh money.

Notwithstanding the absence of fresh funds, the Commission's services did manage to design an investment initiative worthy of the name, in the form of the European Fund for Strategic Investments (EFSI), or the 'Juncker Plan'.[138] Under the complex EFSI construction, a Union budget guarantee of EUR 16 billion, supplemented by an additional European Investment Bank (EIB) guarantee of EUR 5 billion, was used by the EIB to issue bonds and raise a total of EUR 60 billion on the capital markets. These funds were then used to make first-loss investments of up to 20 per cent of the investment capital of selected projects. By investing in those parts of projects that bore the highest risk, the plan aimed to stimulate additional private-sector investments amounting to EUR 315 billion to cover the remaining shares. In order to support the guarantee, an EFSI Guarantee Fund was created and provisioned to a level of EUR 8 billion, within the limits of the MFF, mainly using funds redeployed from

[137] Special Report 5/2023 (n. 39) 6.
[138] See n. 81.

other programmes. EFSI was extended in 2017, before being incorporated into the InvestEU programme for the 2021–2027 MFF period.[139] The EFSI Guarantee Fund has also since been incorporated into the CPF.

In 2017, the EFSI guarantee model was extended to the domain of external development assistance in the form of the European Fund for Strategic Development (EFSD).[140] The EFSD sought to incentivize additional private-sector investments in developing countries. The EFSD was incorporated into the NDICI–Global Europe programme for the MFF period from 2021 to 2027 in the form of the EFSD+.[141] More recently, in the context of the Ukraine Facility, the Commission proposed the creation of a Ukraine Investment Framework, backed by a Ukraine Guarantee, which should follow the EFSI and EFSD models to mobilize additional private-sector investments in the future reconstruction of Ukraine.[142]

Another element of innovation aimed at maximizing the impact of the Union budget in times of crisis is experimentation with new ways of delivering Union funding. A case in point is the implementation of funding through direct management with Member States, based on the achievement of milestones and targets. This innovation is being applied in the context of the Recovery and Resilience Facility (RRF), which is the main instrument through which the proceeds of borrowing under NGEU are invested in the Member States.[143] After the endorsement of national plans submitted by Member States, payments are made under the RRF based on the achievement of the pre-defined milestones and targets. The option to deliver funding rapidly in this way, rather than by traditional methods based on eligible costs under shared management, was made possible by a small but significant amendment introduced into the Financial Regulation in 2018 as Article 125(1)(a)(ii). This sub-paragraph allows Union contributions to take the form of financing not linked to costs, based on 'the achievement of results measured by reference to previously set milestones or through performance indicators'.

At the time of its adoption, few would have imagined that this small sub-paragraph would open the way for a major innovation in how Union

[139] Regulation (EU) 2021/523 of the EP and of the Council of 24 March 2021 establishing the InvestEU Programme and amending Regulation (EU) 2015/1017, OJ 2021 L 107/30.

[140] Regulation (EU) 2017/1601 of the EP and of the Council of 26 September 2017 establishing the European Fund for Sustainable Development (EFSD), the EFSD Guarantee and the EFSD Guarantee Fund, OJ 2017 L 249/1.

[141] Regulation (EU) 2021/947 (n. 10).

[142] See n. 86.

[143] Regulation (EU) 2021/241 of the EP and of the Council of 12 February 2021 establishing the Recovery and Resilience Facility, OJ 2021 L 57/17 (hereinafter the 'RRF Regulation').

contributions are delivered, being used for the delivery of hundreds of billions under the RRF. The European Parliament and the Court of Auditors have expressed concerns about their capacity to exercise budgetary control over the RRF funds delivered in this way.[144] Nevertheless, variants of the same approach will be applied to deliver funding under the SCF Regulation[145] and the European Defence Industry Reinforcement through common Procurement Act (EDIRPA).[146] The use of financing not linked to costs is also proposed by the Commission for the new Ukraine Facility.[147]

A further trend evident over the course of the various post-Lisbon crises is an increased awareness of the potential for the Union budget to function as a policy tool in itself.[148] The burgeoning academic literature on 'governing through funding' and the policy steering potential of Union funds attests to the growing importance of this topic.[149] In particular, cross-cutting and horizontal funding conditionalities have become a notable feature of Union funding legislation over the past two MFF periods.[150] For example, Article 17 of the RRF Regulation, which is a cohesion policy act, adopted on the legal basis of the third paragraph of Article 175 TFEU, requires that national RRF plans must be consistent with the country-specific recommendations issued to Member States under the European Semester process in the domain of economic policy coordination.[151] Under the Structural Funds, meanwhile, Article 15 of the Common Provisions Regulation provides for a series of horizontal and thematic 'enabling conditions' that must be respected as a prerequisite to accessing funding.[152]

Most famously, perhaps, the budget Conditionality Regulation, adopted in the context of a rule of law crisis in certain Member States, seeks to make access

[144] See European Parliament, 'Discharge Approved But MEPs Concerned over Control of EU's Recovery and Resilience Funds', Press Release (10 May 2023); European Court of Auditors, *Design of the Commission's Control System for the RRF*, Special Report 07/2023.

[145] See n. 127.

[146] Proposal for a Regulation of the EP and the Council on establishing the European defence industry Reinforcement through common Procurement Act, COM(2022) 349.

[147] See n. 86.

[148] See Fisicaro, 'Beyond the Rule of Law Conditionality: Exploiting the EU Spending Power to Foster the Union's Values', 7 *European Papers* (2022) 697.

[149] See e.g. papers of the conference 'Governing through Funding in the EU' hosted at Maastricht University on 15–16 May 2023. See also Patrin, 'Governance by Funding: NGEU, Solidarity and the EU Institutional Balance', REBUILD Centre Working Paper 4 (2023).

[150] Vita, 'Revisiting the Dominant Discourse on Conditionality in the EU: The Case of EU Spending Conditionality', 19 *CYELS* (2017).

[151] See MacIver, 'From Cooperative to Coercive Federalism? The Legislative Function under Next Generation EU and the Federal Genus of Union Law', REBUILD Working Paper 10 (June 2023).

[152] See n. 42.

to Union funding conditional on respect for the rule of law.[153] In the context of a challenge to the validity of that regulation, the Court of Justice held that the rule of law 'is capable of constituting the basis of a conditionality mechanism covered by the concept of "financial rules" within the meaning of Article 322(1)(a) TFEU'.[154]

4. Beyond the Galaxy: Towards Consolidation

A. Enhanced Coordination of Funds and Instruments

Looking beyond the current state of flux, this section examines how certain of the innovations developed in response to the various post-Lisbon crises may provide a basis for more lasting evolutions in the Union's public finance architecture. It first looks at how awareness of the benefits of coordinating the various European-level funds and instruments appears to have improved over the course of the various post-Lisbon crises and how funding is increasingly used to drive the Union's policy agenda. It then goes on to assess the future of common borrowing, which is likely to be a central issue in future reforms of the Union's finances. Finally, some observations are made on the institutional dimension of recent trends.

In contrast to the initially uncoordinated European-level policy responses to the early post-Lisbon crises, such as the sovereign debt crisis and the Syrian migration crisis, a striking feature of the more recent responses to the COVID-19 pandemic and the Russian invasion of Ukraine was the manner in which coordinated responses were quickly organized across various European-level institutions and using various different policy tools. For example, when the COVID-19 pandemic hit Europe in March 2020, the European Central Bank (ECB), the EIB, and the ESM adopted immediate measures. The Commission relaxed the state aid rules and the general escape clause of the Stability and Growth Pact was activated. In the framework of the Union budget, urgent measures were prepared to assist the Member States, including a Coronavirus Response Investment Initiative (CRII), and later

[153] Regulation (EU, Euratom) 2020/2092 of the EP and of the Council of 16 December 2020 on a general regime of conditionality for the protection of the Union budget, OJ 2020 L 433I/1 (hereinafter the 'Conditionality Regulation').

[154] Case C-156/21, *Hungary v. European Parliament and Council* (EU:C:2022:97), para. 128.

a CRII+, in cohesion policy.[155] The ESI was also mobilized on the basis of Article 122(1) TFEU.

Two years later, at the end of February 2022, there was almost a sense of déjà-vu as many similar initiatives were rolled out again or extended by the same institutions in response to the Russian invasion of Ukraine. Under the Union budget, the Cohesion's Action for Refugees in Europe (CARE), and later also CARE+, initiative relaxed certain conditions to assist Member States in supporting Ukrainian refugees.[156] Financial assistance for Ukraine was mobilized through borrowing and lending under MFA.[157] Later on, the RRF Regulation was amended by the REPowerEU Regulation so that Member States could update their national plans to take account of the changed circumstances of higher energy costs and inflation.[158]

Overall, the Union now appears better prepared to mobilize all the legal and budgetary resources at its disposal in a coordinated manner in the immediate aftermath of crises. Moreover, initiatives such as Team Europe approach in the domain of external development aid signal an understanding of the need for more permanent coordination and joined-up thinking across all the actors involved in managing European public funds in a given policy domain.[159]

Continuing the 'governing through funding' theme, the experience of the various post-Lisbon crises also served to focus attention on the extent to which the relationship between legislation and budget is not a one-way process. Recent experience shows that, in policy areas where the Union's legislative competences are weak or fragmented, such as health and defence, coordinated funding packages can be used to cluster together initiatives based on different

[155] Regulation (EU) 2020/460 of the EP and of the Council of 30 March 2020 amending Regulations (EU) 1301/2013, (EU) 1303/2013 and (EU) 508/2014 as regards specific measures to mobilise investments in the healthcare systems of Member States and in other sectors of their economies in response to the COVID-19 outbreak (Coronavirus Response Investment Initiative), OJ 2020 L 99/5.

[156] Regulation (EU) 2022/562 of the EP and of the Council of 6 April 2022 amending Regulations (EU) 1303/2013 and (EU) 223/2014 as regards Cohesion's Action for Refugees in Europe (CARE), OJ 2022 L 109/1.

[157] Decision (EU) 2022/1628 of the EP and of the Council of 20 September 2022 providing exceptional macro-financial assistance to Ukraine, reinforcing the common provisioning fund by guarantees by Member States and by specific provisioning for some financial liabilities related to Ukraine guaranteed under Decision 466/2014/EU, and amending Decision (EU) 2022/1201, OJ 2022 L 245/1.

[158] Regulation (EU) 2023/435 of the EP and of the Council of 27 February 2023 amending Regulation (EU) 2021/241 as regards REPowerEU chapters in recovery and resilience plans and amending Regulations (EU) 1303/2013, (EU) 2021/1060 and (EU) 2021/1755, and Directive 2003/87/EC, OJ 2023 L 63/1. See Fama, 'REPowerEU: Next Generation EU's Architecture beyond the Pandemic', REBUILD Centre Working Paper 6 (2023).

[159] Hodson and Howarth, '"Team Europe" or the Battle of the Banks: Explaining the Evolution of the Pan-European Development Finance Architecture', Banking on Europe Working Paper 1/2022, September 2022. See also Report from the Commission to the Council, '2022 progress report on the European Financial Architecture for Development', COM(2023) 299.

legal bases and different sources of revenue and present them as a single and coherent European policy response to the challenges of the day. In this respect, the budgetary nomenclature, whether at the level of the MFF or in the annual budget, can sometimes provide a clearer indication of the Union's current policy priorities than any reading of legal texts.

For example, in the domain of defence, the Juncker Commission presciently proposed the creation of a 'Security & Defence' heading (now Heading 5) in the nomenclature of the MFF for 2021–2027, even though the amount foreseen of just over EUR 13 billion for the seven-year period was very small in comparison with the other MFF headings. In essence, by creating a separate heading for defence, the institutions signalled their ambition to become more active in this policy area of strategic importance. In the meantime, the Russian invasion of Ukraine has prompted a plethora of funding initiatives in the domain of defence that are financed under this heading.

Towards the end of the last MFF, the Commission initiated a pilot project and then a preparatory action, without a basic act (as permitted under Article 58(2)(a) and (b) of the Financial Regulation), known as the Preparatory Action on Defence Research (PADR), to test the ground for funding defence research with the Union budget.[160] Together with the European Defence Industrial Development Programme (EDIDP),[161] PADR paved the way for the creation of a fully fledged programme in the form of the European Defence Fund,[162] established on the legal bases of Articles 173(3), 182(4), 183, and the second paragraph of Article 188 TFEU, for the new MFF for 2021–2027. The financial envelope for the European Defence Fund amounts to almost EUR 8 billion.[163]

In the meantime, the co-legislators have also adopted the EDIRPA,[164] which aims to coordinate cross-border demand in the defence industry, and an Act in Support of Ammunition Production (ASAP),[165] which aims to strengthen the supply side by supporting a ramping-up of ammunition production. Meanwhile, the Secure Connectivity programme falls to be financed under

[160] PADR funded 18 research projects that were selected following calls for proposals in the years 2017–2019.

[161] Regulation (EU) 2018/1092 of the EP and of the Council of 18 July 2018 establishing the European Defence Industrial Development Programme aiming at supporting the competitiveness and innovation capacity of the Union's defence industry, OJ 2018 L 200/30.

[162] Regulation (EU) 2021/697 of the EP and of the Council of 29 April 2021 establishing the European Defence Fund and repealing Regulation (EU) 2018/1092, OJ 2021 L 170/149.

[163] Ibid. Art. 4(1).

[164] See n. 146.

[165] Proposal for a Regulation of the EP and the Council on establishing the Act in Support of Ammunition Production, COM(2023) 237.

the same heading of the MFF,[166] as does the Military Mobility strand of the Connecting Europe Facility.[167] Just over two years into the new MFF, the margins of the new Heading 5 are nearly exhausted, and new solutions will have to be found to continue financing these initiatives. What is clear, however, is that this heading is destined to remain a permanent feature of the MFF nomenclature for a long time to come.

Turning to the domain of health, the Union has rather weak legal competences under Article 168(5) TFEU to adopt incentive measures designed to protect and improve human health. Nevertheless, following the COVID-19 pandemic, the Commission is promoting the creation of a 'European Health Union'.[168] In addition to the EU4Health programme,[169] which is adopted on the legal basis of Article 168(5) TFEU, other funding for health objectives is directed through a variety of different instruments founded on different legal bases. For example, Union support for vaccine purchases was provided on the legal basis of Article 122(1) TFEU through the ESI.[170] The proceeds of borrowing under the EURI Regulation may also be used for different public-health-related purposes, as may funds under the Health Cluster of the Horizon Europe Programme.[171] Funds also go to the health-related agencies and bodies. Vaccinations in third countries were supported under the Civil Protection Mechanism[172] and the NDICI–Global Europe programme.[173]

Overall, by drawing together the health dimension of different policies (crisis support, internal market, digital, etc.) and then giving them a significant funding boost, the Commission has managed to create something akin to a Union health policy, which is likely to endure well beyond the health pandemic.

[166] Proposal for a Regulation of the EP and of the Council establishing the Union Secure Connectivity Programme for the period 2023–2027, COM(2022) 57.

[167] Regulation (EU) 2021/1153 of the EP and of the Council of 7 July 2021 establishing the Connecting Europe Facility and repealing Regulations (EU) 1316/2013 and (EU) 283/2014, OJ 2021 L 249/38.

[168] See Commission Communication, EU Global Health Strategy: Better Health for All in a Changing World, COM(2022) 675.

[169] Regulation (EU) 2021/522 of the EP and of the Council of 24 March 2021 establishing a Programme for the Union's action in the field of health ('EU4Health Programme') for the period 2021–2027, and repealing Regulation (EU) 282/2014, OJ 2021 L 107/1.

[170] Council Regulation (EU) 2020/521 of 14 April 2020 activating the emergency support under Regulation (EU) 2016/369, and amending its provisions taking into account the COVID-19 outbreak, OJ 2020 L 117/3.

[171] Regulation (EU) 2021/695 of the EP and of the Council of 28 April 2021 establishing Horizon Europe—the Framework Programme for Research and Innovation, laying down its rules for participation and dissemination, and repealing Regulations (EU) 1290/2013 and (EU) 1291/2013, OJ 2021 L 170/1.

[172] Regulation (EU) 2021/836 of the EP and of the Council of 20 May 2021 amending Decision 1313/2013/EU on a Union Civil Protection Mechanism, OJ 2021 L 185/1.

[173] See n. 10.

Other illustrations of policy priorities being shaped through funding include the commitment of the Union institutions in the budgetary IIA to promote the climate transition through the 30 per cent climate-related expenditure target for the 2021–2027 programming period,[174] or to respect targets for biodiversity-related expenditure,[175] or to strengthen gender budgeting.[176] The revenue side of the budget is now also used to promote policy objectives, for example in the way the non-recycled plastics-based own resource incentivizes the recycling of plastics.[177]

B. The Future of Common Borrowing

The two main sources of additional financing relied upon by the Union over the course of recent crises, outside the system of own resources, were off-budget borrowing and external assigned revenue. In the longer term, the possibility to receive additional funds in the form of external assigned revenue can continue to serve a useful purpose, for example, in allowing third countries to contribute to Union programmes. However, a long-term financing of Union activities through external assigned revenue coming from additional national contributions or from, for example, the substantial proceeds of ETS allowances, would undermine the integrity of the budgetary system provided for in the Treaties.

Common borrowing, meanwhile, appears destined to remain a permanent feature of the Union's finances, though on what scale and according to what design remains unclear. Instruments such as the Balance-of-Payments Facility and MFA have existed for decades and are likely to endure. Crisis instruments like SURE, NGEU, and the MFA+ assistance to Ukraine were adopted as temporary measures in response to exceptional circumstances, but their budgetary consequences will endure for decades. Moreover, there will certainly be other crises in the future, and borrowing is again likely to form part of the Union's response.

In this respect, the Commission has used the implementation of the large-scale NGEU borrowing to strengthen its expertise, technical capacities, and organizational structures in matters of debt management.[178] A recent, and

[174] See point 16(d) of the budgetary IIA of 16 December 2020 (n. 49).
[175] Ibid. point 16(e).
[176] Ibid. point 16(f).
[177] See Art. 2(2) of Council Decision 2020/2053 (n. 20). See also Neumeier, 'Political Own Resources: Towards a Legal Framework', 60(2) *CMLR* (2023) 319.
[178] See Malůšková, 'Implementation of NGEU Borrowing, Debt Management and Lending Operations', 23 *ERA Forum* (2023) 463.

little-noticed, revision of the Financial Regulation opened up new possibilities in this regard. As part of the package of measures to facilitate the provision of MFA+ assistance to Ukraine in December 2022, the Financial Regulation was amended to introduce a new Article 220a on a 'Diversified funding strategy'.[179] In accordance with this strategy, which builds on the debt management strategy already developed under NGEU, the Commission should aim 'at a regular capital market presence', and the strategy should 'be based on pooling of funding instruments and shall make use of a common liquidity pool'.[180]

In essence, the diversified funding strategy breaks the link between borrowing and disbursements.[181] Pursuant to the traditional back-to-back approach, the Union borrowed for the sole purpose of financing a specific disbursement to a specific beneficiary under a specific borrowing instrument. Now, the Commission can issue single, EU-branded, bonds to raise financing for NGEU and the various different financial assistance mechanisms. This gives the Commission more freedom to manage the issuances and disbursements as it thinks fit, depending on market conditions.[182] The enhanced liquidity of Union debt that results from this new strategy should make Union bonds more attractive to investors, which, in turn, has an impact on the costs of borrowing.

In this latter regard, investors currently perceive Union bonds as belonging in the Supranational, Sub-sovereign and Agencies (SSA) space of the bond market, where it enjoys almost identical credit ratings to other supranational issuers, such as the ESM. If the Union were instead to be treated as a sovereign issuer, its borrowing costs could be significantly reduced, saving tens of billions under the Union borrowing instruments.[183] It should be stressed, of course,

[179] Regulation (EU, Euratom) 2022/2434 (n. 12).

[180] Ibid. See also Commission Implementing Decision of 19 December 2022 establishing the arrangements for the administration and implementation of the EU borrowing and debt management operations under the diversified funding strategy and related lending operations, C(2022) 9700.

[181] See Malůšková (n. 178).

[182] See Commission Implementing Decision (EU, Euratom) 2022/2544 of 19 December 2022 establishing the arrangements for the administration and implementation of the EU borrowing and debt management operations under the diversified funding strategy and related lending operations, C(2022) 9700, OJ 2022 L 328/109. See also the Commission's 'High Level Risk and Compliance Policy', published on 3 July 2023.

[183] See Claeys, McCaffrey, and Welslau, 'EU Borrowing Costs: Drivers and Dynamics in Times of Rising Interest Rates', European Parliament, DG IPOL Briefing (May 2023); Bonfanti and Garicano (2022) 'Do Financial Markets Consider European Common Debt a Safe Asset?', *Bruegel blog* (8 December 2022), https://www.bruegel.org/blog-post/do-financial-markets-consider-european-common-debt-safe-asset (last accessed 4 July 2024). In December 2022, the ECB decided to treat EU bonds in the same way as bonds issued by governments and central banks under its risk control framework. See ECB, 'ECB Reviews Its Risk Control Framework for Credit Operations', Press Release (20 December 2022).

that the amount of borrowing must always remain within the limits laid down in the relevant basic act. Following the introduction of the diversified funding strategy, an annual borrowing decision determines the overall limits on borrowing for the year in question. For 2023, for example, the Commission may borrow up to EUR 170 billion for long-term funding and up to EUR 60 billion for short-term funding.[184]

Alongside the increased borrowing and lending activity of the Union over recent years, the Financial Regulation has also been revised to require the inclusion of more information on borrowing and lending operations in the budget. The Financial Regulation requires that the budget lines for budgetary guarantees must be accompanied by remarks 'giving reference to the basic act and the volume of the operations envisaged, the duration and the financial guarantee provided by the Union'.[185] A document annexed to the Commission's section of the budget must also indicate the 'ongoing capital operations and debt management'. The Commission must also annex to its draft budget a working document setting out detailed information on borrowing and lending operations, including 'an assessment of the sustainability of the contingent liabilities borne by the budget arising from budgetary guarantees or financial assistance'.[186]

These transparency requirements fall well short of the full 'budgetization' of borrowing and lending, which has been resisted in light of the principle of budgetary balance. However, considering the massively increased volume of borrowing and lending over recent years, it may be time to revisit this issue. In fact, on 15 June 1978, the Commission—with Mr Ehlermann at the head of its Legal Service—presented a proposal to amend the Financial Regulation to 'budgetize' all borrowing and lending operations.[187] Under that proposal, borrowing and lending operations would have been entered in a new Part II of the budget. The Commission considered this necessary in order to respect the requirement in Article 199 EEC (now Article 310(1) TFEU) that 'all items of revenue and expenditure ... shall be shown in the budget'. Under the proposal, the proceeds of borrowing would have been regarded as equivalent to revenue, and loans would have been treated as expenditure.

[184] See Art. 1(1) of Commission Implementing Decision of 19 December 2022 establishing the framework for EU borrowing and debt management operations in 2023 under the diversified funding strategy, C(2022) 9702.

[185] See Art. 52(1)(d)(ii) of the Financial Regulation (n. 11).

[186] Ibid. Art. 41(5)(j).

[187] Proposal for a Council Regulation amending the Financial Regulation applicable to the General Budget of the European Communities, OJ C 160 (6 July 1978) 11. For further information on the history of this debate, see Strasser (n. 21) 100–108 and 317–322; and Vitsentzatos, 'Loans and Guarantees in the European Union Budget', 15(1) *ERA Forum* (2014) 131.

More specifically, the annual planned amounts of borrowing and lending operations and the expected annual repayment instalments (principal and interest) would have been entered in the new Part II of the budget. The adoption of the budget would have constituted authorization to the Commission to borrow (within the limits fixed by the basic act), to lend the funds thus received, and to make the annual amortization payments in respect of the principal, interest, and expenses. Any authorizations entered in Part II of the budget that were unused at the end of the financial year would have been carried forward automatically to the following year. This proposal was warmly welcomed by the European Parliament[188] but was ignored by the Council and, over the decades, even appears to have been forgotten by the Commission.

More broadly, the experience of the past decade of crises suggests that the Union could benefit from having a permanent tool at its disposal that would allow it to raise additional funds from the capital markets to address crisis situations and new challenges. In a recent speech in Massachusetts, former ECB President Mario Draghi expressed the view that the Union is increasingly confronted with 'common, imported shocks', such as the COVID-19 pandemic, the Russian war on Ukraine, and the energy crisis, which affect Member States in a symmetric manner, rather than the 'asymmetric, self-inflicted ones' that characterized the sovereign debt crisis.[189] In his view, this 'shifts the problem from supporting struggling states towards addressing shared challenges'.[190] Faced with many shared supranational goals, including the climate transition, a geopolitical transition, defence, and enlargement to Ukraine, Draghi argues for an expansion of the central Union budget 'to deliver specific goals in the public interest'.[191]

In his view, the increased central spending should be financed by issuing more common debt. However, he does not discuss the legal mechanics by which this could occur. In principle, the NGEU model could be replicated to respond to further crises, provided the legal conditions for its creation are satisfied and the necessary unanimity in the Council exists, but this would be another temporary mechanism.[192] The idea of creating some form of Union debt

[188] See e.g. EP Resolution on the draft general budget of the European Communities for the financial year 1981 (Section III—Commission), OJ 1980 C 313/39, paras 24–27.

[189] M. Draghi, 'The Next Flight of the Bumblebee: The Path to Common Fiscal Policy in the Eurozone', 15th Annual Feldstein Lecture, National Bureau of Economic Research, Washington (11 July 2023), https://www.nber.org/lecture/2023-15th-annual-feldstein-lecture-mario-draghi-next-flight-bumblebee-path-common-fiscal-policy (last visited 24 January 2024).

[190] Ibid.

[191] Ibid.

[192] On prospects for an NGEU 2.0, see Fabbrini *EU Fiscal Capacity* (n. 93) 137, 143.

agency, which would be empowered to borrow with the backing of its own capital to support Union initiatives, is also discussed.[193] In 2017, the Commission presented a legislative proposal to incorporate the ESM into the Union framework as a European Monetary Fund, established on the legal basis of Article 352 TFEU, which could be a candidate to perform such a role.[194]

Another option could be to look again at the Own Resources Decision. Could the proceeds of borrowing backed by the Union budget be made an own resource of the Union, functioning as a sort of new last resort resource, within strict limits (possibly including a debt ceiling), to be laid down in the Own Resources Decision? In its legal opinion on NGEU, the Council's Legal Service expressed the view, in a footnote, that the proceeds of borrowing cannot be an own resource, since they constitute a liability that must be repaid, and so they are not allocated to the Union in a final and definitive manner.[195] However, as recalled previously, there is no definition of own resources in Union law, and this matter remains open to debate. Aymeric Potteau, for example, has queried whether the Council Legal Service's view is not overly strict, bearing in mind that the principal objective of the transition to own resources is precisely to make the Union budget autonomous from the national budgets.[196] As Federico Fabbrini says of NGEU, it 'endows the EU with a fiscal capacity independent from state transfers, and suitable to invest on EU programmes to promote EU public goods.'[197] This should also be the purpose of an own resource.

Of course, from a legal perspective, the cleanest way to create a permanent borrowing instrument would be through a revision of the Treaties. The controversies surrounding the legality of borrowing for operational expenditure under NGEU (as illustrated, for example, by the sceptical tone of the recent judgment of the German Federal Constitutional Court)[198] suggest that a revision of the Treaties to create an explicit legal basis for borrowing would bring a great deal of clarity. Obviously, obtaining the necessary unanimity in the Council and securing national ratifications would not be an easy process.

[193] Amato et al., 'Creating a Safe Asset without Debt Mutualisation: The Opportunity of a European Debt Agency', (2022) Centre for Economic Policy Research Discussion Paper 17217.

[194] See n. 69.

[195] See n. 97, 24, fn. 39.

[196] Potteau (n. 94) 675.

[197] Fabbrini, 'Europe's Economic & Monetary Union beyond Covid-19', Report for the Irish Department of Finance (December 2020).

[198] Judgment of 6 December 2022, 2 BvR 547/21, 2 BvR 798/21. See BVefrG, 'Constitutional complaints challenging the Act Ratifying the EU Own Resources Decision ('EU Recovery Package') unsuccessful', Press Release 103/2022 of 6 December 2022.

C. Institutional Considerations

Following the Treaty of Lisbon, legislation establishing almost all Union funding programmes, including in the major 'spending' policy domains of agriculture and cohesion, is adopted in accordance with the ordinary legislative procedure. As a result, the European Parliament and the Council, acting by more or less the same majorities (at least at first reading), decide jointly, as budgetary authority, on the allocation of resources to funding programmes, and, as legislative authority, on the policy objectives and eligibility criteria for beneficiaries to access funding under those programmes. Legislative and budgetary implementation and scrutiny then run in parallel. At all stages, the democratic guarantees laid down in the Treaties apply, such as the requirements for the institutions to deliberate and vote in public. The scheme of dual democratic representation referred to in Article 10(2) TEU is duly respected.

However, the neat symmetry in the composition of the Union's legislative and budgetary authorities tends to break down when recourse is made to extra-budgetary sources of financing, with the result that the role of the European Parliament is diminished. In the context of recent crises, the Parliament has sometimes had to leverage either its legislative or budgetary powers, as appropriate, to compensate for the limitations on its powers on the other side of the legislative and budgetary dualism. For example, the Parliament has no formal role in the adoption of legal acts on the basis of Article 122 TFEU, but it relied on its budgetary prerogatives in the context of the NGEU negotiations to insist on the creation of a new procedure of budgetary scrutiny for future proposals presented on that legal basis, having appreciable implications for the budget.[199] That procedure, which was activated for the first time in February 2021 in respect of the Health Emergency Preparedness and Response (HERA) initiative,[200] grants the Parliament at least a modicum of influence in situations where it would otherwise have been entirely excluded.

On other occasions, Parliament's legislative powers are used to compensate somewhat for its lack of influence on the budgetary side. It is no surprise, for example, that MFA decisions concerning off-budget financial assistance to third countries, which are adopted under the ordinary legislative procedure,

[199] Joint declaration of the EP, the Council and the Commission on budgetary scrutiny of new proposals based on Article 122 TFEU with potential appreciable implications for the Union budget, OJ 2020 C 444I/5.

[200] Council Regulation (EU) 2022/2372 of 24 October 2022 on a framework of measures for ensuring the supply of crisis-relevant medical countermeasures in the event of a public health emergency at Union level, OJ 2022 L 314/64.

include stricter requirements on reporting to the Parliament than do the EFSM or SURE Regulations or other acts adopted by the Council acting alone.[201] In the case of NGEU, meanwhile, the Parliament had no role in deciding on the overall amount of the borrowing, which was fixed by the Council alone in the Own Resources Decision and the EURI Regulation, but it did co-legislate with the Council on the breakdowns of expenditure set out in the sectoral legislative financial envelopes, on the conditions for the use of those funds, and on the rules governing their implementation.[202]

When it comes to external assigned revenue, the Parliament's role is more diminished on the budgetary side, where it has no power to authorize the revenue. However, many legislative acts that provide for external assigned revenue, such as the SCF Regulation, are adopted under the ordinary legislative procedure. This means the Parliament is complicit in the decision to resort to that source of revenue. The Parliament was also co-legislator for other acts that expanded the budgetary galaxy, such as, for example, the regulation establishing the banking union's Single Resolution Fund, which is financed from outside the own resources system.[203] The Parliament is also complicit in granting implementing powers on funding-related matters to the Council under acts such as the RRF Regulation[204] and the Conditionality Regulation.[205] The Parliament is, of course, a very diverse institution, and there may be very different motivations behind the votes cast by its Members on given files, but the political imperative to secure additional funds from the Member States as part of package deals in times of crisis appears to be at least one factor contributing to the Parliament's acquiescence in such choices.

If the symmetrical composition of the legislative and budgetary authorities can be considered a sort of ideal-type decision-making constellation to aspire to, then it may be useful to reflect on the steps that could be taken to minimize the deviations from it. On the legislative side, the use of legal bases that exclude the Parliament, such as Article 122 TFEU, for the adoption of measures having appreciable implications for the budget should be restricted to what is absolutely necessary. On the budgetary side, a full budgetization of

[201] See e.g. Art. 15 of the MFA+ Regulation (n. 85).

[202] See Fasone, 'Fighting Back? The Role of the European Parliament in the Adoption of Next Generation EU', 28 *Journal of Legislative Studies* (2022) 3, 368.

[203] Regulation (EU) 806/2014 of the EP and of the Council of 15 July 2014 establishing uniform rules and a uniform procedure for the resolution of credit institutions and certain investment firms in the framework of a Single Resolution Mechanism and a Single Resolution Fund and amending Regulation (EU) 1093/2010, OJ 2014 L 225/1.

[204] See n. 143.

[205] See n. 153.

borrowing and lending operations, as proposed by the Commission in 1978, would grant the Parliament and Council joint powers as budgetary authority to authorize those operations and control their implementation. Furthermore, the Financial Regulation could also be amended to strengthen the role of the budgetary authority in respect of external assigned revenue, which is a creature of that regulation.

Of course, a major factor in the weaker position of the Parliament in budgetary matters is the deliberate choice of the authors of the Treaties to provide that the Council alone should adopt the Own Resources Decision and the MFF Regulation. Nevertheless, it can be recalled that Article 312(2) TFEU includes a *passerelle* clause that could allow a shift to qualified majority voting for the MFF. It may seem unlikely that Member States would ever agree to activate this *passerelle* in such a sensitive domain, but the antics of certain government leaders who hold urgent MFF revisions hostage for unrelated political reasons and the prospect of enlargement to over 30 Member States in the years ahead might, at some point, prompt a reconsideration of the issue.

Furthermore, several apparent distortions of the institutional balance in matters of funding are linked to the way the MFF is currently organized. For example, the package nature of the MFF deal results in legislative matters that formally fall to be adopted by qualified majority becoming subject to a de facto requirement of unanimity, since the legislative financial envelopes must be aligned with the overall budgetary ceilings.[206] Unblocking the necessary unanimity among governments in the MFF negotiations invariably also requires a political deliberation at the level of the European Council, which then issues detailed conclusions also covering matters falling under the ordinary legislative procedure.[207] In strictly legal terms, the 'political will' of the European Council does not bind the legislative institutions with regard to the contents of legislative acts.[208] However, the dominant influence of the European Council over the major decisions in the MFF process, and most especially the levels of the ceilings, is obvious.[209] Moreover, in the case of the MFF for 2014–2020, the rigid ceilings laid down by the Council for seven years in late 2013 ended up binding a democratically elected Parliament and Commission for the entire duration of their mandates, from late 2014 to 2019.

[206] A point stressed by Julio Baquero Cruz of the Commission's Legal Service at the REBUILD Centre Launch Conference, Dublin City University, 24–25 February 2022.

[207] On the role of the European Council in the pandemic, see Schramm and Wessels, 'The European Council as a Crisis Manager and Fusion Driver: Assessing the EU's Fiscal Response to the COVID-19 Pandemic', 45(2) *Journal of European Integration* (2023) 257; J. Werts, *The European Council in the Era of Crises* (2021).

[208] C-5/16, *Poland v. European Parliament and Council* (EU:C:2018:483), paras 83–90.

[209] On the role of the European Council in NGEU, see De Witte (n. 19) 667–674.

There are no easy solutions for some of these issues, but it should be borne in mind that the seven-year MFF programming model that has been applied for decades now is not cast in stone. It is possible to imagine doing things differently, within the constraints of the Treaties. For example, the structure and duration of the MFF could be reconsidered, notably to align its duration better with the Union's electoral cycle.[210]

5. Conclusion

The Convention on the Future of Europe of 2002–2003, which elaborated many of the reforms that were later incorporated into the Treaty of Lisbon, aimed to establish a lasting constitutional settlement for the Union and thereby bring an end to a period of constitutional 'flux' that had begun with the Single European Act.[211] However, the entry into force of the Treaty of Lisbon coincided with the start of a new era of flux in the Union's public finances. Moreover, that flux shows few signs of abating. Each fresh crisis exposes the limitations of the current budgetary system, while also prompting innovations that may have lasting consequences for the future of the system itself and, potentially, for the Union more generally.

In effect, the pressure of events is obliging the Union institutions and the Member States to pool ever greater volumes of shared resources at European level in order to pursue common policy objectives. However, whether for reasons of political will, convenience, or due to legal constraints, those resources are not always mobilized through the own resources system and within the framework of the MFF. Nevertheless, the experience of the past decade shows that, one way or another, the Union is capable of finding ways to mobilize massive amounts of resources in response to crises, even if it means resorting to extra-budgetary means. The institutions have also innovated to seek ways to do 'more with less' using the Union budget.

Looking to the future, the challenges facing the Union are not diminishing. In fact, it is likely that the demand for resources at European level will only

[210] On the duration of the MFF, see De Feo, 'The Multiannual Financial Framework 2021–2027: Ambition or Continuity?', in B. Laffan and A. De Feo (eds), *EU Financing for the Next Decade. Beyond the MFF 2021–2027 and the Next Generation EU* (2020) 1–14, at 10–12. See also the discussion in Fasone and Lupo, 'The Union Budget and the Budgetary Procedure', in R. Schütze and T. Tridimas (eds), *Oxford Principles of European Union Law, Volume I: The European Union Legal Order* (2018) 809–846, at 826.

[211] As suggested by Professor T. Tridimas at a conference entitled 'The Legal Implications of EU Enlargement' hosted at the Academy of European Law (ERA) in Trier on 26–27 April 2004 (from author's notes).

increase, not least in view of further enlargement. An obvious solution to overcome much of the fragmentation in the Union's finances that has resulted from the crises of the past decade would be to abandon the traditional expenditure limit of around 1 per cent of EU GNI and significantly raise the budgetary ceilings. However, permanently increasing expenditure at European level inevitably has an impact, one way or another, on the resources available at national level. As Mario Draghi recently suggested, any reform aimed at increasing spending through the central Union budget should be accompanied by a fundamental reform of the Union fiscal rules applicable to national budgets, with the aim 'to make use of our fiscal space more effectively'.[212] A holistic approach to reform of the fiscal rules, the own resources system, the MFF, and the rules governing Union borrowing could hold much promise.

Draghi also proposed a revision of the Treaties as part of what he terms a 'rethinking of where fiscal powers should reside'.[213] As he puts it, '[t]he starting point of any future Treaty change must be the acknowledgement of the increasing number of shared goals and the need to finance them together, which in turn necessitates a different form of representation and centralised decision-making'. A revision of the Treaties would certainly open up new possibilities in that regard. However, the wide margin of discretion that the current Treaties already afford the institutions in the design of the Union's budgetary system should not be overlooked. The rigid budgetary ceilings under the current Own Resources Decision and MFF Regulation are blunt instruments that can sometimes obscure the fact that these acts, together with the horizontal financial rules laid down in the Financial Regulation, may also be used in more imaginative ways to shape the budgetary system differently, without revising the Treaties.

Furthermore, it is striking that more than 50 years after the adoption of the first Own Resources Decision, the Union still lacks the budgetary autonomy that was intended for it by the authors of the Treaties, as a complement to the autonomy of its legal order. The Council's hesitant approach to the implementation of the 'Roadmap' for the introduction of new own resources that was agreed as part of the NGEU package, notably with a view to covering the costs of repaying the NGEU debt, suggests that the Member States are still not prepared to take own resources seriously.[214] Meanwhile, maintaining the 1 per cent of EU GNI expenditure limit without addressing the need for new sources

[212] Draghi (n. 189).
[213] Ibid.
[214] See Annex II to the budgetary IIA of 16 December 2020 (n. 49).

of revenue to cover the NGEU repayments would greatly complicate the negotiations on future MFFs. The post-Lisbon era of crises has been characterized by much innovation and even positive consolidation in matters of public finance at Union level, but the rigid MFF model carried over from the pre-Lisbon era continues to restrict the Union's capacity to act.

A common refrain after the fall of the communist regimes of central and Eastern Europe in 1989 was that Europe would finally be able to breathe with both of its lungs, East and West.[215] In the post-Lisbon era, if the Union is to exploit its policy competences to the full and assert the strategic autonomy, or even sovereignty, that some now advocate for it, then it must be able to breathe more freely and autonomously with both its legislative and budgetary lungs. The crises of the past decade have exposed this need and have given rise to various innovations that may, over time, lead to lasting consolidation around a new European public finance architecture more suited to the challenges of our times.

[215] This analogy was frequently used, in particular, by Pope John Paul II. See e.g. his Address on the European Construction delivered to the European Parliament in Strasbourg on 11 October 1988, where he speaks of the Slavic peoples as 'the other "lung" of our common European homeland'.

3

The Politics of European Union Funding

Time for Treaty Change?

*Johannes Lindner and Thu Nguyen**

1. Introduction

European Union (EU) budgetary politics is characterized by stability and path dependence in terms of institutional set-up and distributive order. Although the 2021–2027 Multiannual Financial Framework (MFF) did not fundamentally break with this pattern, it did introduce significant innovations in terms of financing and instruments that, while temporary in nature, may have the potential to durably alter the EU budget and its processes: these are large-scale issuances that will need to be repaid from 2028 onwards and that come with a new system of governance that provides EU financing to Member States in return for fulfilling national investment and reform plans; there is also a link to the compliance with a rule of law framework and an increased own resources ceiling with the commitment to introduce new own resources.

While these innovations were a reaction to the COVID-19 pandemic, the context in which the EU budget is placed has evolved in recent years as successive crises have changed the nature of the EU and raised expectations that the EU should provide effective measures to address common challenges.[1] When taking office in 2019, the EU Commission under President Ursula von der Leyen made the green transition and digital transformation key projects for EU action. Since the end of the pandemic, demands for the EU to take on new tasks have been further intensified by Russia's invasion of Ukraine and the resulting tectonic geo-economic and geopolitical changes. Such new tasks and instruments would imply further spending from the EU budget at a time when,

* Comments from Alfredo DeFeo, Miriam Hartlapp, Markus Jachtenfuchs, Claire Kilpatrick, and Eulalia Rubio are very gratefully acknowledged.

[1] J. Hillje and C. Pütz, 'Selbstverständlich europäisch!? Erwartungen der Bürgerinnen und Bürger an die deutsche Europapolitik im Kontext von Krise und Transformation', study by the Heinrich-Böll-Stiftung (2023).

Johannes Lindner and Thu Nguyen, *The Politics of European Union Funding*. In: *New Frontiers of EU Funding*.
Edited by: Claire Kilpatrick and Joanne Scott, Oxford University Press. © Johannes Lindner and Thu Nguyen 2024.
DOI: 10.1093/oso/9780198940319.003.0003

from 2028 onwards, the EU will have to start repaying the money it had borrowed from the capital markets.

When pitting these new demands and realities against the constraints set by the current procedures and practices of EU budgetary decision-making, the question of significant institutional change, including Treaty reform, arises. We assess this question by drawing on the conceptional and empirical work by Enderlein and colleagues in 2005, which dates from the time the most recent debate on reforming the relevant Treaty provisions took place. While in 2005 the budgetary decision-making seems to have been in sync with the state of political integration and provided an appropriate balance between efficiency and legitimacy concerns, as argued by Enderlein and colleagues, we contend that this is no longer the case today. In dealing with a succession of crises, the nature of the EU has changed. Political integration has further advanced since 2005, and expectations for the EU to act jointly have increased. This provides the scope for justifying and making significant institutional reforms to enhance the efficiency and legitimacy of EU budgetary decision-making.

2. The Conceptual Approach

The 2005 paper by Henrik Enderlein, Johannes Lindner, Oscar Calvo-Gonzalez, and Raymond Ritter[2] provides a useful conceptual starting point for this chapter, as their research question is very similar to our own: how much scope is there for institutional reform in the budgetary sphere? At that time, the Sapir Report had underlined the case for a different EU budget,[3] and the Convention for drafting a Constitutional Treaty provided the occasion to discuss whether institutional reform was not the means to liberate the EU budget from its limits and rigidities. In fact, the project of writing the 2005 paper originated from an initiative by the then Executive Board Member of the European Central Bank, Tommaso Padoa-Schioppa, who had played an important role in the creation of the euro. As a convinced European and convincing intellectual, he asked Henrik Enderlein and his colleagues to write a paper that would ideally make the case for far-reaching reforms. In this respect, the result was disappointing as the paper comes, unexpectedly, to a different

[2] H. Enderlein et al., 'The EU Budget—How Much Scope for Institutional Reform?', European Central Bank Occasional Paper Series 27 (2005).

[3] A. Sapir et al., 'An Agenda for a Growing Europe—Making the EU Economic System Deliver', report of an independent high-level study group established on the initiative of the President of the European Commission (2003) (hereinafter the 'Sapir Report'.

conclusion in that it argues that the 'institutional design corresponds by and large to an equilibrium between all the actors involved' and that '[a]ltering that equilibrium would require a shift in the level of integration'.[4]

The authors make two important claims: first, the state of political integration constrains the scope for institutional reform in the field of budgetary politics, and second, the rules and procedures for EU budgetary decision-making constitute an equilibrium where there is little scope for improvement under the current state of integration.

This equilibrium and the scope for improvement are measured in terms of efficiency and legitimacy. The authors describe efficiency of a budgetary procedure 'as the timely and flexible allocation of resources in order to ensure the appropriate provision of the main public goods required', and they see legitimacy as being derived 'from the degree of democratic control by citizens so that resources are allocated according to the will of the people and that any kind of "rent-seeking" is minimised'.[5] To illustrate these two concepts, one could view efficiency-enhancing reforms as ones that, for example, strengthen the role of the European Commission and the flexibility with which it can allocate resources. Legitimacy-enhancing reforms would be ones that, for example, give the EP a stronger role.

The state of 'political integration' as a constraining factor for institutional reform is described as a 'meta-level' that 'not only overarches but also determines decision-making in the different policy fields of the EU'.[6] While never fully spelled out by the authors, the concept of political integration seems to combine three aspects: first, the overall institutional architecture of the Union and the degree to which other policy fields are integrated, and what types of instruments are used to achieve that (i.e. coordination, regulation, and funding); second, the expectations that citizens and political actors have regarding what the EU should actually do and provide; and third, that citizens and political actors have a sense of belonging to the EU and embrace their European identity, as well as a correspondingly inclusive national identity. Of course, these elements are interrelated.

In describing the constraining impact of political integration, the authors do not distinguish between the normative and positive dimensions. Predominantly, the focus seems to be on the positive dimension when they conclude, 'Given that neither the European Convention nor the IGC

[4] See Enderlein et al. (n. 2) 25.
[5] Ibid. 6.
[6] Ibid. 8.

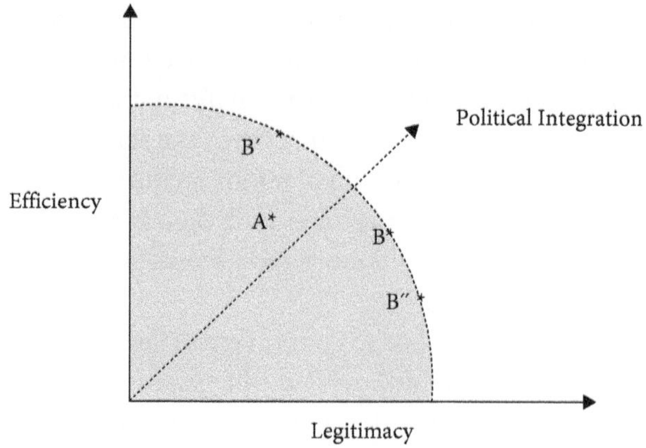

Figure 3.1 The relationship between efficiency and legitimacy
Source: Reproduced from Henrik Enderlein, Johannes Lindner, Oscar Calvo-Gonzalez, and Raymond Ritter, 'The EU Budget: How Much Scope for Institutional Reform?', ECB Occasional Paper Series No. 27/April, 10, Figure 1. Copyright (©) European Central Bank, Frankfurt am Main, Germany. Readers can find the original figure free of charge at https://www.ecb.europa.eu/pub/pdf/scpops/ecbocp27.pdf.

[Intergovernmental Conference] focused on questions related to the general state of political integration, it is not surprising that the calls for far-reaching reforms of the EU budgetary procedure did not result in the desired institutional change.'[7] At the same time, they do not explain how precisely the constraining impact was felt or articulated in the negotiations during the Convention and the Intergovernmental Conference. This corresponds with the more normative nature of the claim: further institutional reform seems to have not been desirable given the state of political integration.

The authors illustrate the relationship between efficiency and legitimacy and the role of political integration in Figure 3.1. Possible institutional arrangements for adopting the EU budget will have both a legitimacy and an efficiency dimension. Solutions are limited by a 'Pareto frontier' determined and constrained by the state of integration. At the frontier, there is a trade-off between legitimacy and efficiency.

Figure 3.1 also illustrates the authors' second claim, namely the limited scope for improvement. The authors argue that the EU budgetary rules and procedures can be depicted as point B, right at the 'Pareto frontier'. This means that there could be ways to increase legitimacy or efficiency, but not both at the same time. As shown with point B′, institutional reforms could increase efficiency but come at the cost of legitimacy. Conversely, B″ would be a point

[7] Ibid. 25.

where reforms increase legitimacy but reduce efficiency. The role of national parliaments can illustrate this point. Eliminating the need for national parliaments to ratify the own resources decisions would be an efficiency gain but would reduce legitimacy. Conversely, their involvement in adopting the MFF could add legitimacy but would certainly reduce efficiency. Against this background, Enderlein and colleagues argued in 2005 that there has been little incentive to deviate from B. They also include A as a point in the figure to explain that, for others (perhaps including themselves originally) who call for significant reform, the budgetary procedure is a situation below the 'Pareto frontier', and thus efficiency-enhancing reforms are possible without an offsetting loss in legitimacy.

In applying their conceptual approach to today's budgetary decision-making, we ask whether political integration has advanced since 2005, thus providing more scope for significant institutional improvements. During this period, the EU had to tackle a number of crises: the financial crisis, the sovereign debt crisis, the migration crisis, Brexit, the COVID-19 pandemic, the war in Ukraine, and the ensuing energy crisis. Many measures adopted in response to these crises have been further steps in integration. Citizens have seen the EU to be an important and often decisive level of state capacity.

While there is ample literature that explains the advancement of the integration process, we find Genschel and Jachtenfuchs[8] particularly instructive as they cover the different aspects of integration previously mentioned and provide insights into how further integration is articulated institutionally. Looking at integration beyond market integration, they analyse the integration of 'core state powers', which they define as the 'increasing involvement of EU institutions in key functions of sovereign government including money and fiscal affairs, defence and foreign policy, migration, citizenship and internal security'.[9] They describe the acceleration in integration following the sovereign debt crisis and show how the initial design of Economic and Monetary Union and the Schengen Agreement made them vulnerable to crisis and shaped policy options during the crises.[10] Further integration does not necessarily make the EU more like a federation, but it does show that new institutional formats and structures can be adopted. Bremer, Genschel, and Jachtenfuchs highlight the

[8] Genschel and Jachtenfuchs, 'More Integration, Less Federation: The European Integration of Core State Powers', 23 *Journal of European Public Policy* (*J. Eur. Public Policy*) (2016) 1; Genschel and Jachtenfuchs, 'From Market Integration to Core State Powers. The Eurozone Crisis, the Refugee Crisis and Integration Theory', 56 *Journal of Common Market Studies* (*JCMS*) (2018) 1.

[9] Genschel and Jachtenfuchs, 'More Integration, Less Federation' (n. 8) 2.

[10] Ibid.

role of national state élites and the public in driving integration and investigate the role of collective identity.[11] They see identity as a strong and fairly consistent predictor for individual variations in support of the integration of core state powers, which is greater and more varied than expected. They conclude that there is considerable room for political agency rather than a general constraining dissensus.[12] Overall, drawing on this literature allows us first to assume that political integration has, in fact, advanced in the 19 years since 2005, and second, that it sheds light on how further political integration provides room for institutional reform.

Adding to the observations of Enderlein and colleagues in 2005, we thus assume that further political integration not only advances the 'Pareto frontier' but also probably directly impacts the institutional choices and options available. This means that efficiency-enhancing reforms are possible without diminishing perceived legitimacy. Furthermore, the nature of crises and challenges, as well as the type of changes to the overall institutional architecture of the EU, narrow the different institutional options (and combinations between efficiency and legitimacy) and create focal points for institutional reform.

In assessing the scope for reform and tracing the institutional evolution, we also ask whether the budgetary procedure has changed either de jure or de facto over these 19 years. Rather than assuming that the rules and procedures have stayed unchanged in the point depicted in the diagram as B, we want to trace any institutional evolutions that may have taken place. Enderlein and colleagues argued in 2005 that the institutional changes introduced by the Draft Constitutional Treaty would not alter the institutional set-up very much as they simply constitutionalized or institutionalized existing practices. While the rejection of the Draft Constitutional Treaty is less relevant in this context since the reformed EU budget provisions were included in the Lisbon Treaty, we want to assess whether the institutionalization did not have an unexpected impact on the efficiency and legitimacy of the budgetary procedures. Even more importantly, we will examine how the innovations brought about by the Next Generation EU (NGEU) has introduced a reinterpretation of the budgetary procedures that de facto created a new institutional reality. Finally, we discuss what type of institutional reforms can be envisaged now and whether, and how, they will bring the current procedures closer to what we expect to be a new 'Pareto frontier'.

[11] Bremer, Genschel, and Jachtenfuchs, 'Juncker's Curse? Identity, Interest, and Public Support for the Integration of Core State Powers', 58 *JCMS* (2020) 1.

[12] Ibid. 56.

3. The Evolution of EU Budgetary Politics

Public finance has played a central yet under-recognized role in the dynamic of European integration. Law has been the major instrument of public power in the EU since its inception, and integration through regulation was, and has remained, a very powerful driver of integration. At the same time, the EU required budgetary resources from the outset. Every major development in integration was facilitated by some financial compensation for Member States expected to profit least from further integration. As a result, the EU budget is more of a by-product of the integration process than the central instrument of political action and prioritization. It is relatively small, and its distributive structure is only slowly evolving.

Budgetary politics has also been central to interinstitutional dynamics in the EU. The Treaties of Luxembourg (1970) and Brussels (1975) were the first treaties to provide the European Parliament (EP) with core powers (i.e. the right to reject, amend, or approve the budget), which justified the subsequent move to direct elections and the EP's role in the legislative process. Before 1970, the EP only had the right to be consulted about the budget. The main reason behind this move was the revision to the system of Community financing by the budgetary treaties, which introduced the Community's own resources based on customs duties, agricultural levies, and value-added tax (VAT). The loss of control by national parliaments over the Community budget was to be compensated through the EP. The Luxembourg Treaty also introduced a distinction between compulsory expenditure and non-compulsory expenditure. Compulsory expenditure was understood as expenditure 'necessarily resulting from [the Treaty establishing the European Economic Community] or from acts adopted in accordance therewith', over which the Council had the final say, while Parliament had the last word on non-compulsory expenditure. This distinction thus had significant consequences for the distribution of budgetary powers between the EP and the Council and was a recurring source of conflict between the two institutions.[13]

Finally, after years of conflict among Member States and between the EP and the Council, the budgetary reform of 1988 brought 'budgetary peace' by creating the system of multiannual bargains around the annual negotiations The introduction of the 'Financial Perspective', fixed over a period of five years (later seven years), was intended to limit the scope of political choice during the annual budgetary procedure by setting an upper limit. Proposed by the

[13] J. Lindner, *Conflict and Change in EU Budgetary Politics* (2006).

Commission and, after discussion in the European Council, adopted unanimously by the Member States and the EP as an Interinstitutional Agreement (IIA), the Financial Perspective was decided through a procedure that Enderlein and colleagues described as an equilibrium that optimizes efficiency and legitimacy.[14] Notably, the Financial Perspective had what was known as a 'semi-voluntary character', whereby the revenue ceilings were fixed in legal acts. Yet, the expenditure ceilings were not binding but dependent on the willingness of the actors to adhere to the IIA. As a consequence, all institutions involved had to cooperate to avoid a breakdown of the MFF.[15] While the new framework was sufficiently adaptive for integrating the new Member States in 2004, the significant increase in political stability came at a cost of reduced flexibility, in particular in between the seven-year renegotiating points.

A. The Lisbon Treaty

The revisions to the budgetary procedure under the Treaty of Lisbon, which entered into force in 2009, had, in hindsight, more of an impact than Enderlein and colleagues had anticipated in their 2005 paper. In the draft Constitutional Treaty, two adjustments were made: the abolition of the distinction between compulsory and non-compulsory expenditure—thus putting Council and Parliament on an equal footing in budgetary matters—and the inclusion of the MFF into primary law. The rejection of the draft Constitutional Treaty in the national referenda and its salvation through the Lisbon Treaty did not affect these changes. Under the Lisbon Treaty, the Union's annual budget is now part of the MFF adopted by the Council following the consent of the EP (Article 312(2) Treaty on the Functioning of the European Union (TFEU)). Thus, the EP has the right to consent to the MFF as well as the power to veto the budgetary procedure for the annual budget (Article 314 TFEU). In cases of disagreement between the Council and the EP, a conciliation committee, composed of the members of the Council and an equal number of Members of the EP, is convened to resolve the problem.

Many observers saw these changes as simply a further institutionalization/formalization of a practice that had been established and laid down in soft law. Over time, however, the changes introduced by the Lisbon Treaty had

[14] See Enderlein et al. (n. 2) 25.
[15] Ibid. 16.

noticeable effects.[16] In particular, there are three aspects in which the revisions were felt in EU budgetary decision-making. First, the pre-Lisbon fragility of the MFF as an arrangement based on soft law had a disciplining impact on the negotiations. Because it was not legally enshrined but only agreed through an IIA, which was not automatically renewed after the end of its period, a refusal to cooperate would have meant risking a return to a system based on annual budgets adopted through qualified majority voting and co-decision, which, in the 1980s, had led to continuous stalemates between the Council and Parliament. This risk of such a return provided a threat, which both the EP and Member States could use against any blocking veto player. Under the Treaty of Lisbon, this threat disappeared: nowadays, failure to agree on a new MFF simply means that the previous MFF will be extended until the new act is adopted (Article 312(4) TFEU). Second, the nature of the MFF pre-Lisbon as a soft law instrument with no legal basis in the Treaties meant that the decision-making rules around the MFF and its interplay with the annual procedure could be flexibly adjusted. This meant that in addition to the negotiations for the MFF, there were also negotiations on the institutional balance between the EP and Council and further adjustments to the framework. While secondary law can still be adjusted in a similar fashion, the institutionalization of the MFF in primary law reduces the flexibility of these institutional adjustments. The ability of the EP to gain institutional concessions, and thus expand its powers in exchange for agreeing to a new MFF, is more limited (even if there is still an IIA connected to the MFF among the institutions). Third, the final veto power of the Council in the Conciliation Committee on the annual budget in the revised procedure gives the Council more of an advantage than had been anticipated. This is explained well by Benedetto in 2015, with the different spending interests of the EP and the Council: the new rules have a bias towards less spending, which weakens the Parliament that tends to prefer a higher budget.[17]

Within the conceptional framework of Enderlein and colleagues of 2005, the Lisbon Treaty thus arguably moved the budgetary decision-making slightly away from the 'Pareto frontier' and reduced both legitimacy (with its effect of the powers of the EP) and efficiency (by reducing flexibility and increasing the power of veto players).

[16] Laffan and Lindner, 'The EU Budget', in H. Wallace et al. (eds), *Policy-Making in the European Union* (2020) 215.

[17] G. Benedetto, 'The Balance of Power over the EU Budget: European Expenditure since the Lisbon Treaty', *Swedish Institute for European Policy Studies, European Policy Analysis* (2015).

B. The Financial Crisis

In parallel to the Lisbon Treaty, the financial crisis in 2008/2009 also marked the starting point of developments that had a significant impact on the state of integration. They shifted the 'Pareto frontier' further out. In dealing with a succession of crises, the EU changed its nature. Political integration has advanced, and expectations for the EU to act jointly have increased. In particular, the sovereign debt crisis led to a number of institutional reforms that deepened integration for eurozone members. New institutions, such as the European Stability Mechanism (ESM), were established and the Banking Union was created. These measures and innovations had financial dimensions. Yet, as they involved only a subset of Member States and (possibly also) due to the rigidity of the MFF, they were addressed largely outside the EU budget in a more intergovernmental format. In the case of the ESM, the EP was largely bypassed. The involvement of national parliaments, which varies from state to state, and very high majority requirements in the decision-making process are sources of legitimacy but come at the expense of efficiency and coherence as regards the overall EU budgetary framework.

While measures adopted in the context of the ESM/International Monetary Fund programmes drew quite some criticism, the relevance of European action to settle the crisis was undisputed and the rise in Euroscepticism receded again in the years after the crisis. When Brexit hit, it did not lead to major integration steps for the remaining 27 Member States, but it created unity amongst them.[18] The deepening of economic integration (outside the EU budget) advanced political integration—raising the expectation that it would be at the European level that responses to new challenges would be provided.

C. The COVID-19 Pandemic

This was further amplified by the EU's responses to the COVID-19 pandemic, which had a profound impact on the EU budget. The perception and framing of this crisis as a one-off exogenous shock that affected the Union and its Member States largely in a symmetrical way contributed to the rapid adoption of large-scale EU measures. In particular, the EU pandemic recovery

[18] As noted above, political integration has also an ideational dimension. We do not trace the evolution of this dimension and its contribution to advancing political integration here in more detail.

instrument, NGEU, marked a decisive shift in the budgetary framework of the Union. Negotiated jointly with the MFF 2021–2027, the EUR 1.8 trillion package represented the most significant MFF negotiations since the original MFF breakthrough. Legally, NGEU is established through three different legal components: first, the Regulation establishing the European Union Recovery Instrument (EURI), based on Article 122 TFEU; second, the EU Own Resources Decision (ORD), based on Article 311 TFEU; and third, various legal acts establishing the spending programmes, with the Recovery and Resilience Facility (RRF) as the centrepiece of the instrument, based on Article 175(3) TFEU. Together, these three parts introduced significant innovations in terms of financing and governance, including a commitment to new own resources for the EU.

In terms of financing, NGEU is hugely innovative in its reliance on common debt issuance that will need to be repaid from 2028 onwards. While not the first in EU history, it constitutes the largest-scale issuance to date. Interestingly, and as De Witte notes, it would have been entirely possible—and procedurally more straightforward—to finance the recovery programme through an increase of the 2021–2027 MFF by EUR 750 billion and a corresponding increase in the ceiling in the ORD.[19] However, politically, increasing the financial burden towards the EU was not an option for the Member States that were dealing with the harsh economic fallout of the COVID-19 pandemic at that time.[20] Repayment of the debt will start in 2028 and last until the end of 2058 (Article 5 ORD). Repayment can be ensured in three different ways:[21] first, the EU can request higher contributions from the Member States to the EU budget, as is also laid down in the 2020 ORD; second, the EU can cut its spending on other programmes in the next MFFs and use the money for the repayments; and third, the EU can introduce additional new own resources. In this regard, NGEU was accompanied by a commitment to introduce new own resources for the EU. The European Council Conclusions of July 2020 include a promise to 'work towards reforming the own resources system and introduce new own resources'[22] based on non-recycled plastic waste, a carbon border adjustment mechanism, a digital levy, and a revised Emissions Trading System-based scheme, possibly extended to aviation and maritime. The IIA on

[19] De Witte, 'The European Union's COVID-19 Recovery Plan: The Legal Engineering of an Economic Policy Shift', 58 *Common Market Law Review* (2021) 3.

[20] Ibid.

[21] There is arguably a fourth option: the repayment of the debt by Member States 'directly' outside the framework of increased own resources.

[22] European Council conclusions of 16–21 July 2020, EUCO 10/20.

budgetary discipline of 16 December 2020,[23] which accompanied the MFF, includes a roadmap towards the introduction of new own resources.

These commitments have the potential to transform a system of own resources that has not changed since 1988, despite the Commission's efforts. The 2020 ORD made a start by introducing a new own resource in the form of national contributions based on unrecycled plastic packaging waste in each country. At the same time, it is not actually an additional own resource as they are offset in the traditional gross-national-income- (GNI)-based contributions by the Member States.[24] And the Council has so far made no progress on the Commission's proposals for new own resources made in 2021 (and updated in 2023).

Also in terms of governance, the Recovery and Resilience Facility (RRF) and its integration into the European Semester has a transformative character for EU economic policy coordination,[25] with potential to drive a strategic agenda for the EU during its lifetime. With the RRF, for the first time, the EU has an instrument that can align national investments and reforms with European interests, including green and digital targets, by providing European money (in the form of grants and loans) in exchange for the implementation of national reforms. Crucially for some Member States, this also includes reforms relating to compliance with rule of law principles, where such clauses have been included in the country-specific recommendations under the European Semester in 2019 or 2020. In the case of Hungary, the rule of law-related milestones in the National Recovery and Resilience Plan (NRRP) have, moreover, been linked to the application of the new rule of law conditionality mechanism.

These three aspects—financing, own resources, governance—constitute a major step in the expansion of the EU budget and are de facto changing budgetary decision-making, despite the temporary nature of NGEU. Long considered an impossibility, the large-scale common debt to be repaid through the EU budget constituted an almost revolutionary step forwards in political integration in Europe. In terms of budgetary procedure, NGEU introduces a new form of financial support linked to the European Semester and has the potential 'to put EU budgetary politics onto a new distributive institutional path',

[23] Interinstitutional Agreement between the European Parliament, the Council of the European Union, and the European Commission of 16 December 2020 on budgetary discipline, on cooperation in budgetary matters and on sound financial management, as well as on new own resources, including a roadmap towards the introduction of new own resources, OJ L 433I (22 December 2020).

[24] Schramm, Krotz, and De Witte, 'Building "Next Generation" after the Pandemic: The Implementation and Implication of the EU Covid Recovery Plan', 60 *JCMS* (2022) 121.

[25] T. Nguyen and N. Redeker, 'How to Make the Marriage Work—Wedding the Recovery and Resilience Facility and the European Semester', Jacques Delors Centre Policy Brief (2022).

as Lindner and Laffan argue.[26] They predict that this 'new distributive and institutional reality [is likely], depending on the economic developments in the Member States, to induce heightened expectations and independencies'.[27] Whether NGEU will be successful in doing so will also frame the debate on a possible successor instrument.

And yet, it should be noted that NGEU was not used to increase European spending programmes but created with the RRF a (temporary) instrument that, within a European framework with targets and monitoring, provides more leeway to Member States in deciding where and how to spend the European grants and loans.

Moreover, the expansion of the EU budget and the de facto change in budgetary procedure did not come with an increase in (democratic) legitimacy. The footing of the legal construction of NGEU on Article 122 TFEU meant a reduction in the role of the EP. Even though the RRF was adopted through the ordinary legislative procedure, Parliament did not manage to negotiate a stronger role for itself in the RRF beyond the 'recovery and resilience dialogue'. This could be seen, if not as a roll-back of EU-level democracy,[28] as a side-step, especially as the Council is involved in the adoption of the NRRPs and the monitoring of their implementation but the EP is not.[29]

These changes in the budgetary procedure took place in a context of changes in European integration. The EU budget operates in an ever-changing political and geopolitical environment, defined by successive crises requiring European intervention. For more than a decade now, the EU's competences have de facto increased to deal with the financial crisis, the migration crisis, Brexit, the rule of law crisis, the COVID-19 pandemic, the war in Ukraine, and the climate crisis, and citizens' assessment of the EU depended on its capacity to handle these crises.[30] The deeper political integration of the EU post-Lisbon also has an effect on the EU budget. The EU must be able to guarantee the continuation of European policies by providing the basic preconditions for them, which is their financing.[31]

The well-established negotiation process of the MFF, in which most conflict points are known, ensures continuity and predictability that allows for an

[26] Laffan and Lindner (n. 16).
[27] Ibid.
[28] L. Guttenberg and T. Nguyen, 'How to Spend It Right—A More Democratic Governance for the EU Recovery and Resilience Facility', Jacques Delors Centre Policy Brief (2020).
[29] N. von Ondarza, 'Die Krisengovernance der Europäischen Union—Mehr Verantwortung braucht mehr demokratische Legitimation' Stiftung Wissenschaft und Politik Studie 2023/S 04 (2023).
[30] Ibid.
[31] P. Becker, *Der Haushalt der Europäischen Union und die deutsche Europapolitik* (2022) 85.

amicable conclusion of budget negotiations and budget stability over seven years. As a result, EU institutions and other actors involved prefer to agree on the lowest common denominator in a tried-and-tested procedure instead of getting entangled in incalculable conflicts that a comprehensive reshaping of the EU budget and an ambitious attempt at reform would entail.[32]

D. New Challenges

Arguably, this will now have to change. From the sizable but as yet unknown costs related to the war in Ukraine, to the concerns on how to respond to the industrial policy strategies in the United States (as well as China), to the financial investments required to meet the growing climate emergency, there is increasing pressure on the EU to deal with tasks that require considerable financial resources, as citizens expect the EU to deliver solutions to mitigate the social and economic effects of the crises.[33] This requires the EU to be able to respond to policy challenges with adequate resources and new spending priorities, which in turn necessitates a more flexible budget. This could be addressed within the EU budget framework or, especially if the MFF proves too rigid, outside with more ad-hoc intergovernmental solution (sidelining the EP and often requiring additional set-up costs).

E. Back to the Conceptual Approach

To translate this into the language of Enderlein and colleagues, the evolution since 2005 shows that political integration has advanced the 'Pareto frontier' and moved the budgetary procedure from B to C and then to D (see Figure 3.2). D represents the increase in efficiency: the EU has made a significant shift in allowing for the possibility of issuing debt for grants, and even though NGEU is temporary in nature, this shift in budgetary procedure and the impact on the EU's crisis management structure will most likely be permanent. Put differently, for future crises of the magnitude of the COVID-19 pandemic, resorting to Article 122 TFEU for large-scale issuance will now be the blueprint. This will not be the case for challenges that do not fall within that definition/category. At the same time, D also illustrates the loss of legitimacy in the

[32] Ibid.
[33] Hillje and Pütz (n. 1).

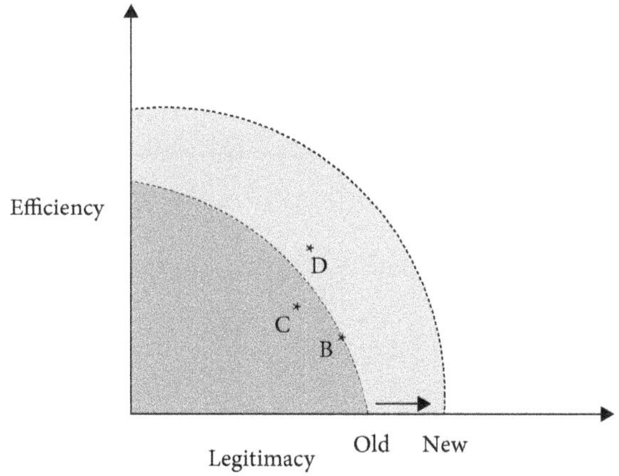

Figure 3.2 Developments since 2005 (updated efficiency–legitimacy graph)
Source: Adapted from Henrik Enderlein, Johannes Lindner, Oscar Calvo-Gonzalez, and Raymond Ritter, 'The EU Budget: How Much Scope for Institutional Reform?', ECB Occasional Paper Series No. 27/April, 10, Figure 1. Copyright (©) European Central Bank, Frankfurt am Main, Germany. Readers can find the original figure free of charge at https://www.ecb.europa.eu/pub/pdf/scpops/ecbocp27.pdf.

reduced role of the EP since the Lisbon Treaty and NGEU. Most importantly, political integration has increased, and thus the 'Pareto frontier' has shifted. This means that further institutional reforms that enhance efficiency and legitimacy seem possible.

Combining these findings with the work of Genschel and Jachtenfuchs, it is important, however, to note that the nature of the crisis conditioned the type of political integration and, in turn, the specific adaptation of the budgetary procedures. The pandemic was regarded as a one-off, external shock and threat that hit the Union (and the world) collectively without prior wrongdoing of individual Member States or citizens. This facilitated the unique move towards a large-scale increase in the budget and the institutional innovations.[34] With the temporary nature of the change (despite its permanent impact on the ability of the Union to react in crisis) and the pandemic-specific rationale, the adjustment of budgetary decision-making was seen as less than a general reform. Moreover, building on the work of Lindner in 2006,[35] NGEU, in its link to the MFF and with the construction of external revenue, could still be described largely as an on-path change of and within the framework, rather than a fundamental break with it. The recourse to borrowed money facilitated a solution

[34] Genschel and Jachtenfuchs, 'Postfunctionalism Reversed: Solidarity and Rebordering during the COVID-19 Pandemic', 28 *J. Eur. Public Policy* (2021) 3.
[35] Lindner (n. 14).

that maintained the existing distributive order of the MFF and was adopted unanimously. The final question is whether the above-described advance of political integration and its nature are such that a real off-path change and far-reaching reform will now be possible.

4. Reform of the EU Budget

The context in which the EU budget is placed in the 2020s is one of successive crises, which have changed the nature of the EU itself and raised expectations that it will be able to provide effective measures to address common challenges.[36] These expectations also have implications for the EU budget and mean that changes are necessary. To allow the EU to efficiently respond to policy challenges and adapt to new spending needs, the budget must be both more flexible and structurally larger than it currently is. This goal, however, becomes more difficult to achieve, if not impossible, with many veto players involved. As long as particular decisions on the spending side are dependent on unanimous agreement between all actors, there remains a strong status quo bias, and efficiency will remain diminished. Following the argument that further political integration not only advances the 'Pareto frontier' but also affects the institutional choices and options available for institutional reform, the increase in political integration provides room for reforms that would make the EU's budgetary framework more efficient, while neither diminishing nor enhancing the legitimacy of the procedure.

There is an increasing recognition that both the EU budget and its adoption process need to change. The final report of the Conference on the Future of Europe in 2022 raises the importance of the EU budget for the future.[37] Most notably, participating EU citizens recommended a strengthening of the EU budget through new own resources and called for 'future-oriented investments

[36] The abstract of the Standard Eurobarometer survey of July 2023 states,

> EU citizens continue to back overwhelmingly the energy transition and to expect massive investment in renewables. They continue to widely approve measures taken by the EU to support Ukraine and the Ukrainian people. They also support stronger EU defence cooperation and increased defence spending. While inflation remains a major concern, perceptions of the economic situation and economic expectations are improving. A majority of Europeans believe that NextGenerationEU, the EU's €800 billion recovery plan, can be effective to respond to the current economic challenges. Support for the euro stays high.

European Commission, *Standard-Eurobarometer* (July 2003).

[37] Conference on the Future of Europe, 'Report on the Final Outcome' (2022), https://wayback.archive-it.org/12090/20220915192132/https://futureu.europa.eu/pages/reporting (last visited 16 December 2023).

focused on the green and digital transitions', taking into account the example of NGEU. They also proposed to 'give further consideration to common borrowing at EU level'. Another recommendation was that the 'European Parliament should decide on the budget of the EU' as a way to bolster European democracy.

Against this background, we see three main areas of reform: first, increasing efficiency on the spending side; second, increasing the scope of the budget to allow for more European funding of European projects; and third, some adjustments to the revenue side.

A. Duration and Structure of the MFF

Increasing efficiency on the spending side relates to both the duration and the structure of the MFF. Regarding the duration of each MFF, there is good reason to argue to reduce it to five years. This would not only increase flexibility, as funds can be reallocated according to new priorities after every five instead of seven years, but it would also allow for the alignment of the long-term budget with the length of the legislature.[38] In particular, for each incoming Commission to have an impact on the negotiations, the parliamentary terms and the period for each MFF should overlap in such a way that the new MFF is always adopted two years into the new legislature. This would leave sufficient time for the new Parliament and new Commission to come into office and establish themselves before negotiations begin. Such a shortened term would not require Treaty change: Article 312(1) TFEU already allows for the MFF to be established for a period of 'at least five years'.[39]

Moreover, failure to adopt a new MFF should not lead to an extension of the previous MFF, as is currently the case under the Treaties. Instead, in such cases, a return to the annual budgetary procedure without an MFF would be preferable (even if the spending programmes are often laid down in multiyear legislative acts) as this reduces the status quo bias and provides the disciplining shadow of qualified majority voting (QMV) (as was the case with the soft law status of the IIA before the Lisbon Treaty). For this, however, Article 312(4)

[38] See the call for a 10-year duration of the MFF: De Feo, 'The Multiannual Financial Framework 2021–2027: Ambition or Continuity?', in B. Laffan and A. De Feo (eds), *EU Financing for Next Decade—Beyond the MFF 2021–2027 and the Next Generation EU* (2020) 10.

[39] See, for similar arguments on how to increase flexibility with the MFF, M. Buti and M. Nava, '"Constrained Flexibility" as a Tool to Facilitate Reform of the EU Budget', European Economy, Economic Papers 326 (2008).

TFEU would have to be amended. It currently reads, 'Where no Council regulation determining a new financial framework has been adopted by the end of the previous financial framework, the ceilings and other provisions corresponding to the last year of that framework shall be extended until such time as that act is adopted.'

Regarding the structure of the MFF, its inflexibility stems from the difficulty of transferring funds from one heading to another and from ceilings that are too low. This forces EU annual budgets to operate with little room to manoeuvre to react to new needs,[40] as any change in the ceilings requires unanimity in Council and an absolute majority in Parliament. This is because the expenditure ceilings are set by the MFF Regulation.[41] This regulation is adopted unanimously by Council and with the consent of the EP (Article 312 TFEU) and can thus only be amended with the same majorities. There are three ways to remedy this lack of flexibility. First, the ceilings could be set higher. The unanimity requirement in Council is not as much of a constraining factor where the ceilings are set sufficiently high from the beginning so as to allow enough leeway in the long-term budget to react to new financial demands in the first place. Second, more flexibility could be achieved by reducing the number of different headings in the MFF. Fewer headings would mean a smaller number of categories to which funds are bound, which would, in turn, increase the flexibility with which the funds can be spent. Neither change would require any Treaty change; they would merely require agreement among the Member States and the consent of the EP. In addition, a further flexibility fund could be created for specific purposes leading to a stronger role in crisis management and in cyclical stabilization. Third, and the most far-reaching option, the *passerelle* clause under Article 312(2) TFEU could be used, whereby the European Council may unanimously authorize the Council to adopt the MFF Regulation by QMV. This would mean that spending ceilings under the MFF would also be adopted by QMV[42] and align MFF adoption more with the procedure of the annual budget.

Overall, these changes would, in effect, have as their objective a reduction of the relevance of the MFF in the EU budgetary framework to increase the

[40] E. Rubio, 'The Next Multiannual Financial Framework (MFF) and Its Flexibility', in-depth analysis requested by the European Parliament's Committee on Budgets (November 2017) 13.

[41] For the period 2021–2027, this is Council Regulation 2020/2093 of 17 December 2020 laying down the multiannual financial framework for the years 2021 to 2027.

[42] Franco-German Working Group on EU Institutional Reform, 'Sailing on High Seas: Reforming and Enlarging the EU for the 21st Century', report (2023).

relevance of the annual budgetary process (with Council and Parliament as two arms of the budgetary authority and QMV in the Council); it would also probably have repercussions for the length and flexibility of the legislative decisions on the spending programmes.

B. Scope of the Expenditure Side

To be able to meet the new demands previously described, the EU budget must not only become more flexible on the spending side but also extend the scope of its reach. Without pre-empting the final evolution of the governance of the RRF and the overall impact of NGEU, we would see benefits in further Europeanization. From the perspective of alignment with other European spending programmes and EU budget items, a possible successor would not be designed as support for national measures with European funds but as funding for European tasks and policies, with a stronger role for the EP. This would not require a change in the Treaty.

To render the overall EU budgetary framework more coherent and stronger, the case can also be made that intergovernmental budgetary formats, such as the ESM, which are currently outside of the EU law framework, should be brought into the community law sphere to increase the scope of the EU budget. More concretely, the ESM could be re-established so that capital paid into the ESM could be transferred to the EU to become a guarantee stock for loan support programmes to be set up.[43] On the one hand, the integration of off-budget instruments such as bringing the ESM back into community law could be seen as reducing flexibility in that it takes away the possibility to meet expenditure demands that cannot, for one reason or another, be met under the regular EU budget. However, as has been argued, not only do such intergovernmental formats come at the expense of the involvement of the EP, but also the (varied) involvement of national parliaments and very high majority requirements in the decision-making process, which provide legitimacy, also come at the expense of efficiency and coherence with the overall EU budgetary framework. Full integration of the ESM into the EU treaties would require Treaty change.

[43] As was argued by L. Guttenberg, 'Time to Come Home—If the ESM Is to Stay Relevant, It Should Be Reinvented inside the EU', Jacques Delors Centre Policy Brief (2020).

C. Issuance of Common Debt

Expanding the scope of the EU budget's expenditure side means that a case should also be made for the institutionalization of a possibility to issue common debt outside of crisis times. This would not only give the EU more flexibility to react to new demands, not least on climate or defence, where there is no more room for manoeuvre left in the budget, but it would also allow the Union to raise money to fund genuinely European tasks at the European level where the need arises. The establishment of such an instrument would necessitate Treaty change. While the use of Article 122 TFEU might become a blueprint for large-scale issuances in times of crisis, as we have argued, it is an emergency article, applicable where Member States find themselves in difficulties caused by 'exceptional occurrences' (Article 122(2) TFEU) and does not seem suitable for more permanent instruments.[44] In any event, we would argue that any such issuance should be decided by unanimity between the Member States to give more legitimacy to the decisions. In addition, and differently than under Article 122(2) TFEU, the EP should have the right to consent in order to further democratically underpin the European dimension of such issuances.

D. Own Resources

A reform of the expenditure side and more common debt issuance necessitates a reform of the EU's revenue and own resources. The unanimity requirement (and ratification according to national procedures) under Article 311 TFEU for changes to the EU's revenue, including revenue ceilings and the structure of the EU own resources, drastically limits its flexibility in this regard. However, at the same time, it also bestows a high level of legitimacy and protection on this core dimension of the distributive order of the Union. Thus, it seems difficult to foresee, given the current state of political integration and as long as revenues are mostly based on Member State contributions, a shift away from unanimity (which would require Treaty change). Less clear is the question of whether the EU would be ready to break with the *juste retour* perspective of Member States by replacing the system of GNI-based quasi-contributions from national budgets with genuine EU own resources. This is relevant also for the question of whether the EU is regarded as a 'sovereign' with genuine taxing powers.

[44] For a further discussion see S. Grund and A. Steinbach, 'European Union debt financing: leeway and barriers from a legal perspective', Bruegel Working Paper 15/2023 (2023).

We would argue that—next to the dominant system of de facto national contributions—the EU could take the revenues that it generates by introducing new systems or policies. This could be similar to the Emission Trading System scheme but would entail taking all the revenues into the EU budget rather than only a share. One could even go a step further to see whether the collection of such revenues would be chiefly done by the EU itself rather than relying on national tax authorities. The EU would get an additional source of income independent of the Member States' budgets, and in itself, such a step would not require Treaty change. Over time, this source could potentially increase in relevance compared to the national contributions. The significant benefits that such a change would entail would need to be set against the conflict-reducing nature of predictability of the current system. If these new own resources became, at some future point in time. the dominant source of revenue, such a shift away from contributions based on national GNIs could then, in turn, justify a move towards QMV also on the revenue side.

In the absence of significant new genuine own resources, and as argued for the spending side, decision-making for the revenue side could also be made less rigid by maintaining higher buffers to the GNI ceiling. The higher the revenue ceiling, the more room there is to increase spending without adjusting the own resources decisions. If the flexibility of adjusting the MFF upwards is also increased, this additional room for manoeuvre becomes very relevant. Moreover, it adds credibility to the Union's ability to repay debt and thus facilitates the issuance of common debt. Such a higher buffer would not require Treaty change.

5. Conclusions: Towards a Significant Reform of the EU Budget?

'As it stands today, the EU budget is a historical relic. Expenditures, revenues, and procedures are all inconsistent with the present and future state of EU integration.'[45] This criticism dates back to 2003 and was one of the key conclusions of the Sapir Report. Despite this devastating verdict, the European Convention and subsequent Intergovernmental Conference did not lead to any significant institutional reforms in the realm of budgetary decision-making. The paper by Enderlein and colleagues in 2005 argued that this was not surprising as, by and large, the existing procedures balanced efficiency and legitimacy concerns with the constraints set by the state of political integration of the EU at that time.

[45] Sapir Report (n. 3).

Has the state of EU integration changed since then? Is it time to overcome the past and change the Treaties? In answering these questions, this chapter has made the following arguments. In line with Enderlein and colleagues in 2005, we see political integration as a key constraining or enabling factor for institutional reform in budgetary decision-making. We show that political integration has advanced significantly since 2005 and that, in order to overcome the successive crises it has faced, the EU has gone beyond market integration and started to integrate 'core state powers'.[46] This has de facto altered the overall institutional architecture of the Union and the tasks that it performs (with implications also for the need to use not only regulatory but also financial instruments). Moreover, it has raised citizens' expectations for what Europe should address collectively; and national identities seem to stand less in the way of providing European responses. However, in line with the work of Genschel and Jachtenfuchs,[47] we argue that further political integration has not (yet, at least) made the EU simply more like a federation. The nature of the crises and type of challenges that the Union faces conditions the institutional choices that follow from them.

An important question for the prospect of reforming budgetary decision-making is thus which types of challenges the EU needs to address and what a corresponding European budget should look like. In a Union that was largely about market integration (and regulation), the EU budget served as a compensation function, and the budgetary procedure was designed in a way to protect the original distributive deals that had enabled the respective integration steps. Yet, the Union has evolved and so have the challenges it faces. The COVID-19 pandemic and NGEU stand for an external shock for which a collective responsibility and common response was accepted, despite their redistributive character.[48] More generally, a fiscal response at the EU level seems likely when the challenge is seen as a common external threat that could affect all Member States in a similar manner or where inaction on the part of some Member States will affect others and fragmented national actions are clearly more costly and less efficient. The current challenges of climate change and increasing geopolitical and geo-economics tensions, we argue, meet these criteria in that they are externally driven.[49]

[46] Genschel and Jachtenfunchs, 'More Integration, Less Federation' (n. 8).
[47] Genschel and Jachtenfuchs (n. 34).
[48] Ibid.
[49] A similar argument is made by M. Draghi, 'The Next Flight of the Bumblebee: The Path to Common Fiscal Policy in the Eurozone', 15th Annual Feldstein Lecture, National Bureau of Economic Research, Washington (11 July 2023), https://www.nber.org/lecture/2023-15th-annual-feldstein-lecture-mario-draghi-next-flight-bumblebee-path-common-fiscal-policy (last visited 4 July 2024).

These challenges require an EU budget that is both more agile in reacting to new developments and structurally bigger. On the expenditure side of the EU budget, a short and less prescriptive MFF will leave more room for the annual budgetary procedure to react in a flexible manner with QMV in the Council and the full involvement of the EP. Funds and arrangements that are currently outside the EU budget could be brought into budgetary procedure and aligned to other EU spending programmes. While deviation from the *juste retour* mindset of Member States would be desirable, we are sceptical about whether a departure from the unanimity principle for changes on the revenue side would, at least at this juncture, not be too challenging to its legitimacy (even if matched by more involvement of the EP). At the same time, more agility will mean that it is desirable for the Union to decide (unanimously) to issue debt even outside very exceptional crisis situations. Moreover, a higher revenue ceiling would provide more flexibility for spending decisions. Furthermore, as small but genuine own resources, the Union could receive in full the revenues that are generated through European policy decisions and by European mechanisms.

Finally, the mixture between the positive and normative dimensions of the main argument advanced by Enderlein and colleagues in 2005 hides the thorny question of how institutional reform in the highly redistributive realm of budgetary procedure can, in fact, be enacted. Many of the issues mentioned in section 4 can be introduced without the need for Treaty change, that is through IIAs, *passerelle* clauses, or simply political agreements for higher margins in the MFF ceilings. Others, however, do require Treaty change.[50] Here, we would argue that Treaty change would only be realistic if it is motivated by a much broader reform agenda. In particular, the enlargement debate following the candidate status of Ukraine, granted in June 2022, presents an opportunity to discuss Treaty change to create an overall EU institutional framework that is capable of maintaining or increasing efficiency and legitimacy even with a significant increase in the number of EU Member States. At the same time, the actual impact of the next enlargement round not only on the EU budget but also on the future of European integration is so far unclear.[51] While the debate

[50] In addition, there are two further relevant questions (that we touch upon partly). First, is it desirable to have detailed provisions laid down in primary law? On the one hand, a prescriptive and very encompassing Treaty provides clarity and certainty. On the other hand, more flexibility is gained when future institutional reforms do not require Treaty change, and institutional stability can also be generated by actors periodically confirming that the procedural arrangements are seen as beneficial. Second, what are the institutional innovations (within and outside the EU Treaty) that will be pursued when the option of Treaty change is not possible?

[51] See, for a first discussion of the impact of enlargement on the EU budget, J. Lindner, T. Nguyen, and R. Hansum, 'What Does It Cost? Financial Implications of the Next Enlargement', Jacques Delors Centre Policy Brief (2023).

on internal reforms of the EU to prepare for enlargement has started, it is not a done deal that the outcome will, in fact, be deeper European integration.[52] And it is, thus, far from certain whether we will not, in 20 years from now, judge that in the mid-2020s we failed to escape a world that, in hindsight, could also be described with the same critical words as in the Sapir Report.

[52] See e.g. the different vision for the future of European integration as explained by then Polish Prime Minister Mateusz Morawiecki in his speech in Heidelberg: 'Europa an einem historischen Wendepunkt' (20 March 2023), https://www.gov.pl/web/deutschland/europa-an-einem-historischen-wendepunkt-premierminister-mateusz-morawiecki-zur-zukunft-europas (last visited 6 December 2023).

4

(Un)Constitutional Conditions

A European Perspective

*Viorica Viță**

1. Introduction

The law of spending conditionality is a novel and rapidly expanding area of European Union (EU) law. In the EU internal legal order, spending conditionality refers to the act of conditioning Member States' access to EU budgetary resources with respect to broader Union objectives, such as the transposition of EU legislation, respect of macroeconomic indicators, or respect of EU values. The most important trait of the law of spending conditionality is its peculiar method of coercion: the withdrawal of EU funds in the case of failure to comply. This non-traditional method of EU coercion makes spending conditionality an important tool of economic statecraft,[1] understood as the EU acting by using economic incentives or disincentives to determine a certain behaviour of its Member States. From this perspective, spending conditionality must be understood as an *EU governance tool* that is economic in nature that has, in practice, important political, legal, and constitutional implications.[2]

In the current context of a general proliferation of spending conditionality across the entire spectrum of EU expenditure, it is ever more important to investigate the constitutional dimension of the tool. The EU budget Multiannual Financial Framework (MFF) for 2021–2027 together with the historic Next Generation EU (NGEU) recovery plan are replete with spending conditionality arrangements that require Member States and private beneficiaries of EU

* The information and views set out in this chapter are those of the author alone and do not necessarily reflect the official opinion of the European Commission.

[1] D. A. Baldwin, *Economic Statecraft* (1985); C. Fabre, *Economic Statecraft: Human Rights, Sanctions, and Conditionality* (2018).

[2] Viță, 'Revisiting the Dominant Discourse on Conditionality in the EU: The Case of EU Spending Conditionality', 19 *Cambridge Yearbook of European Legal Studies* (*CYELS*) (2017) 116–143.

Viorica Viță, *(Un)Constitutional Conditions.* In: *New Frontiers of EU Funding.* Edited by: Claire Kilpatrick and Joanne Scott, Oxford University Press. © Viorica Viță 2024. DOI: 10.1093/oso/9780198940319.003.0004

funds to comply with a wide range of Union standards.[3] The rule of law conditionality complements the generous conditionality packages of both the MFF and NGEU and allows the EU to cut off spending to Member States in breach of rule of law principles with a sufficient link to sound financial expenditure.[4] The impressive development of the EU law of spending conditionality, notably in the 2014–2020 MFF, in the aftermath of the sovereign debt crisis, and its continued expansion in the 2021–2027 MFF shows that conditionality is, and will continue to be, a central piece of the EU's internal governance architecture.

In this chapter, I argue that spending conditionality may have an important constitutional significance when used in purely internal situations. Currently, EU spending conditionality is fully binding and enforceable under EU law and forms an integral part of the EU legal order. This means that it may be legitimately construed only within the framework of EU constitutional law and the fundamental principles underpinning it. Unlike the use of conditionality in external relations,[5] when used inside the EU legal system, spending conditionality gains a firm and special constitutional significance, bearing upon the relationship between the EU, Member States, and—most importantly—EU citizens. Despite its potentially important constitutional remit, EU law scholarship provides little guidance as to how one may construe spending conditionality from a constitutional perspective. The few contributions on the matter are largely concerned with the tool's efficiency as a sanction.[6] Other, more recent, scholarly contributions argue almost exclusively for or against the legality of one specific conditionality type: the rule of law conditionality.[7]

[3] V. Viţă, 'Conditionalities in Cohesion Policy', Research for Committee on Regional Development, the European Parliament (2019); recital (71), Arts 8 and 17(3) of the Regulation of the European Parliament and of the Council 2021/241, OJ 2021 L 57/17.

[4] Regulation of the European Parliament and of the Council 2020/2092, OJ 2020 L 433I; Regulation 2021/241 (n. 2).

[5] Regarding the argument that the EU is guided in external action by the same set of constitutional principles, in particular by its human rights obligations, see V. Kube, 'The EU's Human Rights Obligations towards the Wider World and the International Investment Regime: Making the Promise Enforceable' (2018) (PhD thesis on file at the European University Institute, Florence).

[6] Verhelst, 'Cohesion Policy and Sound Economic Governance: A Loveless Marriage', *Polish Quarterly of International Affairs* (2014) 113–126; Bieber and Maiani, 'Enhancing Centralized Enforcement of EU Law: Pandora's Toolbox?', 51 *Common Market Law Review* (*CMLRev*) (2014) 1057–1092; G. Halmai, 'The Possibility and Desirability of Economic Sanction: Rule of Law Conditionality Requirements against Illiberal EU Member States', EUI Department of Law Research Paper 2018/06 (2018), http:// EUI Working Paper LAW_2018_06.pdf (eui.eu) (last visited 26 January 2024); Sedelmeier, 'Political Safeguards against Democratic Backsliding in the EU: The Limits of Material Sanctions and the Scope of Social Pressure', 24 *Journal of European Public Policy* (2017) 337–351.

[7] K. L. Scheppele, L. Pech, and D. Kelemen, 'Never Missing an Opportunity to Miss an Opportunity: The Council Legal Service Opinion on the Commission's EU Budget-Related Rule of Law Mechanism', *Verfassungsblog* (12 November 2018), https://verfassungsblog.de/never-missing-an-opportunity-to-miss-an-opportunity-the-council-legal-service-opinion-on-the-commissions-eu-budget-related-rule-of-law-mechanism (last visited 24 January 2024). EU Council, Opinion of the Legal Service 13593/18, 'Proposal for a Regulation of the European Parliament and of the Council on the

This chapter aims to remedy this gap by putting forward a constitutional framework for spending conditionality. I argue that the constitutional dimension of spending conditionality must be assessed departing from a broader EU constitutional construction, which balances in a fair manner the constitutional aims of the tool against its competing constitutional limits. It is explained that viewing the legitimate objectives alone or, on the contrary, the competing constitutional interests, does not offer a productive lens of inquiry into the complex constitutional relationships touched upon by the tool. Instead of rejecting all use of spending conditionality at the EU level or fully embracing it, this analysis calls for a continuous constitutional assessment of the still-developing spending conditionality tool, informed also by its performance. I argue that a comprehensive constitutional analysis of the tool is able to offer much more useful guidance to EU institutions, notably the Court of Justice (CJ), in their effort to shape a principled doctrine of spending conditionality at the EU level. It also provides a much broader framework for inquiry to scholars and legal practitioners that could ultimately inform the constitutional debates on the use of the tool, departing from the potential of the tool in practice.

This chapter is structured in five parts. Section 2 situates EU spending conditionality in the context of federal systems (A) and of the EU governance spectrum (B). Section 3 lays out a constitutional framework for spending conditionality departing from some of its constitutional aims goals (A) and competing constitutional limits (B). Section 4 puts forward a balancing test of spending conditionality that aims to provide a model for weighting the overall benefits and limitations of the tool in constitutional terms based on the example of the rule of law conditionality. Section 5 concludes.

2. Spending Conditionality in the Context of Federal and EU Governance

A. Comparative Constitutional Law Perspective

Constitutional questions on spending conditionality are not new in federal systems, such as those of the United States or Canada, where conditional spending has expanded exponentially since the 1960s, together with the growing power

protection of the Union's budget in case of generalised deficiencies as regards the rule of law in the Member States: Compatibility with the EU Treaties' (2019); Rangel de Mesquita, 'European Union Values, Rule of Law and the Multiannual Financial Framework 2021–2027', 19 *ERA Forum* (2018) 287–294.

to tax and the rise of the welfare state in the two federations.[8] Unlike the use of spending conditionality in the EU, the use of federal spending conditionality in these federations has triggered multifaceted constitutional debates over the proper framing of the tool.[9] In particular, it has been argued that the extensive use of spending conditionality may amount to regulation though 'the back door' of the budget, as opposed to 'the front door' of legislation, leading to an expansion of the federal government into areas not reserved to it by the Constitution.[10] In the same vein, spending conditionality has been seen as a 'constitutional workaround', allowing the federal government to circumvent norms requiring a higher level of constitutional consent by finding sufficient basis in other parts of the Constitution.[11] At the other end of the spectrum, scholars have argued that, on the contrary, spending conditionality may enhance the substance of the constitution and may be used to defend constitutional values and individual rights across state lines.[12]

The United States Supreme Court, confronted with questions regarding the constitutionality of the tool, has, for over a century, consistently held that conditionality is constitutional, provided that it meets the four cumulative requirements set out in the *Dole* case,[13] namely that (a) conditionality must advance 'general welfare' as provided for in the US Constitution; (b) must be expressed 'unambiguously'; (c) must be germane to the federal interests in the spending programme; and (d) must not violate any other constitutional provision, including the constitutional rights of individuals.[14] Together, these important

[8] P. E. Trudeau, 'Federal-Provincial Grants and the Spending Power of Parliament, Working Paper on the Constitution' (1969); United States Advisory Commission on Intergovernmental Relations, *Categorical Grants, Their Role and Design* (1978); R. L. Watts, *The Spending Power in Federal Systems: A Comparative Study*, Institute of Intergovernmental Relations, Queen's University (1999).

[9] For a detailed comparative analysis between the EU and the United States, see V. Viţă, 'The Rise of Spending Conditionality in the EU: What Can EU Learn from the U.S. Conditional Spending Doctrine and Policies?', EUI Working Papers 16/2017 (2017) 7–11.

[10] Rosenthal, 'Conditional Federal Spending and the Constitution', 39 *Stanford Law Review* (1987) 1103–1164; Rosenthal, 'Conditional Federal Spending as a Regulatory Device', 26 *San Diego Law Review* (*SDLR*) (1989) 277–288.

[11] On the theory of constitutional workarounds, see Hawkins, 'Constitutional Workarounds: Senate Reform and Other Examples', 89 *Canadian Bar Review* (2010) 513–544; Tushnet, 'Constitutional Workarounds' Harvard Law School, Public Law & Legal Theory Working Paper Series, Paper 09-14 (2009).

[12] Marshall, 'Towards a Nonunifying Theory of Unconstitutional Conditions: The Example of the Religion Clauses', 26 *SDLR* (1989) 243–254; Kotlowski, 'With All Deliberate Delay: Kennedy, Johnson, and School Desegregation', 17 *Journal of Policy History* (2005) 155–192; Congressional Quarterly Almanac, 'Federal Aid Cutoff Prompted Limited School Desegregation' (1965).

[13] Supreme Court (U.S.), *South Dakota v. Dole* 483 U.S. 203 (1987).

[14] Ibid. For a critique of the Dole doctrine as hardly able to meaningfully constrain the US federal government's conditional spending power, see Rosenthal, 'Conditional Federal Spending and the Constitution' (n. 10) 1114; Bagenstos, 'Viva Conditional Federal Spending', 37 *Harvard Journal of Law & Public Policy* 93 (2014); Epstein, 'Foreword: Unconstitutional Conditions, State Power, and the Limits of Consent', 102 *Harvard Law Preview* (1988).

scholarly contributions crystallize the doctrine of '*unconstitutional conditions*', from which the title of this contribution draws inspiration.

I do not intend to rehearse these extremely rich debates here. This is because the constitutional contexts, maturity, and financial power of the US and Canadian federations are significantly different from the EU.[15] Instead, I aim to provoke reflection on what a doctrinal framework for (un)constitutional conditions might look like in the EU.

B. Spending Conditionality within the EU Governance Spectrum

The 2014–2020 multiannual budget opened the door to an unprecedented influx of spending conditionality inside the EU internal budget and legal order.[16] The climate of austerity in Europe, dominated by sovereign-debt conditionality, allowed spending conditionality to find firm legal consecration in EU financial regulations and facilitated its expansion within internal EU budgetary processes.[17] The objective of the 2014–2020 spending conditionally was economic in nature and was coupled with a strong policy remit as these tools were meant to respond to the EU's post-crisis reform of the European Monetary Union. It aimed at enforcing EU fiscal prudence by attaching an elaborate macroeconomic conditionality to 45 per cent of the EU budget (represented by five European Structural and Investment Funds); advancing structural reforms by linking EU spending to the recommendations of the European Semester; and securing efficient spending by ensuring that hundreds of EU legal, policy, and regulatory requirements were complied with before the start of expenditure.[18] A distinct proportion of the budget conditionality is concerned with advancing environmental policy objectives in agricultural aid, upholding the EU fisheries policy in fisheries funds, and with maintenance of the EU Schengen and human rights *acquis* at the EU borders though EU home affairs funds.[19]

The significant internal increase in conditionality and its implementation on the ground posed a number of constitutionally relevant questions, such as

[15] Viță (n. 9).
[16] Viță (n. 2).
[17] V. Viță, 'The Rise of Spending Conditionality in the EU' (2018) (PhD thesis on file at the European University Institute, Florence); Bieber and Maiani (n. 6).
[18] Viță (n. 2).
[19] Ibid.

the legitimate exercise of power by the EU executive, the enforcement of otherwise non-enforceable soft law EU provisions, the shift in treaty basis, the limits of EU competence, variable coercion, and a compliance threshold for Member States.[20] Yet, the 2014–2020 spending conditionality became history even before these questions were fully acknowledged in scholarly debates.

In 2020, a new set of spending conditionalities embedded in the 2021–2027 budgetary perspective caught the public's attention.[21] To understand the scope of the expanding EU law on spending conditionality, it is important to recall that, since 2021, the receipt of all EU Structural and Home Affairs Funds have been tied to a consolidated and expanded set of four horizontal and 16 thematic enabling conditions mandating compliance with EU law and policy objectives throughout the implementation of EU spending.[22] These are further linked to a number of detailed fulfilment criteria that include respect of EU public procurement and state aid rules, compliance with the EU Charter of Fundamental Rights (hereinafter the 'Charter'), correct transposition and respect of thematic EU legislation, and the adoption of numerous strategic frameworks. In addition, a reformed, extensive macroeconomic conditionality clause firmly binds all structural funds to economic governance objectives, including delivery of European Semester country-specific recommendations and the structural reforms therein.[23] A novel infringement conditionality may lead to the suspension of EU payments in case of pending EU law infringement procedures that risk affecting spending.[24] While the disbursement of home affairs funds continue to be conditioned upon consistency with Schengen *acquis* and respect for human rights,[25] even more conditionality has been attached to EU agricultural funds to increase their environmental and social remit.[26] The EU fisheries funds remain conditional upon full compliance with the Common Fisheries Policy.[27]

The novel NGEU funding adopted to support Europe's recovery in the aftermath of the COVID-19 pandemic is no exception to spending conditionality. Access to its largest financial envelope—the Recovery and Resilience Facility,

[20] Viță (n. 17).
[21] Viță (n. 3).
[22] See Art. 15, Annex III and IV of Regulation of the European Parliament and of the Council 2021/1060 (2021) OJ 2021 L 231/159.
[23] Ibid. Art. 19.
[24] Ibid. Arts 73(2)(i), 97(1)(d).
[25] See Art. 4 of Regulation of the European Parliament and of the Council 2021/1149 (2021) OJ 2021 L 251/94; Art. 16(1) of Regulation of the European Parliament and of the Council 2021/1147, OJ L 251/1.
[26] See Arts 12–14, Annex III–IV of Regulation of the European Parliament and of the Council 2021/2115 (2021) OJ 2021 L 435/1.
[27] See Art. 11 of Regulation of the European Parliament and of the Council 2021/1139, OJ 2021 L 247.

representing more than 90 per cent of available funds—requires compliance with structural reforms defined in the European Semester country-specific recommendations and with EU economic governance macroeconomic indicators.[28]

Another notable novelty is the rule of law conditionality.[29] This tool allows the EU to withdraw EU budgetary resources from Member States that fail to comply with rule of law principles and, in so doing, affect, or risk affecting, the sound financial management of the EU budget. The rule of law conditionality is

- the most powerful in financial terms, as it applies to the entirety of EU expenditure in Member States, including the MFF and the temporary NGEU instrument, totalling approximately EUR 1.8 trillion for the period 2021–2027;
- the most robust in legal terms as, in contrast to all other conditionality forms, the rule of law conditionality is a standalone budgetary regulation that is not linked to a specific financial envelope or multiannual budgetary perspective and that will continue to apply beyond the 2021–2027 MFF;
- the most sensitive in political terms, as it marks an important turning point from the traditional EU enforcement toolkit in the area of the rule of law; and
- the most significant in constitutional terms, as it aims to reinforce the EU values that lie at the very heart of the construction of the EU through the route of its budget.

The breadth and depth of the various types of spending conditionality, the detail of their requirements, their impressive thematic reach, and their functional use have already been analysed elsewhere.[30] For the purpose of this discussion, it is essential to reiterate some of its functions and characteristics.

From the functional perspective, spending conditionality may aim to achieve normative aims, and hence, regulate state conduct in similar ways to legislation (*regulatory function*), or seek to enforce existing EU legislation or other soft law measures (*enforcement function*). When conditionality pursues a

[28] Regulation 2021/241 (n. 2). The Recovery and Resilience Facility represents the most significant part of the Next Generation EU financial package, adopted as a response to the COVID-19 pandemic recovery, with a budget envelope of EUR 723.8 billion out of the overall package of about EUR 800 bln.
[29] Regulation 2020/2092 (n. 4).
[30] Viță (n. 2); Viță (n. 3).

regulatory function, the constitutional suspicion is that the tool aims to bypass dedicated legislation, vesting rights, and obligations through the route of the EU budget. When conditionality pursues an enforcement function, the constitutional suspicion is that the tool aims to circumvent traditional infringement procedures, or to render soft law regulation binding through the route of the budget, which could either not have been enforced or could have been enforced with much greater difficulty in its absence. We shall discuss the constitutional implications of these distinctions in section 3 below.

As to its characteristics, it is essential to note that while EU spending conditionality is an innovative governance tool in the EU's internal legal order. it is, however, strongly related to other governance techniques, notably to spending. This leads to several important consequences that strongly impact the effective achievement and reach of spending conditionality in practice. First, EU spending conditionality is, in essence, a condition on spending. However, it goes beyond the strict scope of EU spending action and aims to direct recipients' behaviour towards a distinguishable policy objective. In other words, spending conditionality is an additional condition of spending pursuing distinguishable policy objectives, but spending remains the primary objective of the EU intervention, which will be pursued with reinforced attention by Member States and the Commission alike. Second, the coercive power of EU spending conditionality is intimately linked to the financial power of the EU budget envelope attached to it. The more money at risk of withdrawal, the more attention a Member State would, in principle, pay to the fulfilment of a given spending conditionality. Here, it is worth mentioning that EU spending is unevenly distributed between Member States, with less developed states—net beneficiaries—receiving the lion's share of the EU budget and NGEU resources, and more developed members—net contributors—contributing more to the EU budget than they receive in net terms. As a result of this uneven distribution, spending conditionality is strongly influenced by the distributive tensions between net beneficiary and net contributor Member States, which play out strongly, particularly during its negotiation and enforcement, and are likely to impact the tool's efficiency in practice. Like the vast majority of the EU budget, EU spending conditionality is a tool generally implemented in close cooperation, via shared management proceedings between the European Commission and Member States' administrations, which both have to actively cooperate to ensure that spending and the conditionality attached are successful. However, while the Commission implements the budget in cooperation with Member States, it does so on its own responsibility pursuant to Article 317 of the Treaty on the Functioning of the European Union (TEFU).

In practice, this uneven distribution of responsibility raises important challenges for the Commission, which has to come up with viable solutions to support Member States implementing their share of the EU budget and attached spending conditionality. This is necessary because, ultimately, it is the Commission that is responsible for the sound execution of the budget before the European Parliament. Therefore, enforcement of a spending conditionality is only considered as an option of last resort after all prior efforts to safeguard spending and conditionality attached have failed.

As a result of the above legal, institutional, and financial constraints, as a general rule, spending conditionality is rarely enforced against EU Member States, despite some notable recent enforcements that are discussed in section 4.

3. Constitutional Framework for EU Spending Conditionality

From a constitutional perspective, the crux of spending conditionality is that the EU relies exclusively on its spending power to achieve normative and enforcement objectives. This raises a number of interesting questions in practice. Can the EU act via spending conditionality, even if doing so is not expressly provided for in the EU treaties? If so, what are the legitimate constitutional aims for utilizing spending conditionality in the EU? What are its limits? And most importantly, what is the impact of the use of the tool on the distribution, exercise, and balance of power in the EU?[31]

The sections below show that the EU may use spending conditionality to advance its policy objectives through spending, even though this is not explicitly provided for in the EU Treaties. In doing so, the EU legislator relies on a number of constitutional aims, which may, in turn, be counterbalanced by a number of competing constitutional limits. Regarding those constitutional aims, it is argued that spending conditionality may be constitutionally grounded on the EU's constitutional interest in using European public funds to reinforce European constitutional objectives. Ultimately, it is in the EU's interest to promote effective government at both EU and national level, including effective spending, on theories of necessity, as well as the legitimate interest of promoting and preventing breaches of EU values, including fundamental rights. A robust constitutional assessment of EU spending conditionality cannot be

[31] This contribution develops some of the questions raised in Viță (n. 2) 4–5.

limited to its legitimate objectives. It must also look into the competing constitutional limits that may be adversely impacted as a result. Four competing constitutional limits are discussed below: the legality of EU action, equality of Member States, individual rights, and solidarity.[32]

The discussion is far from exhaustive. It proposes a model constitutional framework that could usefully guide legal scholars, practitioners, and policy-makers in the multiple constitutional aspects raised by spending conditionality in the present and future EU budgetary periods, which could gradually shape the constitutional grounds and limits of spending conditionality in the EU.

A. Constitutional Aims

1. EU Objectives

The first legitimate objective for EU spending conditionality can be found in the EU Treaties. Under Part Six, Title II, Financial Provisions, Article 311(1) TFEU explains that 'The Union shall provide itself with the means necessary to attain its objectives and carry through its policies.'

In light of this provision, all EU revenues have a clear constitutional mission, which is to achieve the EU's *objectives* and assist the Union in effectively executing its policies as set out at Article 3 Treaty on the European Union (TEU), most notably the objective of promoting 'peace, *its values* and the well-being of its peoples'.[33] In this context, a spending conditionality aiming to advance one of the EU objectives or policies is no more than a faithful materialization of the treaty mandate. Whereas the treaties ask the EU to appropriate funds in furtherance of its objectives and policies, a spending conditionality is a spending norm that aims to ensure that these objectives are actually met through spending. The argument for spending conditionality appears even stronger when the tool is designed to ensure that EU public spending is disbursed consistently with EU objectives, laws, and policies and that, above all, EU spending does not go against its constitutional aims. On this point, there is already a long-standing consensus at the EU level that the EU's external spending should be consistent with EU values and objectives and contribute to the progressive realization of the latter.[34] The extension of spending conditionality towards

[32] Other constitutional limits such as accountability, transparency, or legal certainty may be discussed on a case-by-case basis. I shall not discuss these here.

[33] See Art. 3 (1) TEU (emphasis added).

[34] See Art. 236 of Regulation of the European Parliament and of the Council 2018/1046, OJ 2018 L 193/1.

Member States should therefore be seen as an internalization of this external policy stance within the EU internal budgetary processes.

2. Effective Government and Effective Spending

A second legitimation of spending conditionality may be found in the imperative of effective government.[35] Effective government, understood as the capacity of the EU to deliver its treaty mandate and policies, is not a mere economic desire but is the very foundation upon which the legitimation of the entire EU is built.[36] On this point, Gráinne de Búrca argued that the EU derives its legitimacy not only from the democratic process but also from its capacity to deliver policy outcomes and fulfil its founding mission.[37] The main aim of spending conditionality in the 2021–2027 financial perspective is largely to foster effective government at both the EU and at Member State level.[38] At the EU level, a spending conditionality may pursue the aim of effective government in areas where other policy tools are less likely to deliver the policy goal proposed in a satisfactory manner. For instance, if the goal is environmentally sustainable transportation, it may be significantly more difficult to convince EU citizens or Member States to shift to 'green' cars by adopting an EU law obligation on the matter supported by infringement proceedings or other sanctions than by offering budgetary incentives with conditionality attached asking recipients to progressively scrap polluting cars. Regarding effective government at the national level, it should be added that the EU system of government is built around a quasi-federal polity model whereby public functions are exercised jointly and severally on multiple levels of government, and national authorities act as 'agents' of EU integration. In the absence of EU authorities at the national level, the EU relies heavily on Member States' duty of sincere cooperation and solidarity to carry through its treaty mandate and give concrete effect to its rules.[39] Spending conditionality is often designed to encourage full and effective implementation of EU laws and policies, administrative reforms aimed at avoiding government failures, deterring government capture by vested interests, and advancing Member States' capacity to uphold

[35] See, in the same sense, Daintith, 'The Techniques of Government', in J. Jowell and D. Oliver (eds), *The Changing Constitution* (1994) 209–236.

[36] G. de Búrca, 'Europe's Raison D'Etre', Working Paper, EUI AEL, 2013/02 (2013) 8–9; F. Scharpf, *Governing in Europe: Effective and Democratic?* (1999).

[37] de Búrca (n. 36).

[38] Regulation 2021/1060 (n. 22).

[39] Case C-39/72, *Commission v. Italy* (EU:C:1973:13), para. 24 (in which the Court held that the failure to implement EU law must be seen as a 'failure in the duty of solidarity accepted by Member States by the fact of their adherence to the Community [that] strikes at the fundamental basis of the Community legal order').

their EU obligations.[40] Based on the particular importance of Member States' compliance with their treaty obligations and sound governance at the national level for the EU multi-level model of governance,[41] the use of spending conditionality may be clearly legitimated by the objective of effective government.[42]

Effective government includes effective spending. This is, in essence, the most voiced legitimation of spending conditionality in the EU, which is based on the EU legislators' and executive's wide discretion to choose the most appropriate tools to safeguard the financial interests of the EU.

3. Necessity

A third objective of spending conditionality, underlined in particular in federalist constitutional theory, is the potential of the tool to provide ingenious ways to avoid constitutional blockage and help attain desirable policy goals that enjoy a broad and shared consensus, without following the burdensome and costly course of constitutional amendment.[43] In this sense, spending conditionality acts like a 'constitutional workaround'. Constitutional workarounds are routes followed by the legislator to escape a constitutional provision that obstructs the direct achievement of a desired policy goal, in ways that find sufficient support in the other parts of the constitution.[44] Therefore a spending conditionality may assist the higher level of government to work around highly obstructive constitutional provisions to secure desirable constitutional aims, which respond to pressing contemporary needs, enjoy sufficiently wide public and political support, and provide a feasible alternative to the increasingly difficult task of amending the constitution.[45] While it may be argued that, in the case of the EU, treaty revision is still needed, that option may not always be politically feasible. As the EU becomes larger, deeper, and more heterogenous, and the social realities in which it operates change with dramatic speed, the unanimity required by the ordinary and simplified treaty amendment rules may not be easily achievable, even if change is acutely necessary.[46] Similarly,

[40] This is the case for a significant number of *ex ante* conditionalities attached to 2014–2020 European Structural and Investment Funds Regulation 1303/2013 Annex XI and their successor "enabling conditions" in the 2021–2027 Regulation 2021/1060 (n. 22).

[41] von Bogdandy and Ioannidis, 'Systemic Deficiency in the Rule of Law: What It Is, What Has Been Done, What Can Be Done', 51 *CMLRev* (2014) 59–96; Art. 197 (1) TFEU: 'Effective implementation of Union law by the Member States, which is essential for the proper functioning of the Union, shall be regarded as a matter of common interest.'

[42] Art. 197(2) TFEU: 'The Union may support the efforts of Member States to improve their administrative capacity to implement Union law.'

[43] Part 2 A, footnote 11 above.

[44] Tushnet (n. 11); Hawkins (n. 11).

[45] Tushnet (n. 11); Hawkins (n. 11).

[46] See Art. 48 TEU.

the unanimity required by the 'flexibility clause' may not offer a solution.[47] In these cases, spending conditionality may be legitimated by the necessity to adopt acceptable policy solutions for the entire EU, in turn avoiding undesirable treaty ossification or a further fragmentation by differentiated integration or action outside the treaties, which has been frequently observed during the past decade.[48]

4. EU Values

A fourth legitimation, which enjoyed significant traction in established federal systems, relates to the duty of the higher level of government to protect the constitutional rights, equal opportunities, and comparable living conditions to all citizens across state lines.[49] In such a reading, EU spending conditionality—and consequently spending cuts—may be legitimated by the need to safeguard the essence of EU citizenship, such as fundamental and individual rights derived from the EU legal order, including access to independent and impartial courts, when Member States fail to uphold their EU obligations. When these rights are endangered, it may be argued that the EU not only has a right but also a duty to act, by every available means, including spending conditionality.

B. Competing Constitutional Limits

1. Legality of EU Action

When spending conditionality aims to regulate state conduct (regulatory function), the primary constitutional suspicion of spending conditionality is that the tool may seek to escape the constraints of the principle of conferral and its related guarantees, depending on the type of competence exercised.[50] When spending conditionality aims to enforce already existent EU acts or standards (enforcement function), the constitutional suspicion is that the EU circumvents explicit treaty enforcement procedures or effectively adds to the latter. In both cases, the suspicion is that conditionality aims to achieve ends that would have been more difficult or impossible to achieve in the absence of spending conditionality.

[47] See Art. 352 TFEU and Declarations 41, 42.

[48] For an excellent analysis of the current rigidity of the treaty framework and fragmented state of the EU law of integration, see J. Baquero Cruz, 'Rigidity, Fragmentation, and the Allure of International Law' in *What's Left of the Law of Integration? Decay and Resistance in European Union Law* (2018) 169–198.

[49] Kotlowski (n. 12) 166–181.

[50] See Arts 4(1) and 5 TEU.

On the first point, the question of *legal basis* arises when the EU has competence to act within a particular policy domain but where recourse to spending conditionality, as opposed to substantive legislation, switches the initial legal basis towards the budget one; as well as where the EU has no competence to act absent the budget legal basis. The switch in legal basis is not without legal significance, for the choice of legal basis shall dictate, in turn, the legal and procedural guarantees, the level of consent required, the choice of permissible legal acts, the participation requirements of specific stakeholders, and the level of public scrutiny of the proposed act. The Court of Justice has had the chance to pronounce on both points.

1.1 Principle of Conferral and Legal Basis

First, on the EU's competence to act pursuant to the principle of conferral, judging on the assertion that spending and conditionality attached amounts to circumvention of another available legal basis with more stringent procedural requirements, in the *Erasmus* case, the Court stated that

> under the scheme of the Treaty the conditions under which legislative powers and budgetary powers are exercised are not the same. Consequently, the requirements of the budgetary procedure laid down for making available the appropriations needed for the implementation of [EU expenditure] cannot have any implications regarding the procedural requirements for the adoption of [EU legislation], since those requirements fall under a completely separate provision.[51]

The Court has therefore held that even if substantive legislation in a policy area would require more stringent procedural requirements for the adoption of a certain measure, its adoption on the spending legal basis remains consistent with the EU treaties, so long as the EU acts within the limits of its competence in that given area. From this point of view, it must be clarified that EU spending conditionality always follows the legal basis of the financial act to which it is attached and, as a consequence, always takes the form of an EU regulation, binding in its entirety and of direct applicability, and is adopted pursuant to the ordinary legislative procedure.[52]

On the contention that conditionality amounts to regulation through the back door of spending, in areas where the EU would not be able to adopt

[51] Case C-242/87, *Commission v. Council (Erasmus)* (EU:C:1989:217), para. 18.
[52] Viţă (n. 17).

legislation based on another treaty provision, the Court has held, in the recent cases of *Hungary v. Council and Parliament* and *Poland v Council and the Parliament*, that

> it is permissible for the EU legislature, where it has a [spending] legal basis for doing so, to establish, in an act of secondary legislation, other procedures relating to the values contained in Article 2 TEU, which include the rule of law [conditionality mechanism], provided that those procedures are different, in terms of both their aim and their subject matter, from the procedure laid down in Article 7 TEU.[53]

The Court further clarified in the same rulings that the aim of the rule of law conditionality regulation, adopted under Article 322 (2) TFEU, followed a different procedure and had a distinct aim and subject matter, namely 'to protect the Union budget from effects resulting from breaches of the principles of the rule of law in a Member State in a sufficiently direct way, and not to penalise those breaches as such'.[54]

Three important consequences follow. First, the requirement of *sufficiently direct link* between spending and conditionality is critical for the legality of spending conditionality in the EU. Based on the case law above, in the *legal* exercise of its budgetary functions set out under the treaties, the EU may allocate spending based on available treaty legal basis and attach the appropriate conditionality to it, so long as the EU legislator and the executive can show a '*sufficiently direct link*' between a given conditionality and the objectives of spending, even if the EU may not legislate in the policy area of conditionality independent of spending.[55] Second, conditionality has been given a rather limited constitutional construction in the EU, as compared to established federations such as the United States and Canada, where it is commonly agreed that the federal government can deploy spending and attach appropriate conditionality, so long as it remains germane to the objective of government expenditure. As opposed to the EU's 'sufficiently direct link' test, the US 'germaneness' test is construed by the US Supreme Court as being more akin to a relevance test criteria, rather than the rigid cause and effect test suggested by

[53] Case C-156/21, *Hungary v. European Parliament and Council of the European Union* (EU:C:2022:97), para. 168; Case C-157/21, *Republic of Poland v. European Parliament and Council of the European Union* (EU:C:2022:98), para. 207.

[54] Case 156/21, *Hungary v. European Parliament and Council of the European Union* (n. 53), para. 119.

[55] Case C-385/13, *P Italy v. European Commission* (EU:C:2014:2350), para. 60.

the Court of Justice.[56] Although this ruling does not limit the Court to adapting a broader construction of spending conditionality in the future, it is a lost chance to set up a general doctrinal standing for spending conditionality at the EU level. The rule of law conditionality could have served as an example where spending conditionality was intended to advance the respect of EU values, so long as these values appear relevant to spending. Even if, in the aftermath of negotiations, the reach of the rule of law conditionality was significantly limited and the conditionality was firmly linked to sound financial expenditure, it was, in my view, unnecessary for the Court to insist so much on the notion of the 'sufficiently direct link'. By insisting on limiting of the rule of law conditionality—and consequently conditionality in general[57]—to EU values, law, or policy breaches that may demonstrate a direct link to sound financial management or to the protection of the financial interests of the Union, the Court, alongside the legislator, essentially limited the rule of law conditionality to instances that were already to a large extent covered under the general financial regulation.[58] By contrast, if one brings forward the case of conditional spending in the United States, public schools that used to segregate children on the basis of race were not denied public spending in the 1960s simply to ensure sound financial management of federal funds but because the constitutional value of non-discrimination is paramount to all aspects of state action, including through public spending, and the constitutional objective of non-discrimination was seen as sufficiently germane to the objective of spending in education. *Mutatis mutandis*, in this case it should be remembered that spending is not simply better off because financial data shows that when rule of law principles are respected, EU funds are better spent but rather because we, as Europeans, have decided that our EU spending is better off when done in a manner that complies with the rule of law. Likewise, spending is not better off simply because we may quantify the positive economic impact of environmentally friendly spending but rather because we, as Europeans, have decided that our EU spending is better off when done in an environmentally sustainable way. In the absence of a definition of '*sufficiently direct link*', one may still argue

[56] Ibid. paras 136, 138, 147, 242.

[57] The requirement of a 'link' is a general requirement for most conditionality types in the EU. See, for instance, macroeconomic conditionality or enabling conditions in Arts 15 and 19 of the MFF Horizontal Regulation, Regulation 2021/1060 (n. 22).

[58] See Art. 63 of Regulation (EU, Euratom) 2018/1046 (n. 34). EU funds have also long included specific clauses mandating Member States to ensure appropriate remedies during implementation of EU funds, including access to effective complaint mechanisms. Moreover, the Court of Justice has repeatedly stressed that Structural and Cohesion Funds operations must ensure respect of the EU Charter and access to effective judicial review; see Case C-562/12, *Liivimaa Lihaveis MTÜ v. Eesti-Läti programmi 2007–2013 Seirekomitee* (EU:C:2014:2229).

that the notion allows significant discretion in practice to the Commission when deciding upon the enforcement of spending conditionality in general, and of the rule of law conditionality in particular. From this point of view, both the Commission and the Court are expected to gradually crystallize the baselines of the sufficiently direct link test as part of a doctrine of conditionality in the EU, which could turn out to be more generous in practice than either its wording or Commission's guidance suggest.[59]

1.2 Enforcement

As to the claim of a disguised enforcement of EU law, the Court held, in *An Taisce*, that a decision to reduce EU spending and infringement procedures 'are independent of each other, serve different aims and are subject to different rules'.[60]

Furthermore, in *Commission v. Italy*, the Court has usefully clarified that a spending conditionality asking for compliance with EU laws authorizes the Commission to legitimately refuse payments if the latter has established a '*sufficiently direct link*' between the object of the infringement procedure and the EU funding at hand.[61] It appears, therefore, that a functional use of spending conditionality is consistent with the treaties as long as a conditionality aims to enforce EU action that is closely linked to the objectives of spending.

It is therefore settled case law that infringement proceedings and spending withdrawal connected to EU law areas where a Member State has failed to comply may proceed in parallel, without amounting to double punishment, given that the two procedures pursue different aims (i.e. compliance *versus* protection of the financial interests of the EU), are independent of each other, and follow different rules.[62]

While the question of the EU's competence to enforce a certain EU hard law act via conditionality is settled, the conditionality's enforcement function of EU soft law calls into question the *scope of EU competence*. This arises where the EU clearly has the competence to act within a particular policy domain, but the type of EU competence exercised would not allow it to attain the aims that conditionality would. This discussion is particularly relevant for the cases

[59] European Commission, Guidelines on the application of Regulation 2020/2092, C(2022) 1382, para. 61.

[60] Case C-325/94, *P An Taisce, the National Trust Ireland and WWF UK (World Wide Fund for Nature) v. Commission*, OJ JOC_1994_386_R_0009_02, para. 25.

[61] Case C-385/13, *P Italy v. European Commission* (n. 55).

[62] This view is not necessarily embraced by Member States, which may see the two procedures as highly interchangeable in functional use and punitive effect. See Case C-332/01, *Greece v. Commission* (EU:C:2004:496), para. 55, on the claim of Greek government that: 'an action for failure to fulfil obligations would have been more appropriate because the correction may be regarded as a penalty'.

where spending conditionality pursues actions falling under the scope of EU economic, employment, and social competence,[63] as well as EU coordinative, supplementing or supporting action.[64] In these areas, EU legislative powers are limited, and EU action traditionally takes the form of 'soft law' measures.

Even if scholars have questioned the usefulness of the post-Lisbon competence hierarchy from the point of view of its legal consequences,[65] it is clear that EU action enjoys a different level of legitimacy and scrutiny depending on the type of EU competence exercised: exclusive, shared, or cooperative. Arguably, when the EU acts in the *areas of coordinative, supportive, or supplementing competence*, its power is minimal.[66] EU action in economic, employment, and social policy, as well as in areas such as human health, education, vocational training, and administrative cooperation, is largely of a soft nature. In such areas, legislative action is likely to be difficult and politically costly, necessitating a high level of agreement and being subject to closer judicial scrutiny. Spending conditionality has the potential to incrementally challenge the scope of EU competence distribution described above. It may be argued that the distribution of EU spending conditionality along the 'soft' end of EU coordinative, supportive, or supplementary competences may incrementally help the EU to 'harden' some of its powers in these areas. Evidence from the 2014–2020 and 2021–2027 financial periods shows that spending conditionality has an increased potential to mainstream EU soft law measures through the hard law of spending.[67]

Take, for instance, the spending conditionality of the Recovery and Resilience Facility (RRF) requiring that all spending must demonstrate *ex ante* consistency with the challenges and priorities identified in the context of the European Semester, which are essentially soft law policy recommendations

63 See Art. 5 TFEU.

64 Ibid. Art. 6.

65 P. Craig and G. de Búrca, *EU Law: Text, Cases, and Materials* (2011), 84–89. The authors argued that it is generally difficult to distinguish between the type of competence exercised, given the intertwining objectives of EU acts, and that irrespective of the competence exercised, the EU may adopt legally binding acts.

66 See Art. 2(3) and (5) TFEU: EU powers are limited in scope to acts facilitating the exercise of power by Member States, excluding harmonization acts. It follows that when the EU acts in the areas of *exclusive competence*, its power is at its highest. Hence, EU legislative, regulatory, or soft law acts in areas of, for example, customs or trade, shall encounter minimum resistance from Member States and the legislator is generally granted the largest discretion by the judiciary. When the EU acts in the areas of *shared competence*, its powers are in a twilight zone, blurring with the powers of the Member States. Therefore in areas of, for example, the internal market, agriculture, or the environment, the resistance to EU legislative, regulatory, or soft law acts shall depend on particular imperatives that shape the majority position of EU institutions and Member States on a given issue.

67 In 2014–2020, the vast majority of spending conditionality takes shape along the lines of EU shared competence and EU coordinative action. In both areas, it aims primarily to support soft law policy acts.

addressed to Member States by the EU that are not legally binding and lack a dedicated enforcement mechanism.[68] This conditionality effectively hardens the European Semester soft law recommendations and gives them significant normativity by bringing them under the umbrella of spending. The case of Hungary is particularly telling in this respect. Through the RRF spending conditionality, the EU imposed a set of 27 remedial measures ('super milestones') in the rule of law area,[69] which Hungary must comply with in order to draw expenditure from its country-specific allocation of approximately EUR 6 billion. The super milestones include, and outnumber by 10, the initial set of 17 remedial measures required under the legally binding and directly applicable rule of law conditionality regulation.[70] The reach and detail of the conditionality requirements are impressive, including inter alia, the adoption of legislation and government decisions on effective functioning of a newly established an Integrity Authority; submission to the National Assembly of acts on the establishment of an Anticorruption Task Force and repealing prior decisions relating to it; and proposing draft legislation on the fight against corruption, 'including draft legislation including on: Extension of the personal and material scope of asset declarations (including to relatives living in the same household with the person concerned)', effective from November 2022.[71] This list of measures stemming from RRF conditionality further extends to the rule of law challenges that even the legally binding rule of law conditionality regulation could not reach, due to its limited construction and strict direct link to spending discussed above.[72] These measures refer notably to judicial independence, specifically the independence of the National Judicial Council, limitations of political influence on the Supreme Court, removing the Constitutional Court's review of final judicial decisions upon request of public authorities, and removing the veto of the Supreme Court

[68] See Art. 17(3) of Regulation 2021/241 (n. 2): 'The recovery and resilience plans shall be consistent with the relevant country-specific challenges and priorities identified in the context of the European Semester.'

[69] Reuters, 'EU Approves Hungary's Recovery Plan But Withholds Cash, Moves to Freeze Other Funds; EU Approves Hungary's Recovery Plan, But Withholds Cash, Moves to Freeze Other Funds' (2022) (last visited 26 January 2024).

[70] European Commission, Annexes to the Explanatory Memorandum of the Commission proposal for a Council implementing decision on measures for the protection of the Union budget against breaches of the principles of the rule of law in Hungary Brussels, COM(2022) 485 final (2022) https://eur-lex.europa.eu/resource.html?uri=cellar:9473778e-372b-11ed-9c68-01aa75ed71a1.0001.02/DOC_1&format=PDF (last visited 13 February 2024).

[71] Ibid.

[72] Ramona Coman, 'Rule of Law Conditionality in the Framework of the MMF 2021–2027 and Next Generation EU', ULB Institute of European Studies (2020) https://www.iee-ulb.eu/en/blog/news/rule-of-law-conditionality-mmf-2021-2027-next-generation-eu (last visited 26 January 2024).

upon the preliminary references of ordinary judges.[73] I shall discuss the issue of compliance with conditionality and some difficulties therein in section 4. However, irrespective of Hungary's degree of future compliance with these measures,[74] this case clearly illustrates the undeniable normativity that spending conditionality confers on a previously soft law EU mechanism, lacking in enforcement.

Here, it is important to mention that the EU is not as restrained in its authority to put in place policy frameworks as it is in its ability to enforce them at the domestic level.[75] As the EU is increasingly confronted with Member States failing systemically to comply with EU law under the radar of infringement procedures, and is mandated to act increasingly though soft law measures in areas where it lacks legislation but where coordinated action at EU level is clearly of added value—such as the area of structural reforms, spending conditionality may assist the EU to enforce its action in a more effective manner. Given the peculiar normativity and impact of spending conditionality in each Member State, it is hard to generally claim that an active use of spending conditionality in areas of 'soft' EU competences could amount to harmonization and hence to unconstitutional exercise of EU powers.[76] Nevertheless, it is realistic to claim that continuous, and eventually increased, conditional financial allocations in these areas may credibly increase the EU's influence on Member States' policy choices in areas traditionally reserved to Member State action. From this perspective, spending conditionality may have an impact on the competing interests of Member States and their citizens to avoid unwarranted regulation that may affect their pre-existing rights if there is not sufficient clarity on the source of the regulation or the equivalent tools to challenge such EU 'soft law' action implemented through spending conditionality.

[73] Annexes to COM(2022) 485 final (n. 70).

[74] For a comprehensive summary, see BBJ, 'EC Clears Hungary RRF Plan But Links Payouts to "Super Milestones"' (2022) (last visited 26 January 2024). For the most recent state of compliance, see European Commission, 'Commission Considers That Hungary's Judicial Reform Addressed Deficiencies in Judicial Independence, But Maintains Measures on Budget Conditionality', Press Release (13 December 2023), https://ec.europa.eu/commission/presscorner/detail/en/ip_23_6465 (last visited 13 February 2024).

[75] Bieber and Maiani (n. 6).

[76] Court of Auditors, 'Ex Ante Conditionalities and Performance Reserve in Cohesion: Innovative But Not Yet Effective Instruments', Special report 15/2017 (2017), https://op.europa.eu/webpub/eca/special-reports/partnership-agreements-15-2017/en/ (last visited 26 January 2024); European Commission, 'The Value Added of Ex Ante Conditionalities in the European Structural and Investment Funds' (2017), https://ec.europa.eu/regional_policy/en/information/publications/studies/2017/the-value-added-of-ex-ante-conditionalities-in-the-european-structural-and-investment-funds-esi-funds (last visited 26 January 2024).

2. Equality of Member States

The question of the adverse impact of spending conditionality on the equality of Member States has been recently addressed by the Court of Justice in the cases concerning Hungary and Poland previously mentioned.[77] In reply to the assertions of Hungary and Poland that the rule of law conditionality infringes the principle of equality of Member States under Article 4(2) TEU, the Court, relying exclusively on the text of the contested regulation, concluded that the latter sets out important procedural guarantees, including the principle of proportionality and the requirement for the Commission to conduct an objective and diligent analysis prior to ordering any spending cuts.[78] The Court was thus satisfied that these procedural and legal guarantees contained in the financial regulation are sufficient to protect the equality of Member States.[79]

Although it is difficult to disagree with the legal judgement of the Court, if one puts conditionality in the broader economic perspective of spending to which conditionality is inextricably linked, a different picture emerges.

As anticipated in section 2, EU budgetary transfers to Member States are inherently unequal.[80] And there are extremely good reasons for this.[81] The unequal budgetary distribution reflects the socio-economic and territorial disparities and distinct development needs not only between Member States but also within their territories. The unequal distribution of the EU budget, therefore, pursues an equity and solidarity objective, aiming to create a level playing field for all individuals, which would enable them to access the opportunities offered by the European integration project. Another important reason for the unequal distribution of the budget is its efficiency objective—hence, its objective to stimulate economic growth and support sectors at an economic disadvantage in specific areas of interest for the EU (e.g. the shift to green energy, research and innovation, and support for farmers and fishermen) that are

[77] Case C-156/21, *Hungary v. European Parliament and Council of the European Union* (n. 53); Case C-157/21, *Republic of Poland v. European Parliament and Council of the European Union* (n. 53).

[78] Case C-156/21, *Hungary v. European Parliament and Council of the European Union* (n. 53), paras 168, 316–317.

[79] Ibid.

[80] See, for the current 2021–2027 MFF budget distribution, https://commission.europa.eu/strategy-and-policy/eu-budget/long-term-eu-budget/2021-2027/spending-and-revenue_en (last visited 26 January 2024). See also the distribution of Recovery and Resilience Facility (RRF) per Member State, https://ec.europa.eu/economy_finance/recovery-and-resilience-scoreboard/index.html (last visited 26 January 2024). The RRF allocations as a share of gross domestic product (GDP) are Greece (16 per cent), Romania (12 per cent), Croatia (11 per cent), Italy (10 per cent), Bulgaria (9 per cent), Portugal (8 per cent); as opposed to Luxembourg (0.1 per cent), Ireland (0.2 per cent), Denmark (0.4 per cent), Netherlands (0.5 per cent), Sweden (0.6 per cent), and Germany (0.7 per cent).

[81] R. W. Boadway and A. Shah, *Fiscal Federalism: Principles and Practices of Multiorder Governance* (2009).

embraced by each Member State and each EU region pursuant to their particular development needs and goals.[82]

Therefore, withdrawal of funds from Member States in case of non-compliance with a spending conditionality would primarily affect Member States at the receiving end of the EU budget, as opposed to more developed Member States—the so-called EU budget beneficiaries *versus* contributors. Here, it is important to bear in mind that the law of spending conditionality requires respect of certain EU standards, which are to be observed in an equal manner by all Member States, for example respect of rule of law or macroeconomic indicators. However, in case of non-compliance, the financial sanction of a spending conditionality shall have a fundamentally more severe economic impact for a very clear set of less developed Member States and their most vulnerable communities.

Contrary to infringement procedures, where the eventual financial penalties and lump sums are calculated using sophisticated formula to ensure the deterrent effect of the sanctions based inter alia on Member States' economic power and capacity to pay,[83] in case of spending conditionality, the deterrent effect is economically credible only in a subset of clearly identifiable less developed Member States.[84] For more developed Member States, the deterrent effect is significantly lower and, at best, may be resented in the form of political or reputational damage. The proportionality requirement or the procedural guarantees, stressed by the Court in its recent rulings against Hungary and Poland, is not likely to change this objective outcome.[85]

3. Individual Rights

One question regarding the protection of fundamental rights arises in situations where Member States put in place normative frameworks in the implementation of a given spending conditionality that may limit or otherwise affect individual rights but do not present a sufficiently clear link to the EU law act of spending, thus calling into question the applicability of the EU Charter of Fundamental Rights. The Charter has a limited scope of application at national

[82] For a critique of EU record in balancing the equity and efficiency objectives of budgetary transfers, see F. Barca, *An Agenda for a Reformed Cohesion Policy. A Place-Based Approach to Meeting European Union Challenges and Expectations* (2009) 94–98, An agenda for a reformed cohesion policy—Publications Office of the EU (europa.eu) (last visited 26 January 2024).

[83] In particular with regards to the state's GDP, seriousness, duration, and importance of infringement, the impact of the sanctions on the general and particular interests at stake, and the State's capacity to pay. See Commission Communication C(2018) 5851 final.

[84] Ibid.

[85] Case C-156/21, *Hungary v. European Parliament and Council of the European Union* (n. 53), paras 168, 316–317.

level. Pursuant to Article 51(1) therein, the rights and provisions referred to apply 'to Member States only when they are implementing Union law'. On this point of law, the Court has so far held that the Charter shall apply to national acts implementing EU funds each time there is an applicable and traceable EU law obligation or where a Member State is implementing EU funds acts in derogation from an EU single market freedom.[86] The Court has nevertheless denied the Charter's applicability in situations where national acts implement EU soft law policy orientations or recommendations, even if the latter measures may be financed from the EU budget.[87] In *Florescu*, the Court found that the Charter does apply to the provision of a memorandum of understanding, implemented pursuant to a binding EU law act (decision), so long as the conduct proscribed is sufficiently detailed and precise to allow the inference that the latter was an implementation of EU law, and irrespective of the fact that a certain degree of discretion was exercised by the Member State in adoption of the said action, that is reform of the pensions system.[88] It follows that in cases where sufficiently detailed and precise national measures are adopted pursuant to spending conditionality that can be traced back to the binding text of an EU law act—a spending regulation—the Charter would be applicable to Member States. This leaves open the question of insufficiently precise and detailed national measures adopted based on a conditionality requirement. As demonstrated in full detail elsewhere, the implementation of certain spending conditionalities on the ground leaves significant discretion to Member States, which, in turn, may lead to important departures from the established EU legal framework.[89] In this sense, Member States may adopt additional implementing action, going beyond the requirements of the EU funding regulations (e.g. changes triggered by public procurement ex ante conditionality led to the establishment of specialized court chambers in Romania in the 2014–2020 MFF).[90] Moreover, certain spending conditionalities, such as macroeconomic conditionality,[91] not only ask for compliance with existent measures but also continuous compliance with future EU measures and recommendations, that

[86] For a detailed analysis on the Charter applicability to EU funds implemented at the national level, see V. Viță and K. Podstawa, 'When the EU Funds Meet the Charter of Fundamental Rights: On the Applicability of the Charter of Fundamental Rights to EU Funds Implemented at the National Level', Global Campus Working Papers (2017) 10–18, https://repository.gchumanrights.org/items/11435ca1-8d8c-4aa9-a646-2d393a2dbfc4 (last visited 13 February 2024).
[87] Case C-117/14, *Grima Janet Nisttahuz Poclava v. Jose María Ariza Toledano* (EU:C:2015:60), para 42.
[88] Case C-258/14, *Florescu and Others v. Casa Județeană de Pensii* (EU:C:2017:448) 48.
[89] Viță (n. 17).
[90] Ibid.
[91] See Art. 19 of Regulation 2021/1060 (n. 22).

is compliance with future European Semester recommendations. In these situations, the implementation of spending conditionality at the national level may lose connection to the legal norms of the EU funds regulations. In the light of the Court's doctrine of Charter applicability to EU funds at national level, spending conditionality is an extremely interesting case study. The latter shall inevitably add complexity in discerning the situations covered by the protection of the Charter at national level, which shall require the continued special vigilance of EU legislators and scholars as well as further clarification from the Court.

A further question, and an important element in this discussion on the protection of individual rights, is the potential risk the funding cut-off poses to individual rights and legitimate expectations. Even if the primary addressees of EU spending cuts are states, ultimately the disadvantage is felt most strongly by EU citizens (i.e. researchers, the unemployed, farmers, fishers, and small and medium-sized enterprises), who may see their grants or subsidies are no longer available or may be indirectly impacted by failure to enjoy the result of spending actions, that is, green and accessible energy, roads, health or education infrastructure, clean environment, social inclusion, ICT connectivity, rural development, and research and development. In this respect, the rule of law conditionality is the only spending conditionality of the EU budget that includes a safety clause which states that the impositions of withdrawals of funds shall not affect the obligations of Member States towards final recipients and beneficiaries of funds and confers an obligation on the Commission to ensure that individual rights are safeguarded.[92] Furthermore, even in this singular case, while this obligation may sound reassuring in law, in practice, such an obligation inevitably places the burden of enforcement on the individual and raises the prospect of the beginning of complex litigation at national and EU level that ultimately EU citizens need to undertake on their own.[93]

[92] See Art. 5(2) of Regulation 2020/2092 (n. 4):

> the imposition of appropriate measures shall not affect the obligations of government entities referred to in point (a) of paragraph 1 or of Member States referred to in point (b) of paragraph 1 to implement the programme or fund affected by the measure, and in particular the obligations they have towards final recipients or beneficiaries, including the obligation to make payments under this Regulation and the applicable sector-specific or financial rules. The Commission shall verify whether applicable law has been complied with and, where necessary, take all appropriate measures to protect the Union budget, in line with sector-specific and financial rules.

[93] O. Ceran and Y. Guerra: 'The Council's Conditionality Decision as a Violation of Academic Freedom?', *Verfassungsblog* (28 March 2023), https://verfassungsblog.de/the-councils-conditionality-decision-as-a-violation-of-academic-freedom (last visited 13 February 2024). Regarding the case of Hungarian universities challenging the Council decision on enforcement of rule of law conditionality,

4. Solidarity

As previously argued by Marise Cremona, the notion of solidarity in EU internal action is predicated on the notion of economic and territorial cohesion, unity of purpose based on mutual trust, and loyalty to the EU project as a whole and to the values it stands for.[94] She further argued that as an expression of solidarity within the EU, failure to fulfil an obligation does not lead to retaliation or countermeasures by other Member States but is resolved by independent and impartial courts, whose rulings are generally accepted by Member States.[95] Moreover, the fact that the treaties entrust the vigilance of enforcement primarily to the Commission further enhances solidarity internally and limits the space for adversariality between Member States, which rarely bring a case against each other to court. Another important finding is that infringement fines and economic sanctions are rarely deployed internally, even if they are increasingly available in EU internal action.[96] This is not because the EU lacks the courage or capacity to deploy sanctions, as commentators have argued,[97] but because sanctions depart from what Bieber and Maiani call the EU's 'constitutional template' of enforcement, which is premised primarily on a culture of cooperation and negotiation between the EU and the Member States with the primary goal of compliance (not imposing sanctions).[98]

The law of spending conditionality sheds new light on all these important constitutional distinctions in the unique and complex context of spending. There is an inevitable friction between the solidarity-enhancing aim of the EU budget and the significant increase in spending conditionality therein, which has been referred to in recent years as the nexus of 'solidarity–responsibility'. Given the deep interdependencies and the advanced stage of EU integration, the enforcement of EU objectives through spending conditionality may credibly add adversariality and invite the retaliation of Member States concerned. As a result, and in consistency with the EU's constitutional template of enforcement, the spending conditionality addressed to Member States is, as a general rule, rarely enforced in the EU.[99] Evidence from the operation of spending

see Case T-138/23, Action brought on 13 March 2023, *Semmelweis Egyetem v. Council* (case in progress).

[94] Cremona, 'EU Enlargement: Solidarity and Conditionality', 30(1) *European Law Review* (2005) 3.
[95] Ibid.
[96] Bieber and Maiani (n. 6).
[97] Pech and Scheppele, 'Illiberalism within: Rule of Law Backsliding in the EU', 19 *CYELS* (2017) 3–47; Halmai (n. 6); Wennerås, 'Sanctions against Member States under Article 260 TFEU: Alive, But Not Kicking?', 49(1) *CMLRev* (2012) 145–175.
[98] Bieber and Maiani (n. 6).
[99] Viță (n. 2).

conditionality in the EU shows that in practice, enforcement of spending conditionality is a measure of last resort taken only when all the previous measures aimed at cooperation and negotiation have failed.[100] The very fact that conditionality is enforced denotes a system failure, meaning that compliance has not been achieved and solidarity is already affected. In these rare instances where conditionality is enforced, the question that arises is whether conditionality ultimately helps stem the haemorrhaging solidarity and restore lost solidarity or whether the enforcement of the tool is leading the EU farther from its foundational aspiration of a 'de facto solidarity' between the people of Europe.[101]

4. The Balancing Test

In the previous sections, it has been shown that there are important ways in which the expanding law on spending conditionality may reinforce the constitutional aims of the EU treaties and, at the same time, weaken a number of the legitimate interests therein. As such, I have argued—in a non-exhaustive manner—that spending conditionality may be constitutionally legitimated as a tool that can be used to reinforce the EU's objectives, ensure effective government, including efficient spending, provide flexible legal solutions in times of necessity, and enhance the protection of EU values. At the same time, I have argued that spending conditionality may call into question a number of competing constitutional limits, for instance the legality of EU regulatory and enforcement action, the equality of Member States, the protection of individual rights, and the principle of solidarity.

This section argues that the true constitutional bearing of spending conditionality may be construed only after a comprehensive balancing test of both the constitutional aims and the competing constitutional limits raised by spending conditionality. The rule of law conditionality, and its unique recent enforcement in the case of Hungary, will be used to illustrate this point (see Table 4.1).

At the outset, it is important to clarify that at the end of 2022, the Commission put in motion an unprecedented triple enforcement of conditionality against Hungary, adopted by the Council in December 2022, concerning a highly significant total amount of approximately EUR 30 billion in cohesion and RRF funds, which represented a quarter of the country's GDP in 2019 figures. On

[100] Viţă (n. 17).

[101] R. Schuman, Declaration of 9 May 1950: 'Europe will not be made all at once, or according to a single plan. It will be built through concrete achievements which first create a de facto solidarity.'

Table 4.1 The balancing test of conditionality

Legitimate constitutional aims	Competing constitutional limits
EU objectives	Legality of EU action
Effective government	Equality of Member States
Necessity	Individual rights
Protection of EU values	Solidarity

12 December 2022, EUR 5.8 billion in RRF funds were suspended for Hungary subject to the fulfilment of 27 'super milestones' related to the rule of law.[102] Furthermore, on 22 December 2022, EUR 6.3 billion in cohesion funds commitments were suspended by a Council decision based on rule of law conditionality, subject to the complete fulfilment of 17 remedial actions, already included in the 27 super milestones of the RRF.[103] Finally, on the same day, the Commission announced the approval of the partnership agreement with Hungary regarding EUR 22 billion in EU cohesion policy funds, whereby future disbursements are conditional on the fulfilment of enabling conditions, detailed in a roadmap which has very strong links, yet again, with both the RRF super milestones and the rule of law conditionality remedial actions.[104]

Returning to our analysis of the rule of law conditionality instrument: from the point of view of the constitutional aims pursued, the tool has, in principle, strong constitutional legitimation.

First, the conditionality has the potential to strengthen the EU's objectives, and notably the EU's aim to promote its values,[105] by putting in place a mechanism that allows the withdrawal of EU funds in case of breaches of certain principles of the rule of law. The very act of adopting the rule of law conditionality regulation emphasizes the sense of importance that the EU attaches to the respect of the rule of law. However, if one looks at the actual record of the rule of law conditionality in action, the recent and only enforcement of the tool Hungary has managed to partially achieve thus far is incomplete and symbolic compliance with the EU values at stake.[106] As the explanatory memorandum

[102] Council of the EU, 'NextGenerationEU: Member States Approve National Plan of Hungary', Press Release 1041/22 (2022) (europa.eu) (last visited 26 January 2024); Council implementing decision available at http://Consilium (europa.eu) (last visited 26 January 2024).

[103] Council Implementing Decision 2022/2506, OJ 2022 L 325.

[104] European Commission, 'Brussels (2022) EU Cohesion Policy 2021–2027: Hungary', Press Release (2022) (europa.eu) (last visited 26 January 2024).

[105] See Art. 3 TEU 'The Union's aim is to promote ... its values.'

[106] Explanatory Memorandum, Proposal for a Council implementing decision on measures for the protection of the Union budget against breaches of the principles of the rule of law in Hungary, Brussels

to the Council decision on the suspension of EUR 6.3 billion in cohesion funds destined for Hungary illustrates, the Commission states that despite the actions taken, Hungary did not adequately address the 17 remedial measures and 28 correlative key implementation steps to which it had committed itself in the context of rule of law conditionality procedures.[107] For instance, based on the Commission's assessment, amendments to public procurement law do not seem to have led to improvements in practice.[108] Furthermore, the concentration of powers in the hands of the Prosecutor General's Office and systematic lack of investigations in cases of corruption involving high-level officials remain a challenge.[109] Although an anti-corruption strategy has been adopted, it is not being effectively implemented.[110] The new legal rules on asset declarations provide for even less stringent requirements than before.[111] The Commission thus concluded that 'pending the details and the correct, full and effective implementation of all the key implementation steps of these measures', the risk to the EU budget persists.[112] This limited compliance is even more striking as the enforcement of the rule of law conditionality feeds into the unique, triple enforcement of spending conditionality for Hungary explained above: first by enforcement of the rule of law conditionality mechanism,[113] second by enforcement of the general enabling conditionality on the respect of the Charter blocking access to the entirety of 2021–2027 cohesion funds,[114] and third by enforcement of the RRF conditionality relating to European Semester recommendations on the rule of law.[115] Given that none of the above cuts imply an immediate halt in EU funds to Hungary, it remains to be seen to what extent the rule of law conditionality will be able to promote the EU's objectives in the years to come. Thus far, the repeated pattern of incomplete achievement confirms the limitations of conditionality as a compliance tool identified in the 2014–2020 MFF[116] and, hence, questions the capacity of the tool to effectively address the EU's objectives.

(18 September 2022), COM(2022) 485 final, https://eur-lex.europa.eu/resource.html?uri=cellar:9473778e-372b-11ed-9c68-01aa75ed71a1.0001.02/DOC_1&format=PDF (last visited 13 February 2024).

[107] Ibid. Section 7.2.
[108] Ibid. para. 20.
[109] Ibid. para 43.
[110] Ibid. para 52.
[111] Ibid. para 55.
[112] Ibid. para 122.
[113] Council Implementing Decision 2022/2506 (n. 103).
[114] European Commission (n. 104).
[115] Council of the EU (n. 102).
[116] Viță (n. 17).

Second, the tool appears well equipped to promote effective government, notably in the form of effective spending, by ensuring that serious rule of law breaches do not adversely affect EU expenditure. As discussed, while the rule of law conditionality alone managed to secure EUR 6.3 billion from potential irregularities and risk of corruption in the case of Hungary,[117] the highly significant total of EUR 30 billion in EU expenditure has been safeguarded upfront if one accounts for all the other spending conditionalities. In this context, it is important to stress that as time passes, the pressure to spend the withheld EU funds may be mounting, leading to further compromises on the part of both the EU and Hungary. Evidence from the 2014–2020 financial period shows that, in most instances, the Commission adopted a light approach to enforcement and ultimately did not suspend any of the payments linked to an unfulfilled conditionality.[118] From this point of view, it will be important to follow what happens in Hungary closely to gather more insights on the dynamics of the tool in times of mounting political pressure.

Third, in the absence of unanimity for treaty change, conditionality is justified by the urgent need to tackle the failure of some Member States to uphold the rule of law, which weakens the very basis of the EU as a project, albeit limited to instances presenting a sufficiently direct link to spending. If ultimately effective, the tool has the potential to indirectly protect EU values by incentivizing compliance with the rule of law under the threat of future spending withdrawal or actual withdrawal. As discussed, the effectiveness of the rule of law conditionality is still to be observed in practice. If the tool proves ineffective, the question of what alternative action can be taken arises. Baldwin argued that as far as international economic sanctions are concerned, they are deployed not because policymakers are naïve, and not because they work, but because all the other tools have failed, and they remain the best policy choice in the absence of better policy alternatives.[119] The case of spending conditionality seems to confirm these arguments in the area of the rule of law, where

[117] Annex, COM(2022) 485 final (n. 106).

[118] Viță (n. 17) 349–350; Court of Auditors (n. 76) paras 8–9. In the 2014–2020 MFF, no suspensions of funds have been ordered in case of non-compliance, even though approximately 700 *ex ante* conditionalities and their corresponding action plans attached to the European Structural and Investment Funds were not completed by the legal deadline, affecting about 27 per cent of cohesion policy spending: Viță (n. 3) 26–27. Macroeconomic conditionality enforcement against Spain and Portugal in 2016 failed due to the European Parliament's strong opposition to the tool. These countries ultimately adopted sufficient measures to tackle their excessive imbalances.

[119] Baldwin, 'The Sanctions Debate and the Logic of Choice', 86 *International Security* 24 (2000) 3, at 80–107. Baldwin further noted that 'If the menu of choice includes only the options of sinking or swimming, the observation that swimming is a "notoriously poor" way to get from one place to another is not very helpful.'

the EU is uniquely limited in its capacity to act. From this point of view, the ultimate act of withdrawal of funds may not necessarily denote the potency of the EU but rather its impotence in the area. However, as opposed to the case of international sanctions, or deployment of conditionality in external relations,[120] inside the EU policy choices and alternatives do exist. From this point of view, a continued limited added value of spending conditionality to secure compliance may signal that possibly the time is ripe for a robust treaty basis for the rule of law within the EU, with an even more central role for the Court of Justice, as opposed to the EU Council.

Fourth, regarding the role of the rule of law conditionality in protecting EU values, including enjoyment of fundamental rights across the EU, as already shown above in our discussion on the promotion of EU objectives, such capacity is directly dependent on the capacity of conditionality to achieve genuine compliance with the conduct prescribed. To date, as shown by the example of Hungary, compliance is only partial in the absence of genuine commitment to the EU policy objectives pursued by conditionality and has led to little actual effective improvement of EU fundamental rights protection, such as freedom of speech and access to an independent and impartial tribunal, despite the approval of a significant number of legal acts and strategies by the government.[121]

At the other end of the scale, first, the Court has already held that the EU has competence to enact a rule of law conditionality departing from the budget legal basis, so long as the rule of law principles breached present a sufficiently direct link to spending.[122] Departing from the criterion of a sufficiently direct link between spending and the respect of the principles of the rule of law, the Court has held that the enforcement of a rule of law conditionality does not constitute a sanction for failure to respect EU values but rather a measure aimed at the protection of the EU budget, which is distinct from infringement proceedings.[123] Second, as to the question of equality of Member States, the Court has held that the procedural safeguards of the rule of law conditionality regulation are able to ensure formal equality.[124] However, as argued in section 3, substantive equality will be difficult to achieve given the inherent inequalities of budget distribution within the EU, which means that enforcement of

[120] E. Fierro, *The EU's Approach to Human Rights Conditionality in Practice* (2003).
[121] COM(2022) 485 final (n. 106).
[122] Case C-156/21, *Hungary v. European Parliament and Council of the European Union* (n. 53); Case 157/21, *Republic of Poland v. European Parliament and Council of the European Union* (n. 53).
[123] Case C-156/21, *Hungary v. European Parliament and Council of the European Union* (n. 53); Case 157/21, *Republic of Poland v. European Parliament and Council of the European Union* (n. 53).
[124] Case C-156/21, *Hungary v. European Parliament and Council of the European Union* (n. 53); Case 157/21, *Republic of Poland v. European Parliament and Council of the European Union* (n. 53).

the tool will inevitably hit Member States at the receiving end of the EU budget, such as Hungary, harder. Third, regarding the potential risk of conditionality enforcement to individual rights, so far no real risk has arisen as the recent enforcement of rule of law conditionality under the current 2021–2027 MFF concerned only future commitments of funds, or future programmes, which effectively implied blocking EU money upfront, before any right or legitimate expectation was conferred upon EU citizens.[125] Until the end of 2023, Hungary was still drawing on payments from the 2014–2020 financial framework resources, thus securing the individual amounts already committed. Finally, regarding the principle of solidarity, the recent enforcement of rule of law conditionality inevitably limits—or at least clearly does not enhance—the degree of solidarity between the EU, its Member State Hungary, and most importantly, EU citizens. The tension raised by the enforcement of spending conditionality for the principle of solidarity is evident. On the one hand, rule of law conditionality is attached to the EU budget and NGEU funds, which are the most direct expression of solidarity between EU Member States and their peoples, notably in times of health crises and economic downturn. On the other hand, enforcement of the rule of law conditionality mechanism,[126] in and of itself, is not likely to increase the solidarity between European peoples at either end of the budget distribution scale.

If the withdrawal of EU funds from Hungary continues over the next few years, the lack of EU budget disbursements to Budapest are likely to be felt not only by the government but also by the country's citizens. As discussed, solidarity in EU internal action is predicated not only on the notion of economic solidarity (economic cohesion) but also on the unity of purpose based on mutual trust, as well as Member States' loyalty to the EU project as a whole and to the values it stands for. It is clear from the long-standing confrontation between the EU and Hungary on the rule of law that the unity of purpose, mutual trust, and loyalty to EU values suffered a major setback. One may even argue that enforcement of rule of law conditionality is simply the EU's natural response. This may well be true. However, if we question to what extent the rule of law conditionality is able to remedy this setback and further reinforce the foundational treaty objective of increased solidarity within the EU, the capacities of conditionality appear limited. In addition, the enforcement of rule of law conditionality raises a question of solidarity with the EU citizens concerned and the pressing question of the EU's interest in advancing equal opportunities

[125] Council Implementing Decision 2022/2506 (n. 103).
[126] Ibid.

and comparable standards of living for all its citizens across state lines, which is unlikely to be strengthened as a result.[127]

Furthermore, the fact that the rule of law conditionality is enforced by the Council upon a proposal by the Commission and not by the Commission alone added significant adversariality between Member States and concrete counteractions adopted by Hungary in the form of temporarily blocking the attainment of important EU objectives, such as the release of aid to Ukraine or the adoption of the Corporate Tax Directive.[128] This type of confrontation is corrosive to the achievement of an 'ever deeper Union', characterized by a very high degree of integration and interdependence of its Member States. Ultimately, the result of this confrontation reinforced the EU's constitutional template of enforcement, which is premised primarily on a culture of cooperation and negotiation between the EU and its Member States with the primary goal of compliance—not sanctioning, as discussed above. Of the four issues put before the Council in December 2022, all have been adopted but are subject to significant changes, thus securing a win–win solution for both sides.[129] Hungary gave its positive vote on EU aid to Ukraine and the Corporate Tax Directive and agreed to fulfil 27 rule of law milestones (conditionalities) linked to its Recovery and Resilience Plan. In addition, for the first time ever, the EU managed to enforce the rule of law conditionality, suspending 55 per cent of future commitments to Hungary—not actual disbursements—under the cohesion funds, worth EUR 6.3 billion.[130] In turn, Hungary secured an exception under the Corporate Tax Directive to the 9 per cent corporate tax applicable in Hungary from the fixed EU minimum corporate tax of 15 per cent. Hungary also secured the approval of its Recovery and Resilience Plan worth EUR 5.8 billion, 70 per cent of which would have been lost to Hungary if the plan had not been adopted before 31 December 2022.[131] Of course, Hungary still has to comply with 27 rule of law 'super milestones' before it may draw on these funds, but it has until 31 August 2026 to do so, giving it plenty of time for continued symbolic and piecemeal compliance.[132] Equally important, Hungary also managed to reduce the rate of commitments suspended from the 2021–2027

[127] See section 4.1 above.

[128] EU Observer, 'EU Secures Deal with Hungary, Unblocks Joint Aid to Ukraine' (2022) (euobserver.com) (last visited 31 May 2023).

[129] EU Council, 'Outcome of Written Procedure on Aid to Ukraine, Minimum Tax, Hungary's Recovery Plan and the Conditionality Mechanism', Press Release (2022) http://Consilium (europa.eu) (last visited 31 May 2023).

[130] Council Implementing Decision 2022/2506 (n. 103).

[131] Council Implementing Decision on the approval of the assessment of the recovery and resilience plan for Hungary, Brussels, 15447/22 (9 December 2022).

[132] Ibid. Art. 2(3).

cohesion funds under the rule of law conditionality mechanism from the initial 65 per cent proposed by the Commission to 55 per cent.[133]

In the final analysis, when one assesses the constitutional bearing of the rule of law conditionality, limited to the criteria analysed above, a mixed picture emerges. The rule of law conditionality has been declared legal by the Court and has managed to generally promote EU objectives, even though actual compliance with the latter has proven incomplete. with very limited actual improvements regarding the rule of law. The tool has been successful so far in safeguarding the EU's financial interests, but in so doing it is able to preserve only formal equality due to the inherent inequalities in EU funds distribution to Member States. Although the rule of law conditionality was necessary to address systemic challenges to the rule of law in certain Member States in light of the EU's very limited rule of law enforcement toolkit, its limited capacity to achieve compliance beyond sound spending weakens its justification in constitutional terms and calls for reflection on more robust constitutional avenues. Equally important, individual rights that have not yet reached fruition may translate into a limited enjoyment of EU membership rights if there is a lack of disbursement from the EU in the years to come. Finally, while conditionality has so far been shown to be constrained in its capacity to effectively protect EU values, at the same time, its enforcement has limited potential to reinforce or otherwise address weakened solidarity.

This constitutional balancing test clearly shows that the constitutional legitimation of conditionality relies strongly on its capacity to deliver genuine compliance with the EU policy objective sought. This is why it is so important to look into the underlying factors that enable compliance with a spending conditionality. From this perspective, it is essential to distinguish between the capacity of spending conditionality to safeguard expenditure and its capacity to achieve compliance. As this analysis shows, spending conditionality is well equipped to assist the EU in protecting its financial interests by promptly and expediently withholding access to the EU funds at risk. However, the capacity of spending conditionality to secure Member States' compliance is less straightforward. The latter necessarily depends on a set of economic, social, and political factors such as Member State's commitment to the policy objective pursued by conditionality, the economic leverage of EU funds, the availability of alternative financial resources, the expected social impact of spending cuts, the likelihood of retaliation, the political costs involved, and domestic public

[133] COM(2022) 485 final (n. 106).

opinion. Commitment, in particular, is crucial to the success of conditionality on the ground, as vividly shown by the experience of spending conditionality in previous financial periods.[134] As paradoxical as it sounds, conditionality seems to work best in cases of willing Member States, where it is used to guide and steer national authorities towards reform. Conversely, conditionality is destined to fail if Member States are unwilling to bring about change. Where the commitment is symbolic or partial, the compliance is partial, with little to no qualitative impact on the policy end pursued by conditionality. Where the commitment is lacking, there is no qualitative improvement in the policy area pursued by conditionality, irrespective of numerous measures adopted on paper. The combination of these factors will ultimately inform the outcome of compliance. As such, genuine compliance may be achieved if the Member State is committed to achieving the conditionality criteria attached to EU spending; the financial envelope linked to a given conditionality is significant and the economic leverage of EU funds in that particular Member State is high; no alternative financial sources are immediately available; the expected social impact of withdrawal of EU funds is high; the likelihood of retaliation is low and can, in any case, be avoided by recourse to enhanced cooperation; the political costs are prohibitive for the elected leaders of the Member State concerned; the political cost for the EU is not higher than the benefits of EU funds withdrawal in the Member State concerned; and domestic public opinion, both in the EU as a whole and the Member State concerned, is supportive of the aim pursued. Only if all these critical and important considerations are carefully accounted for can one assess whether a spending conditionality, including the rule of law conditionality, may credibly lead to compliance.

5. Conclusion

Spending conditionality is a novel, developing area of EU law. As spending conditionality constantly expands and touches upon increasingly important constitutional questions, a more comprehensive and multifaceted constitutional discussion about the potential and actual reach of the tool appears necessary. In this chapter, I have laid out a constitutional framework of spending conditionality in the EU. In a systematic manner, I pointed to a number of constitutional aims that may be used as a basis for spending conditionality in the EU and contrasted them with the constitutional limits that may be called

[134] Viță (n. 17).

into question by the tool. I have argued that spending conditionality may be constitutionally legitimated departing from its potential to promote the EU's constitutional objectives; from its ability to promote effective government at the EU and national level; and from theories of necessity, protection, and promotion of EU values. I have also suggested that spending conditionality may be constrained by constitutional limits such as the principle of legality of EU's legislative and enforcement action, equality between Member States, certain aspects of the protection and distribution of EU values, and by the principle of solidarity. In so doing, I have argued that the constitutional questions raised by spending conditionality must be assessed, starting with a balancing test, which weighs the legitimate constitutional aims of the tool against the competing constitutional interests. Considering the example of rule of law conditionality, it was demonstrated that the constitutional legitimation of spending conditionality relies to a crucial extent on its capacity to achieve genuine and meaningful compliance with the policy objective pursued. From this point of view, the experience of the rule of law conditionality thus far confirms the findings on the operation of spending conditionality in the EU and attests that the tool is well equipped to safeguard EU spending, but it is less effective in securing genuine compliance with the policy goal pursued, that is the rule of law. The commitment of Member States is a key factor in enabling compliance. In this context, perhaps one of the most fascinating areas of future scholarly inquiry is to distil with a higher degree of accuracy the factors that enable commitment to the policy objective pursued by a spending conditionality, as opposed to focusing excessively on spending efficiency and cuts. At the other end of the balancing test, it has been shown that the most provocative questions on the legality of EU legislative and enforcement action through spending conditionality have already been usefully clarified by the Court of Justice. On the contrary, the impact of a spending conditionality on substantial equality between Member States, the enjoyment of individual rights, and the principle of solidarity have not yet received the due attention of the Court and will require further careful consideration.

The constitutional framework for conditionality and the balancing test described earlier aim to encourage continuous holistic scrutiny of the tool, which will guide EU lawyers, scholars, and EU institutions towards the development of a mature constitutional doctrine for spending conditionality. A robust doctrinal stance on spending conditionality would better equip the EU institutions to continuously assess the constitutional opportunity of conditionality seen individually, on a case-by-case basis, and also holistically, departing from the overall construction of the treaties and the actual results achieved by the tool in practice. In doing so, when adopting, enforcing, adjudicating, and measuring the impact of spending conditionality, the EU institutions may weigh the constitutional aims and limits at stake and assess whether conditionality is capable of reinforcing EU constitutional ends; risks weakening them; or will, most likely, turn out to be a zero-sum game.

The performance of spending conditionality so far points to a neutral constitutional balance. It remains to be seen whether the performance of the significantly reinforced law of spending conditionality in the 2021–2027 MFF and its implementation can change the current record.

5

The Emergence of New Own Resources to Strengthen the European Union Budget and Achieve Green Policy Objectives

A Win–Win or a Difficult Fit?

Ioanna Hadjiyianni

1. Introduction

Under the European Union's Multiannual Financial Framework (MFF) for 2021–2027 and the temporary recovery instrument known as the Next Generation EU (NGEU), there is an impetus to move away from a strong focus on Member State national contributions to common sources of revenue that simultaneously serve common European Union (EU) objectives.[1] The new own resources (ORs), including national contributions on non-recyclable plastic packaging waste and the ORs based on revenues from the EU Emissions Trading System (ETS) and the Carbon Border Adjustment Mechanism (CBAM), represent a significant shift in the EU's funding architecture to 'purposeful sources' of revenue. EU funding thereby serves EU policy objectives not only in allocating expenditure but also in *raising* revenue by putting a price on products/activities. The purposes and sources of EU funding thus more clearly emerge as two sides of the same coin, aligning new ORs with the EU's priorities to better focus expenditure on common public goods and priority areas, including the green transition.

This chapter explores the ways in which the purposes and sources of EU funding become inextricably linked and how the COVID-19 crisis and the need to repay the recovery fund have created a renewed momentum for restructuring the alignment between the revenue and expenditure of EU funding,

[1] The analysis in this chapter reflects legal developments as they were on 20 June 2023.

Ioanna Hadjiyianni, *The Emergence of New Own Resources to Strengthen the European Union Budget and Achieve Green Policy Objectives*. In: *New Frontiers of EU Funding*. Edited by: Claire Kilpatrick and Joanne Scott, Oxford University Press.
 DOI: 10.1093/oso/9780198940319.003.0005

particularly by creating economic incentives for introducing new ORs. It focuses on the emergence of 'green' sources of EU funding, which aim to deliver key policy objectives of the European Green Deal, thereby embodying environmental integration in the EU's funding. The analysis draws on different criteria developed in EU policy and legal documents and existing literature and categorizes these into three factors—suitability, genuineness, and fairness—using them as benchmarks for assessing the new green ORs. While the chapter adjusts and applies these criteria to the specific characteristics of the green ORs, they could also be relevant more broadly for additional ORs proposed in the future.

The 'greening' of the EU budget is also determined by horizontal mechanisms through which EU funding seeks to reconcile environmental and climate objectives with economic development and social equity by attaching 'green strings' on the expenditure of EU funds. They include targets to ensure that sufficient funds are spent on green objectives and compliance with the 'Do No Significant Harm' (DNSH) principle, which seeks to ensure that recovery and resilience measures and action under the cohesion policy funds are not harmful to environmental objectives. Green conditionalities as well as the establishment of policy-specific funds, such as the Social Climate Fund, set the broader context within which the new ORs will operate and ultimately influence their legitimacy.

Section 2 explores the context of the emergence of new 'purposeful sources' of EU funding. It discusses how addressing the consequences of the COVID-19 pandemic and repaying NGEU without unduly burdening the Member States emerge as significant new purposes of EU funding, which create a pivotal moment for the introduction of new ORs. Discussed for some years, the introduction of new ORs, based on EU policies and serving EU common objectives, signals a shift towards the EU's budgetary autonomy, which gains a renewed momentum.

Section 3 analyses the potential of the green transition, which serves as the first and predominant policy reason for introducing new, purposeful sources of EU funding, exhibiting clear European Added Value in the context of the European Green Deal. This section also sets out the roadmap and discusses the criteria that are used in this chapter for the assessment of the new ORs, focusing on their suitability, genuineness, and fairness, with both internal and external implications. Strategically creating economic incentives to promote EU priorities presents a significant tool for furthering EU integration while testing the foundations of solidarity among Member States. At the same time, from the perspective of the rest of the world, unilaterally raising revenue for the EU's budget and recovery from global issues such as climate change, on which international negotiations are ongoing, can harm the EU's international credibility. In this context, section 4 analyses each of the new green sources of EU funding (the plastic levy, the ETS, and the CBAM) and assesses their legitimacy against these criteria, presenting their overall performance in summarizing tables. The analysis also draws attention to the inter-relationship between the internal and external implications of the policy instruments underlying the EU's new ORs, which affects the legal complexity of their introduction as well as their political acceptability.

2. The Emergence of 'Purposeful' Sources of EU Funding: The Momentum of COVID-19 and NGEU

The need to move away from the high dependence on national contributions in the EU budget and the culture of *juste retour* had already emerged during the negotiation of the previous MFF, particularly with pressure from the European Parliament, which only gave its consent to the 2014–2020 MFF on the condition that an interinstitutional high-level group would examine reform options for the OR system. This led to the creation of the High-Level Group on Own Resources, which issued its final report in December 2016 on new ORs.[2] However, the need to raise revenues to recover from and address the effects of the COVID-19 pandemic crisis led to the Commission being authorized to borrow on the international markets on an unprecedented scale. Subsequently, the need to repay the recovery debt has created novel incentives and a renewed commitment to introducing, for the first time since 1988, new ORs of EU funding.

A. Moving Away from *Juste Retour*: Achieving EU Policy Priorities and Repaying a Common Debt

For a long time, the EU budget centred on the logic of *juste retour* or 'I want my money back',[3] with Member States seeking to achieve a balance between what they contribute to the EU budget and what they get back. This logic persisted

[2] M. Monti et al., 'Final Report and Recommendations of the High-Level Group on Own Resources' (December 2016) (hereinafter the 'Monti Report').

[3] Famously, Margaret Thatcher, when negotiating the United Kingdom's European Community budget rebate in 1979, declared 'We want our own money back' at the press conference after the Dublin European Council.

because the national contributions to the EU's annual budget, consisting of a proportional share of national budgets based on Member States' relative economic strength,[4] prevailed as the single largest source of the EU's revenues. While initially conceived as a residual source of revenue, to balance the budget in case other ORs did not cover the EU's expenditure, ultimately, national contributions, known as the gross national income (GNI)-based resource, ended up accounting for roughly two-thirds of the EU's revenue.

Proceeds that accrue directly to the EU budget (as an obligation under EU legislation) are considered genuine ORs, even if the collection of the funds is done at the national level.[5] On this basis, of the existing ORs, only traditional ORs relating to customs duties qualify as truly 'genuine'. This is because the decision-making underlying the customs policy is largely based on the community method. Therefore, the incidence and proceeds from these resources cannot be easily attributed to any particular Member State, and the largest part of proceeds accrues directly to the EU budget (even if collected nationally) and is not accounted as expenditure in national budgets. Notably, similarly to some of the new ORs, the traditional ORs also involve 'taxing foreigners' to raise revenue for the EU budget.

On the contrary, although classified as an OR, the GNI-based resource is not founded on an EU common policy, and the amounts are essentially taken out of the general income of national budgets. As Schratzenstaller-Altzinger aptly put it, both the GNI-based and the OR calculated as a percentage of the estimated value added tax (VAT) collected by the Member States are transfers that Member States 'provide' and not resources 'owned' by the EU.[6] There has been a tendency to seek to reduce national contributions on the revenue side, particularly given that the benefits and purposes served by the EU budget are often not clearly visible and cannot be easily measured. This led to the creation of correction mechanisms in the form of rebates for those Member States contributing excessively to the EU budget in relation to their relative prosperity, to compensate for the difference between their contribution and what they got back from the EU budget. While the GNI-based resource is generally favoured because it is seen as reflecting fair burden-sharing, calculated on the basis of each Member State's ability to pay, the correction mechanisms and reductions

[4] This is calculated on the basis of their gross national income.

[5] ORs are defined as as 'revenue allocated irrevocably to the Union to finance its budget and accruing to it automatically without the need for any subsequent decision by the national authorities': Monti Report (n. 2).

[6] M. Schratzenstaller-Altzinger, 'The Next Multiannual Financial Framework (MFF), Its Structure and the Own Resources', in-depth analysis requested by the European Parliament's Committee on Budgets (October 2017).

granted to certain Member States call into question the fairness achieved.[7] They rather lead to a 'regressive' system in the sense that the contributions are not proportional to the GNI per capita of each Member State.[8]

Overall, the predominance of GNI-based resources rendered the discussion around EU funding highly political, focusing on net balances and not on the European Added Value of raising common revenues that also serve in achieving European common goals.[9] Within this context, discussions on reforming the OR system had already been ongoing, particularly taking into account Brexit and the need to create supplementary sources of revenue, as well as in light of the need to phase out the rebates. Following the Monti Report,[10] the European Commission proposed a basket of new ORs in 2018, which consisted of a national contribution based on non-recycled plastic packaging waste, an OR based on ETS revenues, and an OR based on the Common Consolidated Corporate Tax Base (CCCTB).[11] Overall, Member States had been reluctant to introduce new ORs, hesitating to surrender their tax sovereignty to the EU. Also, the requirement of unanimity for the adoption of certain economic instruments that would form the basis of new ORs renders agreement particularly complex given that different kinds of ORs affect the Member States in different ways. As further explained below, the emergence of the COVID-19 pandemic and the subsequent raising of funds collectively at EU level created a different momentum for the introduction of new ORs. As Heber notes, 'the EU's enormous debt financing of the recovery fund has reshuffled the cards and new ORs will be needed in the future to avoid placing a too high burden on national budgets'.[12]

B. Spending and Repaying NGEU: A Pivotal Moment for Restructuring EU Funding

For the first time ever, funds are being raised on the financial markets as EU debt, including for providing non-repayable support to the Member States.

[7] Monti report (n. 2) 8.

[8] Ibid. 38.

[9] C. Fuest and J. Pisani-Ferry, 'Financing the European Union: New Context, New Responses', paper for presentation at the Informal Economic and Financial Affairs Council under German presidency (September 2020).

[10] Monti Report (n. 2).

[11] 'Commission Proposal for a Council Decision on the System of Own Resources of the European Union', SWD (2018) 172 final.

[12] C. Heber, 'European Legal Limits for the Recovery Fund', Max Planck Institute for Tax Law and Public Finance Working Paper 2020-16.

In a remarkable effort, described as 'creative legal engineering',[13] which stretches conventional understandings of key budgetary principles,[14] the Member States authorized the Commission to borrow on the international financial markets on behalf of the EU on an unprecedented scale to assist the Member States' recovery from the consequences of the COVID-19 crisis. In particular, the EU Commission has been authorized to borrow up to EUR 750 billion in 2018 prices. NGEU, which is financed by this borrowing, provides a new and significant source of revenue. At the same time, NGEU involves two new significant types of expenditure. On the one hand, in the short term, spending the NGEU funds by 2026 emerges as a priority and immediate purpose. This is limited in time and confined to the consequences of the pandemic.[15] On the other hand, repaying NGEU, both capital and interest, by the end of 2058 emerges as a significant purpose, mainly, for future EU budgets. The repayment of NGEU costs is meant to be at least partly covered by the new ORs, thereby creating a pivotal moment for the restructuring of the EU's OR system.

The architecture of NGEU, particularly as regards its spending, raises questions regarding its compatibility with core budgetary principles. NGEU funds are assigned as 'other revenue' in the sense of Article 311(2) of the Treaty on the Functioning of the European Union (TFEU), consisting of sources of revenue for the EU budget, which, unlike 'own resources', do not require unanimity in the Council or national ratification.[16] The fact that such large-scale funds are assigned as 'other revenue' may call into question the integrity of the own resource system as provided in Article 311(2) TFEU, whereby ORs should be the predominant source of EU revenue. However, arguably, the guarantees of its exceptional nature, limited in time and scope, ensure that this is *additional* to ORs. The complementary nature of the NGEU funds is reflected in the guarantees of its temporary nature, as they are to be used solely for addressing the consequences of COVID-19 and not for operational expenditure.[17] NGEU is thus characterized

[13] De Witte, 'The European Union's COVID-19 Recovery Plan: The Legal Engineering of an Economic Policy Shift', 58(3) *Common Market Law Review* (*CMLRev*) (2021) 635.

[14] The reinterpretations of key principles and legal competences needed to establish NGEU are considered by some to be situated 'in the grey zone between creative legal engineering and illegality': Leino-Sandberg and Ruffert, 'Next Generation EU and Its Constitutional Ramifications: A Critical Assessment', 59(2) *CMLRev* (2022) 433, at 439.

[15] See Art. 5(1) of the Council Decision 2020/2053, OJ 2020 L 424/1 (Own Resources Decision, hereinafter 'ORD').

[16] The requirements set out in Art. 311(3) TFEU for introducing new ORs are of a quasi-constitutional nature as the resulting decision only enters into force after approval by all Member States in accordance with their national constitutional requirements. On the other hand, other revenue only requires modification of the underlying policy.

[17] Restricting the use of the NGEU funds as 'other revenue' to specific purposes was deemed important by the German Federal Constitutional Court (*Bundesverfassungsgericht*), which held that the

by 'additionality' in the sense that it is a supplementary source of revenue to normal ORs relating to the exceptional situation of the pandemic recovery and is not considered a normal spending programme. Alternatively, NGEU's exceptional character and additionality justifies a derogation from the normal understanding of Article 311 TFEU, in the context of dealing with the pandemic crisis.[18] The flexibility of using 'other revenue' to supplement the EU's ORs in setting up NGEU is not similarly reflected in the introduction of new sources of revenue as discussed below, which instead take the form of 'own resources'.

At the same time, restricting the use of the funds to purposes related to COVID-19 may be seen as problematic in light of the principle of universality governing the EU budget. According to this principle, all revenue should be used to finance all expenditure without distinction.[19] However, the Financial Regulation (which sets out the rules according to which the EU budget is spent) provides for the possibility of indicating that revenue is earmarked for specific purposes (either as internal or as external assigned revenue to the EU budget).[20] In applying this exception, the EU Recovery Instrument (EURI) acts as the basic act, based on the 'crisis' competence embedded in Article 122 TFEU, and designates the NGEU funds as external assigned revenue.[21] As De Witte notes, this technique had been traditionally employed for Member States wishing to contribute additional amounts to certain programmes or external aid schemes. In the NGEU context, it is employed for 'compartmentalizing' the proceeds of the loans taken by the Union on the financial markets.[22] While this derogation from the principle of universality emerges as a novel and broadened use of assigned revenue, it seems confined to NGEU for now. As discussed below, the proposed ORs are usually not earmarked and will accrue to the general EU budget, partly for repaying the NGEU debt.

Apart from spending the NGEU funds, repaying both capital and interest by the end of 2058 also emerges as a significant new purpose for future EU budgets.[23] The loans are to be repaid by individual Member States unless the

2020 ORD does not evidently violate the principle of conferral of competences, neither does it affect the constitutional identity of the Basic Law, Judgment of 6 December 2022, 2 BvR 547/21, 2 BvR 798/21.

[18] De Witte (n. 13); De Gregorio Merino, 'The Recovery Plan: Solidarity and the Living Constitution', 50 *EU Law Live Weekend Edition* (6 March 2021).

[19] See Art. 20 of the Parliament and Council Regulation 2018/1046, OJ 2018 L 193/1 (hereinafter the 'Financial Regulation').

[20] Ibid. Art. 21(5).

[21] See Art. 3 of the Council Regulation 2020/2094, OJ 2020 LI 433/23 (EU Recovery Instrument, hereinafter 'EURI').

[22] De Witte (n. 13).

[23] See Art. 5(2) of ORD (n. 15).

EU budget guarantee is called on in the event of a default, using contingent liabilities. The grants component will be repaid directly from the EU budget, with Member States remaining responsible for their future contributions to the EU budget. In order to guarantee the repayment through the EU budget, the maximum level of resources that can be called from Member States (the OR ceiling) has been temporarily increased by 0.6 per cent, devoted exclusively to repaying the NGEU costs.[24]

Against this background, the extent to which the Member States will have to contribute to the repayment of NGEU from national budgets depends on whether the EU will establish new resources to strengthen its own budgetary capacity.[25] First, repayment could be achieved by reducing funding for other EU policies, an option to which the European Parliament would unlikely consent. Second, repayment could be covered through the increase of the OR ceiling provided under the ORD, thereby increasing national contributions to the EU budget. Third, the introduction of new ORs, ensuring that sufficient revenue from EU policies accrues to the EU budget, would ensure timely repayment of the NGEU debt without unduly burdening the Member States. Although the creation of new ORs for the EU budget may mean a reduction of certain revenue for the Member States, such as revenue from most auctioned EU ETS revenues, ensuring that the EU budget is based on sufficient ORs shields the Member States from increasing their GNI-based contributions (by triggering the application of the default guarantee). The discussion on the new ORs proposed on 22 December 2021 thus emerges in a spirit of 'agree or pay the money yourselves'.[26]

The interconnection between the COVID-19 pandemic recovery package and the introduction of new ORs was initially made in the July 2020 Council Conclusions, a political agreement on the EU budget and recovery fund, which provided the EU Commission with a clear mandate to introduce proposals for new ORs with a specific timeline.[27] With a catalytic role played by the European Parliament, this mandate was subsequently included in the preamble to the new ORD[28] and into a legally binding roadmap in the 2020 Interinstitutional Agreement on the EU budget.[29] The Interinstitutional Agreement clarifies that the repayment of the principal and interest of NGEU will be financed by

[24] Ibid. Art. 6.

[25] De Witte (n. 13).

[26] K. Taylor, 'New "ORs" for EU Budget Will Come from Carbon Market, Executive Says' (2021), https://www.euractiv.com/section/energy-environment/news/new-own-resources-for-eu-budget-will-come-from-carbon-market-executive-says (last visited 1 December 2022).

[27] European Council Conclusions (17–21 July 2020) EUCO 10/20.

[28] See recitals 6–8 of ORD (n. 15).

[29] Parliament Council and Commission Interinstitutional Agreement of 16 December 2020, OJ 2020 L 433 I/28 (hereinafter the 'Interinstitutional Agreement'). Such an agreement on the budget and

the general budget of the EU, including new ORs. New ORs should cover the NGEU costs, and any excess is to be assigned to the EU general budget in accordance with the principle of universality.[30] It also stresses that repayment of the EURI should not lead to an undue reduction in programme expenditure or investment instruments under the MFF as well as mitigate increases in the GNI-based OR from the Member States.[31] The Interinstitutional Agreement thereby embodies and further clarifies the new momentum for the introduction of new ORs, partly to repay NGEU. This new momentum carries with it a sense of urgency as expressed in a commitment by EU institutions to take the necessary steps to facilitate a swift decision on legislative proposals on new ORs.[32]

In this context, the roadmap set out in Annex II of the Interinstitutional Agreement incorporates a timeline for the introduction of a variety of new ORs. Notably, the Agreement is based on Article 295 TFEU, which provides the possibility for institutions to conclude interinstitutional agreements that may be binding. Also, the Preamble of the Agreement itself indicates that it is binding on the institutions for as long as it is in force. The European Parliament can now claim that the Commission has a legal duty to come forward with proposals for the creation of new ORs, and the Council may be required to discuss these within a specific time frame, but the actual creation of new ORs requires a unanimous decision of the Council.[33] The existence of the roadmap in the Interinstitutional Agreement cannot force individual Member States to approve the creation of a specific new OR. In light of the strict requirements for the introduction of ORs, new sources of EU funding could have been introduced as 'other revenue'. Apart from NGEU, 'other revenue' ranges from fines to surpluses and contributions from EU staff. According to the Monti Report, other revenue that stems directly from EU policies and concerns funds that would not have been otherwise raised represents a genuine source of income that is directly linked to EU policies and competences. It is also more legally flexible, as it is based on a modification of secondary legislation (the relevant policy instrument) rather than requiring a ratification by all Member States according to national rules, as is the case with the introduction of ORs under Article 311(3) TFEU. While this flexibility was used in relation to NGEU, the

interinstitutional cooperation is typically concluded at the start of a new MFF. It did not usually involve agreement on new ORs.

[30] Interinstitutional Agreement (n. 29) Annex II, Preamble, para. F.
[31] Ibid. Annex II, Preamble, para. E.
[32] Ibid. Annex II, Part A, para. 3.
[33] De Witte (n. 13).

potential of 'other revenue' to supplement the EU's ORs has not been leveraged by the Commission in introducing other new sources of EU funding. Presumably, this choice avoids violating Article 311(2) TFEU, maintaining ORs as the predominant source of the EU budget. It also reflects the intended permanent and long-term contribution of the new sources of revenue to the EU budget.

Overall, NGEU has been designed on the basis of a novel understanding of key budgetary principles, which may reshape the future operation of EU funding. This understanding is founded on the guarantees of its exceptional and temporary character as well as the targeted increase of the ceiling, providing for a potential increase of GNI-based contributions as a default guarantee for repaying the NGEU costs. This will be triggered if sufficient ORs are not created in time. NGEU's architecture therefore provides the context for new sources of EU funding, creating the urgency for their swift adoption.

3. Roadmap and Criteria for New ORs: The Momentum of the Green Transition

According to the timeline set out in the Interinstitutional Agreement, the first batch of new ORs includes the plastics tax, which has already been introduced, followed by ORs based on the EU ETS, the CBAM, and a digital levy, which were meant to be proposed by June 2021 and introduced by January 2023. For these, the Council had to 'deliberate'[34] by 1 July 2022 at the latest in view of their introduction by January 2023.[35] The timeline was politically motivated, aiming to avoid the introduction of new ORs, apart from the plastic levy, in the 2020 ORD. This Decision had to be quickly ratified to allow for the necessary increase in the OR ceiling that would enable the EU Commission to start borrowing on the international markets. Incorporating new ORs at that stage would have further complicated things, potentially preventing a swift ratification. The second batch of ORs could include a financial transaction tax and a contribution by the corporate sector, possibly based on a new CCCTB, to be proposed by June 2024 and introduced by January 2026. These additional ORs will increase revenue flow to the EU budget and potentially complement the green ORs that are due to decrease as the EU's environmental and climate goals

[34] While the Interinstitutional Agreement (n. 29) does not specify what 'deliberate' means in this context, it likely refers to legislative deliberations on draft legislative acts proposed by the Commission.

[35] Interinstitutional Agreement (n. 29) Annex II, Part B, para. 9.

are reached. This chapter focuses on the green ORs included in the first batch, which are relevant for the reform of new ORs within the current MFF and demonstrate the potential (and challenges) in establishing purposeful ORs with significant regulatory implications both internationally and externally.

A. Criteria for the Introduction of New ORs: An Overview

Different sets of criteria have been advanced for the introduction of new sources of revenue for the EU budget. According to the Monti Report, some candidates for ORs or 'other revenue' are more genuine and suitable than others. Genuineness relates to European Added Value,[36] based on a common policy and contributing to the achievement of common policy objectives, while suitability relates to the stability, long-term contribution to the EU budget, and the legal complexity for agreeing and implementing the OR.[37] Fuest and Pisani-Ferry put forward a different combination of criteria for assessing the candidates for new ORs: whether the origin of revenue can be assigned to a particular Member State, whether corresponding revenue can be raised in isolation or requires pan-European tax coordination, whether the introduction of new resource can help tax distortions in the EU, and whether the resource is related to EU policies.[38]

The Interinstitutional Agreement on the EU budget also reflects some of these criteria in Annex II. Among the most important is the *alignment* of the sources of revenue with EU policy objectives and priorities (purposeful sources). They are thus meant not only to serve as sources of revenue but also to create economic incentives to achieve policy priorities. The Interinstitutional Agreement sets out such priorities relating to climate change, the circular economy, Europe for the Digital Age, fair taxation, the fight against tax fraud, and tax evasion. The underlying rationale for such policy-based 'owned' resources also relates to creating and strengthening the autonomy of the EU budget as proceeds are *not easily attributed to particular Member States* (moving away from *juste retour*). When the underlying policy is EU based, it is more difficult to attribute to particular Member States. (That, of course, varies in relation to the different candidates for new ORs.) This links to and reinforces the argument that ORs exhibit *European Added Value*, with policy issues better

[36] This is determined as the value resulting from an EU intervention that is additional to the value that would have been otherwise created by Member State action alone: Monti Report (n. 2).

[37] Ibid.

[38] Fuest and Pisani-Ferry (n. 9).

addressed by pooling resources at the EU level rather than through national expenditure. Special attention is also drawn to the *fairness* of ORs, which links to the fair distributions of costs among the Member States. This leads to the need for a mix of different ORs, which would affect different Member States to different degrees due to structural differences. For example, France, Germany, and Italy are more impacted by the plastic levy, whereas Poland would be more heavily affected by the reform of the ETS. The *predictability and stability* of revenue flow is also highlighted in the Interinstitutional Agreement, as is the need to raise additional *'fresh' revenues* rather than redirecting existing funds from national budgets, which would not assist in moving away from a logic of *juste retour* and would not avoid an undue burden on the Member States.

B. The Green Transition as an Underlying Objective of EU Revenue: Potential and Limitations

Against this background, various features of environmental protection and climate change make these policy issues relevant and attractive for EU funding both on the expenditure and revenue sides. Climate change and many environmental problems are inherently transboundary, exhibiting features that necessitate collective action and justify a coordinated EU response.[39] The EU has a clear democratic mandate for increased EU action in this domain, with environmental and climate action presenting clear European Added Value and a potential for the EU to take a global leadership role. The green transition emerges as a reinforced policy priority at the EU level, particularly within the context of the Commission's flagship policy instrument, the European Green Deal, which, among other aims, seeks to align EU policy priorities with EU funding.[40] The reinforced priority is also expressed in relation to the climate mitigation target, which has been embedded in a legally binding obligation in the EU climate law with an aim to achieve net-zero greenhouse gas (GHG) emissions by 2050 and a strengthened target for reducing emissions by at least 55 per cent by 2030.[41] The Member States therefore share increasingly ambitious climate and environmental objectives and, in delivering such common goods, pooling and leveraging resources at the EU level can prove more

[39] D'Alfonso, 'Climate Action: A Policy with the Potential to Redefine the EU Budget', in B. Laffan and A. De Feo (eds), *EU Financing for Next Decade, Beyond the MFF 2021–2027 and the Next Generation EU* (2020) 145.

[40] Commission Communication, 'The European Green Deal', COM(2019) 640 final.

[41] See Art. 4(1) of Parliament and Council Regulation 2021/1119, OJ 2021 L 243/1.

efficient and effective than uncoordinated action by Member States through their national budgets. In this context, Member States are more likely to accept the adoption of new green sources of EU funding.

Green taxes and economic instruments have been emerging as useful tools for delivering the environmental objectives of the European Green Deal, with the potential to provide the necessary price signals and incentives to instigate behavioural change and stimulate innovation, as well as presenting the potential to simultaneously reduce taxes in other areas, through cost-effective policies. The revenue side of EU funding has been identified as a significant policy tool for some time, but its contribution to policy priorities is not straightforward. There is an inherent danger with green economic instruments serving as ORs for the EU budget. They may bring inflow of revenue to the EU budget while not achieving the primary policy objective relating to the environment/climate and ensuring the burden is not borne by the poorest and most vulnerable. It is important to be cautious not to 'greenwash' the EU budget with ORs based on policy instruments, which may not ultimately contribute to the achievement of the underlying policy goal, offering the 'wrong trousers' for addressing wicked problems, such as climate change,[42] while seemingly offering the right (and easier to agree on) instruments to establish revenue sources for the EU budget. As Kendrick notes, certain ORs are inherently designed in a way that the success of one initiative (raising sufficient ORs to repay the NGEU debt by 2058) is dependent on the failure of another (decarbonization).[43] However, the need to increase the revenue-raising capacity, which is meant to be a secondary purpose of these measures, cannot be given priority over the primary environmental objectives. To deliver the perceived policy benefits of economic instruments serving green objectives, revenue sources should be carefully designed and monitored to deliver the rationale behind the 'polluter pays' principle rather than removing the moral stigma from environmental pollution and giving companies a way to buy out their obligations by passing on the costs to consumers. Their potential to serve as genuine 'purposeful resources' thus depends on their legal design and implementation in the broader policy context.

Overall, despite its attractiveness for EU funding, the green transition also presents challenges. The strategic use of EU funding to achieve green

[42] G. Prins and S. Rayner, 'The Wrong Trousers: Radically Rethinking Climate Policy', Joint Discussion Paper of the James Martin Institute for Science and Civilization, University of Oxford and the MacKinder Centre for the Study of Long-Wave Events, London School of Economics (2008).

[43] M. Kendrick, 'NextGenerationEU: Will the Debt Be Repaid by EU Own Resources or Member State Taxpayers?', 48(1) *European Law Review* (2023) 29.

objectives unilaterally through economic instruments can give rise to global implications that might constrain the EU's ability to adopt purposeful sources. Furthermore, if green sources are successful in delivering results (i.e. reducing plastic waste or GHG emissions), they will inherently lead to a reduction of the calculation base, calling into question the long-term stability, predictability, and contribution of such revenue to the EU budget. It therefore seems that a significant number of new sources of EU funding—three out of the four new ORs—are characterized by a temporal mismatch, serving as temporary solutions to the long-term autonomy of the EU budget, particularly in light of the ambitious goals set in the European Green Deal, which, if successful, would lead to a reduction of revenue. Nonetheless, the green transition will not happen overnight, and in the meantime, green policies provide promising new sources of revenue that can be supplemented by other types of ORs.

An additional layer of complexity relates to the alignment between policy-based sources of revenue and what the proceeds from those sources are spent on. How the money will be used is a controversial issue, with both internal and external implications. While the principle of universality indicates that revenues cannot be appropriated for specific spending purposes, and the Interinstitutional Agreement stresses the need to follow the principle of universality, the Financial Regulation allows, by way of exception, for a basic act to earmark revenues as 'internally or externally assigned revenue' to be spent on specific purposes (as the EURI does for the NGEU funds).[44] While earmarking revenues may not always significantly affect the potential of an OR to contribute to a specific policy priority (i.e. its potential to be 'purposeful'), it may influence its fairness and ultimately the likelihood of its acceptability and legitimacy. At the same time, earmarking funds for corresponding policy purposes might raise questions as to the sufficiency of new ORs in repaying NGEU. In light of the three options for repaying NGEU explained above, if revenue from new OR is earmarked as assigned revenue for specific policy purposes and there is not sufficient money left to repay NGEU, there will have to be either a reduction of current funding instruments (such as Horizon funding for research and innovation, etc.) or the default guarantee enabling the increase of GNI-based sources will be triggered. There is therefore a conflicting tension between assigning revenue and ensuring that sufficient funds are available to repay NGEU without reducing existing funding allocations.

Additional mechanisms for aligning EU funding with green policy priorities may, to a certain extent, mitigate any potential mismatches between the

[44] Ibid.

policy-orientated character of new ORs and the purposes on which the funds will be spent through earmarking of revenue. As shown in Table 5.1, alongside the introduction of green purposeful resources, three types of conditionalities aim to further 'green' the EU budget and align the EU's funding with the policy priorities relating to the green transition.

First, spending targets embody what can be termed as 'positive' environmental integration[45] by ensuring that a sufficient proportion of funds furthers environmental and climate objectives. This is usually done through environmental and climate 'tracking'. For example, 30 per cent across the current MFF and NGEU is devoted to climate objectives, and this translates into different targets in sectoral legislation and in national recovery and resilience plans. Even in the context of the Recovery and Resilience Facility (RRF), where individual national recovery and resilience plans have to achieve a target of 37 per cent towards climate purposes,[46] concerns have been raised about the use of markers in inflating climate spending. It is particularly problematic that while green tracker organizations that assessed the submitted recovery and resilience plans concluded that a large number fell short of the target, the Commission approved them.[47] Much will depend on how rigorously targets and milestones associated with the targets are examined for the disbursement of the funds, but this should have been much more rigorous from the outset. Notably, the Interinstitutional Agreement notes that in case of insufficient progress to ensure this target, the EU institutions are to consult each other on appropriate measures to be taken to ensure its achievement.[48]

Second, the DNSH principle applies horizontally in different kinds of EU funds to avoid harm to environmental objectives, thereby embodying what can be characterized as 'negative' environmental integration. It aims to integrate a spectrum of environmental objectives[49] by ensuring that actions falling within EU structural funds and the RRF do not negatively impact these objectives.

[45] The principle of environmental integration, set out in Art. 11 TFEU requires environmental protection requirements to be integrated into the definition and implementation of the Union's policies and activities.

[46] See Art. 18(4)(e) of Parliament and Council Regulation 2021/241, OJ 2021 L 57/17 (hereinafter the 'RRF Regulation').

[47] See e.g. the country reports by the Green Recovery Tracker project (2021), https://green-recovery-tracker.webflow.io/ (last visited 19 August 2024) and Climate Action Network (CAN) Europe, 'Reaching for a Green Recovery: What Holds Back Progress in Ten EU Recovery and Resilience Plans' (2022), https://caneurope.org/reaching-for-a-green-recovery-what-holds-back-progress-in-ten-eu-recovery-resilience-rrf-plans-covid-climate (last visited 14 June 2023).

[48] Interinstitutional Agreement (n. 29) Part II, A(d).

[49] These objectives are set out in Art. 17 of Parliament and Council Regulation 2020/852, OJ 2020 L 198/13: climate change mitigation and adaptation, sustainable use and protection of water and marine resources, transition to a circular economy, pollution prevention and control, protection and restoration of biodiversity and ecosystems.

Table 5.1 Mechanisms for aligning EU funding with EU policy priorities in relation to the green transition

Mechanisms for aligning EU funding with policy priorities	Key developments in relation to the green transition
Purposeful sources of revenue	Plastic levy, ETS revenues, and the CBAM
Spending targets	30% of MFF and NGEU to climate objectives
Complementarity, coherence, and synergies	Do No Significant Harm
Policy-specific budgetary instruments	Just Transition Fund and Social Climate Fund

Source: Data in left column adapted from A. D'Alfonso, 'Matching Priorities and Resources in the EU Budget', European Parliament Briefing (May 2021).

It thereby aims to increase coherence and synergies between different parts of the EU budget. However, it is not clear how demanding the DNSH is in practice, particularly in light of the exception created for natural gas according to Commission Guidance on the principle's application in the context of the RRF[50] and the overall lack of transparency and participation by civil society in the assessment process of national recovery and resilience plans.

Third, the creation of new dedicated budgetary instruments, such as the Social Climate Fund[51] and the Just Transition Fund,[52] further seeks to achieve a balance between the different pillars of sustainable development within the EU encompassing specific social aspects of a just transition. This is to be realized by redistributing some of the funds raised by climate-related sources of revenue among the Member States in ways that increase their fairness. The former, as further discussed below, aims to alleviate the burdens placed on transport users, micro-enterprises, and vulnerable households as a corollary to the new ETS on road transport and buildings. The latter focuses on regions and sectors most affected by transition, given their dependence on fossil fuels or GHG-intensive industrial processes, provided they align with the EU's climate targets (see Table 5.1).

Even though revenue raised from green ORs may not be earmarked for specific green purposes, the spending targets indirectly ensure that sufficient funds from the EU budget are devoted to environmental objectives, the DNSH principle ensures that funds will not go to environmentally degrading

50 See Annex III of Commission technical guidance on the application of the DNSH under the RRF Regulation, OJ 2021 L C 58/1.

51 Parliament and Council Regulation 2023/955, OJ 2023 L 130/1.

52 Parliament and Council Regulation (EU) 2021/1056, OJ 2021 L 231/1.

purposes, and dedicated funds aim to mitigate inequalities and unfairness of environmental policies that may raise revenue for the EU budget while detrimentally impacting vulnerable individuals and households.

While the mismatch between where the money is coming from and where it is going in terms of the underlying policy objective may be somewhat alleviated internally through a solidarity-based redistribution of funds to related purposes (e.g. by allocating part of the ETS revenues to the Social Climate Fund), it is not clear whether a similar redistribution will be ensured externally towards affected third countries. This raises fairness concerns relating to *international distributive justice*, particularly when EU unilateral measures that serve as ORs impose obligations on third-country actors. The extent to which the EU's policies on global issues are accepted internationally might ultimately determine the likelihood and sustainability of each new OR. Earmarking or redistributing some proportion of revenues to international funding can externally show that the EU is aware of concerns arising from the introduction of unilateral policies on global issues like climate change, as well as increase the likelihood of compliance with the law of the World Trade Organization (WTO). This arguably provides a more direct and visible way of showing that funds raised from unilateral EU policies on international issues go to related policy goals of global concern rather than exclusively serving the EU's recovery needs.

C. Adjusted Criteria: Assessment Benchmarks for New 'Green' Sources of Revenue

Drawing on the discussion of different criteria for assessing new ORs and on the peculiarities of serving the green transition through the revenue side of the EU budget, this chapter adopts the criteria of 'genuine', 'suitable', and 'fair', as set out in Table 5.2, for carrying out an assessment of the three green new ORs.

Table 5.2 Criteria for the Introduction of New Green Own Resources

Assessment criteria	Description
Genuine	Not easily attributed to individual Member States, based on EU policy, incentivizing potential, European Added Value
Suitable	Long-term stability of revenue, fresh revenue, legal complexity, and international implications
Fair	Solidarity among the Member States and international distributive justice

These criteria combine features deemed important in the literature and in the interinstitutional understandings. They are also adapted to the distinct complexities of green sources of revenue.

These criteria are interrelated to some extent and could be categorized in different ways. This classification reflects key controversies; enables a comparative analysis of the different new ORs; and provides a benchmark for assessing their legitimacy, both internally and externally, in light of the broader operation of EU funding. The extent to which specific ORs are genuine, suitable, and fair depends on the design of each OR and the broader regulatory framework, as well as additional (horizontal) mechanisms of integrating EU funding with EU policy priorities, such as spending targets, the DNSH principle, and allocations to specialized funds serving related policy purposes. Earmarking funds raised by green sources to matching green purposes also cuts across all three criteria.

As a preliminary observation, a spectrum of genuineness emerges, with the initial 1970s understanding relating to customs duties on one end and national GNI-based contributions on the other. The new ORs exhibit a 'hybrid' quality of genuineness, in between these two models. The suitability of the new green ORs is also particularly distinct in light of the unavoidable reduction of the calculation base as climate targets and environmental goals are reached. Finally, in terms of fairness, the new ORs raise novel issues internally relating to solidarity among Member States but also externally, given that a large portion of the money, at least in relation to the ETS and CBAM ORs, comes from outside the EU. Taxing foreigners established outside the EU is a theme already present in the traditional ORs, such as customs duties, but the new ORs present additional and distinct complexities considering their scale, the countries affected, and the legal context, which includes external implications (including WTO law, the Paris Agreement on Climate Change, and the principle of Common but Differentiated Responsibilities and Respective Capabilities (CBRRC)).

4. Assessing the New Green ORs: Different Shades of Genuine, Suitable, and Fair

In terms of the timeline of implementation, although the proposals for the underlying policies on the revision of the ETS and the introduction of a CBAM were announced in July 2021 as part of the 'Fit for 55' package, the package on the corresponding ORs was delayed, as the work on a new digital levy was put on hold in the aftermath of a long-awaited agreement at the Organisation for Economic Co-operation and Development (OECD)/G20 level on the reform of the international taxation. The three new ORs were finally proposed as a 'Christmas present' on 22 December 2021.[53] The package on all three new ORs is necessary to generate sufficient funds and limit the revisions of the ORD. According to the legally binding timeline under the Interinstitutional Agreement, the Council had to 'deliberate' on these by 1 July 2022 with a view for their introduction by 1 January 2023. The introduction of all new ORs first requires the adoption of the underlying sectoral policy instruments and, second, the ratification of the new ORD by all Member States, in accordance with national procedures. The timing of the proposal on the Next Generation of ORs, while negotiations on the underlying policy instruments were ongoing, created additional pressure for their swift adoption at EU level.

Drawing on the criteria set out in Table 5.2, the following analysis examines the extent to which the three green ORs provide genuine, suitable, and fair ORs that align the EU's sources of funding with the achievement of EU policy priorities. The following sections analyse the three new green ORs by setting out the regulatory problem to be addressed as well as the basic design of both the underlying regulatory measure and the OR itself. In light of this, the analysis then evaluates the incentivizing potential of each OR in terms of its extent to serve as a purposeful source of revenue that contributes to the achievement of the underlying policy objective. Attention is also drawn to any mismatches between the source of revenue and where that money is going to be spent, which may complicate its introduction from both an internal and an external perspective. This assessment also draws on the broader operation of the EU budget and the mechanisms for aligning the EU budget with the green transition set out in Table 5.1, which may address this mismatch indirectly.

A. The Plastic Levy as a Source of EU Revenue

The so-called 'plastic levy' represents the first new OR introduced in the EU since 1988 and was already agreed as part of the 2020 ORD. It is based on the EU's existing policy on plastic packaging waste (in terms of calculating the amount of plastic packaging waste not recycled in each Member State). Presumably, this rendered it easier to agree on, but inevitably carries forward existing problems of implementation and may not have a substantial,

[53] Commission Communication, 'The Next Generation of Own Resources for the EU Budget', COM(2021) 566 final.

additional incentivizing potential towards decreasing non-recyclable plastic packaging waste.

Its basic design stipulates that from 1 January 2021, Member States are to pay for all non-recycled packaging plastic waste placed on their market. The national contribution is, therefore, proportional to the quantity of plastic packaging waste generated in each Member State that is not recycled. The levy is multilevel in nature; it consists of a uniform call rate, with each Member State having to pay a rate of EUR 0.80 per kg of plastic packaging waste generated in its territory that is not recycled[54] while reflecting subsidiarity according to the discretion of the Member States on how to implement it. The charge is not a tax as it is payable at state level, not by individuals or corporations. Member States could seek to recover the cost of the charge through taxation, but this is up to individual countries. They could decide to recoup the cost of meeting the charge from differing parts of the supply chain, leading to potential regulatory divergence. Rather than providing a truly genuine OR, the plastic levy emerges as a different kind of national contribution. The proceeds do not accrue directly to the EU budget from a common EU policy, but the national contribution transferred to the EU budget should create additional incentives to comply with existing EU obligations on plastic packaging. Additionally, the funds are easily attributed to individual Member States, which limits the possibilities of moving away from a logic of *juste retour*.[55]

France, Germany, and Italy are expected to pay the highest national plastic contributions.[56] In order to ease the financial burden on poorer Member States, an adjustment mechanism with an annual lump sum reduction is applied to Member States with below EU average GNI per capita in 2017. The reduction corresponds to 3.8 kg of plastic packaging waste per capita and 17 Member States will be entitled to this reduction applied to their respective contributions. Anticipating issues of *fairness* that may arise between Member States, this adjustment mechanism is embedded in the design of the measure and appears like the 'reverse' lump sum reduction similarly applied to GNI-based OR. Its long-term contribution to ensuring solidarity among Member States remains to be seen, as both national GNI and EU recycling targets change.

Questions are also raised regarding its European Added Value, with some claiming that it reduces a primarily local environmental issue.[57] Although the amount of the contribution is directly proportional to the amount of plastic

[54] See Art. 2(1)(c) of ORD (n. 15).
[55] Fuest and Pisani-Ferry (n. 9).
[56] Based on available data from Eurostat.
[57] Fuest and Pisani-Ferry (n. 9).

packaging waste not recycled in a specific Member State, this levy presents European Added Value by supplementing the EU Plastics policy and the Circular Economy policy, particularly ensuring that no displacement of plastic waste occurs within the EU. Additionally, reducing and potentially eliminating plastic packaging waste in seas and oceans is not a localized issue, nor is the carbon emitted from plastic production and treatment. Inherently, the treatment of plastic packaging waste presents significant transboundary and global elements that can be better addressed through coordinated action at the EU level. Nonetheless, the interconnection of the plastic levy with the EU's broader policy on recycling and the circular economy should be more systematically pursued.

The Packaging and Packaging Waste Directive (PPWD) sets legally binding recycling targets for plastic packaging waste, aiming to reach a recycling target of 50 per cent by 2025 and 55 per cent by 2030.[58] Member States are legally obliged to take the necessary measures to reach the binding targets, but they have discretion on the kinds of measures to reach them. Member States may apply measures to ensure that producers of products bear the cost of respective waste management, including through extended producer responsibility schemes. They could also, or alternatively, levy a real plastic tax on the production or use of plastic packaging. The national contribution is *not* linked to a legal obligation for Member States to introduce additional measures targeted at the reduction of non-recycled plastic packaging waste. Although it provides indirect incentives, these are complementary to direct incentives already set in EU environmental legislation.

The Commission is currently assessing options to review the PPWD; this review will contribute to reaching the objective of the European Green Deal and the new Circular Economy Action Plan (CEAP) to ensure that 'all packaging on the EU market is reusable or recyclable in an economically viable way by 2030'.[59] It will also contribute to the objective of the 2018 European Strategy for Plastics, in which the Commission committed to ensure that 'by 2030 all plastics packaging placed on the market can be reused or recycled in a cost-effective manner'.[60] Beyond the PPWD, the single-use Plastics Directive aims to reduce plastic litter and ban certain products with readily available alternatives.[61] Member States had to transpose it by July 2021, but

[58] Parliament and Council Directive 94/62/EC (as amended), OJ 1994 L 365/10.
[59] Commission Communication, 'A New Circular Economy Action Plan', COM(2020) 98.
[60] Commission Communication, 'A European Strategy for Plastics in a Circular Economy', COM(2018) 28.
[61] Parliament and Council Directive (EU) 2019/904, OJ 2019 L 155/1.

its correct implementation has presented multiple obstacles. In this context, the plastic levy could function as a complementary measure to further incentivize Member States to comply with existing obligations, but it does not solve any of the problems in this regime, particularly how to increase recycling capacity and increase the recyclability of products. It rather carries with it the weaknesses of the existing regime, demonstrating that the legal complexities of the underlying policy instrument ultimately influence its *suitability* as an OR.

The rate for the national contribution will be proportional to the weight of non-recycled plastic packaging waste generated in each Member State, calculated as the difference between the weight of plastic packaging waste generated and the weight of plastic packaging recycled in that Member State. The calculation is dependent on the calculation of plastic packaging waste reported as recycled under PPWD Directive 94/62/EC. Up to 2019, the amount of plastic packaging waste recycled was measured at different points of the value chain and based on inaccurate estimations of plastic packaging put on the market. According to the Court of Auditors, this was due to a combination of reasons.[62] First, Member States had the discretion to measure the amount of recycled plastic at different points in the value chain after plastic packaging had turned into waste—collection, sorting, or recycling. Second, the amount of plastic packaging put on the market was actually higher than that reported by the Member States. This inaccurate estimation was due to the incomplete inclusion of packaging from online sales, from small manufacturers, and of reusable packaging put on the market for the first time. The underestimation of the actual amount of plastic packaging waste was roughly proportional to an overestimation of the actual recycling rate. To improve the quality and accuracy of the data reported, an amendment in 2018 introduced a harmonized calculation method and EU-wide requirements for the calculation, monitoring, and reporting of data. Following these revisions, the weight of packaging waste deemed to be recycled is measured at the point where packaging waste, after having been collected, sorted, shredded, and cleared, enters the actual recycling operation (input). The implementation of this harmonized method of calculation is expected to lead to a decrease in the EU-wide recycling rate by 10 per cent.[63] This means there will be a considerable gap between current rates and strengthened recycling rates for 2025 and 2030.

[62] Court of Auditors Report, 'EU Action to Tackle the Issue of Plastic Waste', 4/2020.

[63] The new rules are expected to lead to a downward correction in the EU's average reported plastic packaging recycling rate from 41 per cent (2017) to as low as 32–39 per cent: ibid.

Furthermore, plastic packaging waste will become subject to the stricter controls of the Basel Convention and thus not as easy, or even possible, to export outside the EU for recycling, reflecting the proximity principle. From January 2021, most plastic packaging waste has been considered hazardous waste under the Basel Convention.[64] The EU amended the Waste Shipment Regulation to reflect the changes introduced by the 14th Conference of the Parties (COP) to the Basel Convention, with the effect of banning exports of certain types of hazardous plastic waste to non-OECD countries and subjecting a broader range of plastic waste to prior informed consent procedures requiring the application of equivalent standards of recycling in the third countries.[65] These changes are significant given that shipments for recycling outside the EU account for 27–30 per cent of reported shipments, and for the period 2012–2017, shipping for recycling outside the EU played a significant role in reaching plastic packaging recycling targets. The introduction of the plastic levy does not anticipate or directly address the impacts on transnational waste trade and on the adjustments that third-country facilities need to implement to ensure that their recycling standards are equivalent to those set in EU legislation.

In light of the stricter 2025 and 2030 legally binding recycling targets, the Member States will have to increase their capacities to respond to changes both in the calculation of non-recycled plastic packaging waste and in relation to controls on exports under the Basel regime,[66] which necessitate higher recycling capacity within the EU. The extent to which the plastic levy is going to help or incentivize Member States to deal with the challenges ahead is questionable. It does not solve infrastructure shortages and legislative barriers that limit the ability of the market to increase recycled material suitable for food-grade packaging and hazardous material packaging. Instead, until chemical recycling matures and provides enough volume of material to tackle shortages, the implementation of the national contribution, at least in the short term, will probably be passed on to consumers.

An additional concern that may reduce the plastic levy's incentivizing potential relates to the fact that, in accordance with the principle of universality, proceeds are not earmarked for objectives relating to the circular economy or in supporting waste management infrastructure. It will therefore not *directly* increase recycling capacities. It will rather accrue to the general EU budget,

[64] 'Basel Convention Plastic Waste Amendments' (2020), http://www.basel.int/Implementation/Plasticwaste/Amendments/Overview/tabid/8426/Default.aspx (last visited 18 January 2024).

[65] Commission Delegated Regulation 2020/2174, OJ 2020 L 433/11.

[66] Court of Auditors Report 4/2020 (n. 62).

to be partly used to repay NGEU costs, while any financing of relevant purposes may be achieved through established EU spending programmes (e.g. cohesion funds, LIFE, Horizon Europe, etc.). Funding actions under the cohesion policy and the RRF are governed by the DNSH principle, which includes the objective of a transition to a circular economy. At the same time, the circular economy and waste management form part of the purposes on which EU funds are spent through the Member States. However, there are significant divergences between EU countries in terms of how much is invested in waste management.[67]

Ultimately, the incentivizing potential of the plastic levy to achieve the underlying environmental objective and its *genuineness and suitability* as an OR will depend on how each Member State finances this contribution. In the first years at least, a majority of Member States will pay it out of their national budget, which limits its incentivizing potential for further reductions of plastic packaging waste. Some countries will pay it out of their national budget irrespective of whether they set up a new tax system to collect the contribution (Austria and Belgium will do this at least for the first year). Other Member States, including Italy and Spain,[68] have introduced plastic levies nationally and others are considering the possibility. These include Austria, Bulgaria, Croatia, Cyprus, Germany, and Finland.[69] Depending on how each Member State sources the funds for this contribution, the levy does not necessarily constitute 'fresh' revenues, thereby detrimentally affecting its *suitability* as an OR, given that for many Member States, funds from their general budget will be redistributed to the EU budget in the form of the plastic-related national contribution. As more national tax policies on plastic waste are rolled out, its incentivizing potential is likely to increase in the medium term.

The long-term stability of the plastic levy, as with any green source of revenue, is called into question. The Commission estimates that the levy will finance, on average, 4 per cent of the annual EU budget (7 billion euros) for the

[67] European Commission, DG Environment, Study on Investment Needs in the Waste Sector and on the Financing of Municipal Waste Management in Member States' (2019), https://op.europa.eu/en/publication-detail/-/publication/4d5f8355-bcad-11e9-9d01-01aa75ed71a1 (last visited 18 January 2024).

[68] EY Webcast Summary, *Plastics and Packaging Taxes in Europe* (2021), https://assets.ey.com/content/dam/ey-sites/ey-com/en_gl/topics/tax/tax-pdfs/ey-plastics-and-packaging-taxes-webcast-summary.pdf (last visited 18 January 2024).

[69] WTS Global, 'Plastic Taxation in Europe: Update 2023' (2023), https://wts.com/global/publishing-article/20230522-plastic-taxation-europe-update-2023~publishing-article?language=en (last visited 18 January 2024).

period 2021–2027. However, this does not take into consideration the potential change in behaviour (reducing plastic packaging waste as a result). The lack of recognition in this respect can be problematic in light of the levy's dual purpose: to create incentives to reduce the consumption of single-use plastics, foster recycling, and boost the circular economy as well as generate revenues for the EU budget and repay the NGEU costs.[70] If the levy does actually incentivize Member States to reduce plastic packaging waste, then it will not be a continuous, reliable source of revenue. As put by Perissich, 'the idea to transfer to the EU the revenue of part or the entirety of a tax on recyclable plastic is little more than a gimmick. It would concern goods that we are busy eliminating from the market.'[71] However, moving to higher recycling rates and viable alternatives will take time. According to a Commission analysis carried out following a request from the Court of Auditors in 2018, at least within the current MFF, the revenues from the plastic levy are expected to remain relatively stable.[72]

The diversity in the implementation of the plastic levy at the national level is also likely to complicate things for transnational trade. It may ultimately influence trade in terms of additional costs incurred, as well as leading to implications at different levels of the supply chain, impacting exports of waste to third countries. However, these external implications do not seem to have played a significant role in the legal design of the measure. The plastic levy is not an EU-wide measure, for example, imposing an import tax on plastic packaging producers exporting products to the EU or a tax on waste management when plastic packaging waste is exported to be treated in foreign facilities. Rather, the external implications emerge as unavoidable and indirect, borne out incrementally, as the plastic levy is implemented variously throughout the EU and across the global supply chain. This is a significant differentiating factor of the plastic levy in comparison with the other two new ORs discussed below, which strategically implicate direct obligations on third-country actors that will contribute towards raising funds for the EU budget. The choice of the level of regulatory interference by the EU plastic levy at the Member State level and not at the level of individual operators follows the existing structure of the PPWD, which the EU did not

[70] See recital 7 of ORD (n. 15); Interinstitutional Agreement (n. 29).

[71] R. Perissich, 'Did We Say "New Own Resources" for the Recovery Fund?' (2020), https://www.ceps.eu/did-we-say-new-own-resources-for-the-recovery-fund (last visited 18 January 2024).

[72] Commission Staff Working Document, 'Financing the EU Budget: Report on the Operation of the Own Resources System', SWD (2018) 172 final.

Table 5.3 The Plastic Levy as a New Own Resource

Criterion	Assessment
Genuine	National contributions based on the amount of non-recycled plastic packaging waste can be easily attributed to individual Member States. The plastic levy is based on an EU policy but partly addresses a localized issue. Its incentivizing potential is dependent on how each Member State implements it, and its European Added Value relates to its interconnection with the EU-wide plastic packaging targets and the circular economy package.
Suitable	The long-term stability of revenue is likely to reduce as recycling targets are met. The freshness of revenue depends on how Member States implement it and whether they impose national taxes. Its legal complexity relates to implementation challenges in calculating waste that is recycled and in controlling exports. International implications will depend on how transnational trade is affected (but this is incidental).
Fair	Solidarity among the Member States is built into the measure through a GNI-based reduction, but its long-term effects will have to be reassessed. Fairness questions may be raised if costs are passed on to consumers, as well as international distributive justice concerns in light of impacts on waste treatment facilities abroad.

seek to alter when introducing a new source of revenue for the first time in 32 years. Altering the regulatory structure, with EU law directly imposing obligations on operators/producers would likely have involved longer and more contentious negotiations, as well as giving rise to significant external implications if such obligations were extended to imports. This difference, as to the type and extent of external implications for operators outside the EU, partly explains why the plastic levy was easier to agree on already in the 2020 ORD, whereas the other ORs have been the subject of intense negotiations, complicated by the looming impacts on the EU's relations with its trading partners and its credibility as a cooperative actor in international fora (see Table 5.3).

Overall, while the incentivizing potential of the plastic levy very much depends on how it is implemented and sourced at the national level, for the time being, it can provide an additional source of funding that is expected to contribute substantially, at least to the current MFF. If it simultaneously provides indirect incentives for the Member States to comply with existing EU legal obligations on the calculation of recycled plastic packaging waste, as well as recycling and elimination targets, including putting the Single Use Plastics Directive in place correctly, it already provides a purposeful source of revenue that contributes revenue flows to the EU budget alongside a combination of other ORs.

B. The EU Emissions Trading System as a Source of EU Revenue

The second new source of revenue is based on a policy instrument, the ETS directive,[73] which has been operational for some time, so, in principle, its introduction as an OR should be straightforward. However, the EU's flagship climate measure has struggled to create a functional carbon market through a top-down approach. Also, establishing an OR based on ETS revenues involves redirecting funds from the Member States to the EU and is based on a revised version of the ETS that expands to additional sectors of the economy, covering a broader scope of emissions from aviation and emissions from maritime transport, as well as creating a separate ETS for road transport, buildings, and other industrial sectors not currently covered by the ETS.[74] It is therefore likely to raise concerns both internally, in relation to the disproportionate impact on certain Member States and the impact on vulnerable households and transport users, and externally in relation to the EU's trading partners. The climate debate is a 'contest over what values are going to shape the global society in the future'.[75] The unilateral extension of the EU's regulatory choices, favouring carbon-pricing and covering activities partly taking place outside its territorial borders, can raise legitimacy concerns. It has to be carefully designed alongside the introduction of the CBAM in order to be acceptable both within and outside the EU. Assessing the genuineness, suitability, and fairness of the OR based on the ETS requires an explanation of the basic operation of the ETS and the proposed OR, the ETS's recent revision in 2023, as well as the ways in which ETS revenue is being used and will be used following its revision and its designation as an OR.

The EU ETS is (or is meant to be) the 'cornerstone' of the EU's climate change response. It currently covers about 10,000 installations in the power sectors and manufacturing industry, as well as airlines operating between European Economic Area (EEA) countries, covering about 45 per cent of emissions in the EU. It is a 'cap-and-trade' ETS, which requires all covered installations to surrender one EU allowance (EUA) for each tonne of carbon emitted. Within the limit of emissions, operators are allowed to buy and sell allowances as they

[73] Parliament and Council Directive 2003/87/EC, OJ 2003 L 275/32.
[74] Commission Proposal on the Revision of the ETS Directive, COM(2021) 551 final; Commission Proposal on the Revision of the ETS Directive as regards aviation's contribution, COM(2021) 552 final. The legislation amending the ETS was published in the OJ in May 2023 and entered into force on 5 June 2023. Amendments will apply from 1 January 2024. The relevant legislative instruments are available at https://eur-lex.europa.eu/legal-content/EN/TXT/?uri=OJ:L:2023:130:TOC (last visited 6 July 2024).
[75] Prins and Rayner (n. 42).

require. Since 2013, the cap has been set at EU level and linearly reduced each year. The mitigation target that contributes to the overall EU target is currently set at 43 per cent reduction by 2030 compared to 2005. Since January 2009, a mechanism known as the 'Market Stability Reserve' automatically reduces allowance auction volume in case of surplus to increase resilience of the system to shocks and deal with the surplus of allowances that emerged because of the economic crisis in 2009.

The Monti Report had already identified ETS-based revenues for the EU budget as a promising source, albeit sporadic and unpredictable.[76] The ETS-based OR presents clear European Added Value as it links to the common, transboundary aim of the fight against climate change, as well as relating to the better functioning of the single market. According to Fuest and Pisani-Ferry, among the candidates for new OR, ETS revenues should be the main source of new ORs given that it is based on a truly European policy.[77] Additionally, while revenues from allowances can be easily allocated to the Member State where emissions are emitted, they argue that there is no reason why proceeds from auctions should be given to that country. The emitting industry does not impose any particular damage on that country in terms of its carbon dioxide emissions. Taking the EU cap on emissions as a given, an additional emission in a particular Member State should be regarded as a 'negative externality' by other Member States in light of the common mitigation objectives.[78] The ETS revenues should therefore be allocated to the EU as the underlying corresponding policy is fundamentally a common policy as well.

Looking more closely at the proposed ETS-based OR, 25 per cent of most revenues generated from allowances auctioned from emissions trading are to accrue to the EU budget.[79] This would include revenues from the current ETS for stationary installations and aviation (for which additional allowances will be auctioned rather than allocated for free following the revision) and its extension to the maritime transport, as well as from the introduction of the new ETS for road transport and buildings.[80] The proposal includes a temporary solidarity adjustment mechanism to mitigate the regressive distributional impacts of the ETS-based OR. It provides for a maximum contribution for

[76] Notably, the Monti Report (n. 2) suggested its introduction as 'other revenue' that would have only required a revision of the ETS and not the more demanding modification of the OR decision. However, both the 2018 and the 2021 Commission proposals put forward ETS revenues as a new OR.

[77] Fuest and Pisany-Ferry (n. 9).

[78] Ibid. 11.

[79] COM(2021) 566 (n. 53).

[80] This would exclude allowances auctioned by the European Investment Bank for the Innovation Fund and the initial endowment of the Modernisation Fund.

lower-income and carbon-intensive Member States until 2030 and a minimum contribution for typically higher-income and low-carbon Member States. This will ensure that Member States do not contribute disproportionally to the EU budget in comparison to the size of their economy during the period of transition to more sustainable economies and societies and, overall, achieve a just contribution for all. Similarly to the plastic levy, the ETS OR anticipates *fairness* concerns and reduces, albeit temporarily, the effect of the OR on certain Member States, depending on their income level and the carbon intensity of their economy, thereby granting them more time to transition to low-carbon solutions. Apart from this adjustment built into the ETS OR, additional mechanisms, such as the Social Climate Fund and the Just Transition Fund, also contribute to ensuring the just transition by allocating additional financial resources to carbon-intense economies and affected actors.

The Commission estimates that the revenues from the ETS will be around 9 EUR billion per year over the 2023–2030 period.[81] The Commission highlights the pan-European nature of the ETS servicing common EU objectives of reducing GHG emissions at the lowest cost, a policy that requires action at EU level and thereby constitutes an appropriate base for EU ORs.[82] In brief, the ETS-based OR proposed by the Commission in December 2021 will partly redirect revenues from the Member States to the EU budget in the context of the current ETS, thereby not creating any new fresh revenue. Also, it will partly be based on the revised, strengthened existing ETS ('ETS 1') and the new proposed ETS for road transport and buildings and other sectors ('ETS 2') to be operational from 2027, both of which would produce additional 'fresh' revenue. While some funds will be taken away from the Member States, overall the revisions will increase the number of allowances auctioned, including from additional sectors. The importance of the ETS-based OR for the EU budget and for ensuring sufficient funds are available for repaying NGEU has created additional incentives to move the contentious negotiations on the ETS's revision forward.

In terms of its regulatory ambition, the revised ETS Directive tightens the emissions cap to 62 per cent by 2030 compared to 2005 levels,[83] in line with the overall increase in the EU's ambition to reduce emissions by 55 per cent by 2030 compared to 1990 levels and achieve carbon neutrality by 2050 under the EU Climate Law.[84] This should be realized with the linear reduction factor increased from 2.2 per cent to 4.3 per cent for the period 2024–2027 and to 4.4 per

[81] COM(2021) 566 (n. 53).
[82] Ibid.
[83] See recital 39 of Parliament and Council Directive 2023/959, OJ 2023 L 130/134.
[84] COM(2021) 551 (n. 74).

cent for 2028–2030 combined with two one-off adjustments of the cap reducing it by 90 million allowances in 2027 and by another 27 million allowances in 2026.[85] The strengthened targets require further reductions and are likely to lead to a higher number of auctioned allowances, at least in the medium term. At the same time, as climate targets are strengthened and met, the revenue will incrementally decrease, calling into question its *suitability* as an OR.

As to the scope of the ETS, the coverage of aviation and maritime emissions raises significant legal challenges, particularly in light of coexistence with applicable international regimes, which may influence the *suitability* of the ETS as an OR. In relation to emissions from aviation, the revised ETS provides that the ETS will not cover flights between the EEA and third countries until 31 December 2026. Flights between third countries and the EU will be covered by the international market-based instrument known as the Carbon Offsetting and Reduction Scheme for International Aviation (CORSIA) under the International Civil Aviation Organization (ICAO)[86] for those states that implement it. The revised ETS requires the Commission to report on the progress of implementation and the environmental integrity of CORSIA consistently with the objectives of the Paris Agreement and proceed with a legislative proposal where appropriate. From 2027, departing flights from the EEA to third countries will be included in the ETS if the Commission's report shows either that the ICAO Assembly has not strengthened CORSIA in line with the long-term aspirational goal by 31 December 2025 towards meeting the Paris Agreement goals or that the list compiled by the Commission of those that have implemented CORSIA in a certain way[87] represents less than 70 per cent of international aviation emissions.[88] The revised ETS also indicates that flights to/from least developed countries (LDCs) and small island developing states (SIDS), as defined by the United Nations, other than those listed in the implementing act on states that apply CORSIA for the purposes of EU law, and other than those with gross domestic product (GDP) per capita that equals or exceeds the EU average, will be exempted from the ETS and CORSIA

[85] See Art. 1(13) of Directive 2023/959 (n. 83) amending Art. 9 of Directive 2003/87/EC (n. 73).

[86] COM(2021) 552 final (n. 74).

[87] See Art. 1(9) of Parliament and Council Directive 2023/958, OJ 2023 L 130/115, amending Art. 25a of Directive 2003/87/EC (n. 73):

> The Commission shall adopt an implementing act listing States other than EEA countries, Switzerland and the United Kingdom which are considered to be applying CORSIA for the purposes of this Directive, with a baseline of 2019 for 2021 to 2023 and a baseline of 85 per cent of 2019 emissions for each year from 2024.

The choice of baselines corresponds to the latest ICAO decisions for the operation of CORSIA.

[88] See Art. 1(10) of Directive 2023/958 (n. 87) replacing Art. 28b of Directive 2003/87/EC (n. 73).

indefinitely.[89] This exemption seeks to incorporate distributive justice concerns as embedded in the principle of common but differentiated responsibilities (CBDR).

The European Parliament's position on 8 June 2022 was, overall, more demanding in relation to the interaction of the ETS with the international instrument.[90] It considered that CORSIA is already not aligned with the level of ambition required to keep the temperature goals of the Paris Agreement. Therefore, the ETS should apply to all departing flights to third countries from an EU airport as of 2024. The money spent on credits used for CORSIA for flights to countries that are implementing CORSIA should be deductible from the financial obligations under the EU ETS. This, according to the European Parliament, strengthens CORSIA, while the EU safeguards its legislative autonomy to regulate global aviation emissions.[91] Therefore the European Parliament wished to adopt a stricter 'penalty default' approach to climate 'contingent unilateralism',[92] not giving carte blanche approval to CORSIA but maintaining the ETS in case CORSIA is not considered sufficient on the basis of the EU's ambitions.

Overall, under the revised ETS, the default position is thus the application of the international market-based instrument until 2026, and the ETS will apply from 2027 in case the global measure is evaluated by the EU as not being stringent enough or the extent of global implementation is not sufficient. While the revised ETS therefore extends the 'stop-the-clock' approach to the coverage of global aviation emissions, the original scope of the ETS is to fully cover global aviation emissions, but this is postponed repeatedly to allow international negotiations to move forward while maintaining the 'threat' of EU unilateral action.[93] Effectively, the EU's unilateral approach through the ETS emerges as a 'penalty default' in case of insufficient international progress. This is considered problematic by some as the EU's unilateral (and subjective) evaluation of CORSIA's progress compared to the EU's gold standard in the ETS may potentially undermine international negotiations.[94] The international

[89] See recital 21 of Directive 2023/958 (n. 87) and Art. 1(9)(b) of Directive 2023/958 (n. 87) inserting Art. 25a(6) to Directive 2003/87/EC (n. 73).

[90] Revision of the EU Emissions Trading System for aviation, Amendments adopted by the European Parliament at first reading (8 June 2022), P9_TA(2022)0230.

[91] The application of the ETS to arriving flights is to be re-examined at a later stage in light of CORSIA's implementation.

[92] Scott and Rajamani, 'EU Climate Change Unilateralism', 23 *European Journal of International Law* (2012) 469; Scott, 'Extraterritoriality and Territorial Extension in EU Law', 62 *American Journal of Comparative Law* (2014) 87; I. Hadjiyianni, *The European Union as a Global Regulator for Environmental Protection, A Legitimacy Perspective* (2019).

[93] On this approach, see Scott (n. 92) 117; Hadjiyianni (n. 92) 37.

[94] Rafael Schvartzman, International Air Transport Association Regional Vice President for Europe, 'EU ETS Reform Destabilizes International Consensus for Aviation Carbon Reductions' (2023),

implications and reactions overall call into question the suitability of the ETS-based OR.

Additionally, the scope of the revised ETS is broadened to cover maritime transport of intra-EU voyages, 50 per cent of the emissions from extra-EU voyages (arriving from or departing to a third country), and emissions from ships while at berth in an EU port.[95] Surrendering of allowances for maritime transport will be phased in from 40 per cent of verified emissions for 2024, increasing gradually to 100 per cent by 2026.[96] Given that there is no global market-based action in relation to maritime emissions (unlike aviation), the Commission proposed to cover parts of global emissions in line with the CBDRRC principle and allowing third countries to decide on appropriate action in respect of the other share of emissions. The inclusion of global maritime emissions is again formulated in contingent terms providing for the Commission to review the ETS application to maritime emissions in light of future international developments and efforts to achieve the Paris Agreement objectives, including within the auspices of the International Maritime Organization (IMO) and negotiations concerning a global market-based measure.[97] It is meant to encourage third countries to take appropriate action on the share of emissions from extra-EU voyages not covered by the ETS or support the development of global market-based mechanisms. The incentivizing element was even more prevalent in the European Parliament's position, which clarified that IMO developments are not sufficient, and in the meantime, the EU should include 10 per cent of emissions from international shipping trips from 2027 with possible derogations if an IMO market-based measure is put in place.[98] The IMO measure should be in line with the Paris Agreement and at least comparable to the reductions resulting from EU measures. It calls for a proportionate reduction of the scope of application of EU measures while keeping at least 50 per cent of international shipping trips within the EU ETS. The European Parliament's position was more demanding and involved a greater scope of coverage. It ranges from simply accepting any international action on GHG emissions in the maritime sector as sufficient to withdraw the EU unilateral measure to a requirement that would include assessing the sufficiency of

https://www.iata.org/en/about/worldwide/europe/blog/eu-ets-reform-destabilizes-international-consensus-for-aviation-carbon-reductions (last visited 18 January 2024).

95 See Art. 1(7) of Directive 2023/959 (n. 83) inserting Art. 3g (a) to Directive 2003/87/EC (n. 73).
96 Art.1(7) of Directive 2023/959 (n. 83) inserting Art. 3g (b) to Directive 2003/87/EC (n. 73).
97 See recital 18 and Art. 3(g)(e) of COM(2021) 551 (n. 74).
98 Amendments adopted by the European Parliament at first reading on 22 June 2022 on the proposal to revise the EU Emissions Trading System, P9_TA(2022)0246.

international action and requiring for at least comparable ambitions, thereby exhibiting 'contingent unilateralism'[99] that is *reactive and persistent*.

The final compromise covering 50 per cent of extra-EU voyages with incremental consideration of further coverage in light of international developments and third-country action amounts to less demanding unilateralism. The revised ETS provides for the Commission to review the coverage of maritime transport emissions if a global market-based measure is adopted, examining its ambition in light of the objectives of the PA, its overall environmental integrity compared to the ETS, and any issues relating to its coherence with the ETS.[100] In this context, the Commission may propose amendments that would be consistent with the Union's 2030 climate target and the climate neutrality objective of the EU Climate Law as well as preserve the environmental integrity and effectiveness of EU climate action 'while avoiding any significant double burden'.[101] Additionally, if the IMO does not adopt a global market-based measure by 2028 at least comparable to the reductions resulting from the ETS, the Commission will examine the need to extend the ETS coverage to more than 50 per cent of emissions from extra-EU trips to/from foreign ports, in light of the objectives of the Paris Agreement. It will also examine progress at IMO level and any third-country, market-based measures equivalent to the ETS.[102]

Whatever the eventual geographic scope of the ETS regarding aviation and maritime emissions looks like pending future reviews of international developments, its extraterritorial reach and the fact that revenues raised through allowances surrendered by operators established outside the EU are not earmarked for international climate purposes raises concerns from the perspective of third countries and can harm international negotiations under the ICAO/IMO. These legal complexities call into question the *suitability* of the ETS-based OR and make it difficult to predict the level of revenues from auctioned allowances that will accrue to the EU budget in the long term on the basis of differentiated geographic scope.

The 'Fit for 55' revision also includes the introduction of a new, separate ETS on road transport, buildings, and additional industrial sectors not currently covered by the ETS ('ETS 2').[103] The new ETS will focus on upstream

[99] Scott and Rajamani (n. 92).
[100] See Art. 1(7) of Directive 2023/959 (n. 83) inserting Art. 3g(g) to Directive 2003/87/EC (n. 73).
[101] See Art. 1(7) of Directive 2023/959 (n. 83) inserting Art. 3g(g) to Directive 2003/87/EC (n. 73).
[102] See Art. 1(7) of Directive 2023/959 (n. 83) inserting Art. 3g(g) to Directive 2003/87/EC (n. 73).
[103] Additional sectors that correspond to industrial activities not covered by Annex I of Direct 2003/87/EC (n. 73), such as the heating of industrial facilities.

fuel suppliers and not on householders and road transport users. While not directly imposing obligations for surrendering allowances to fuel consumers in these sectors, it is expected to lead to price increases for consumers, with varying effects in different Member States and exposing vulnerable households to the risk of energy poverty, and it was met with significant resistance by certain Member States. For this reason, the Social Climate Fund has been introduced, which seeks to mitigate the impacts of this regime on vulnerable households and urge investments in cleaner mobility, which is further discussed below.[104] ETS 2 will have its own cap that will be set from 2027 with a linear reduction factor to achieve a 42 per cent reduction in these sectors by 2030 compared to 2005 levels,[105] and all allowances will be auctioned. The operation of the new ETS may be delayed until 2028 if energy prices are deemed exceptionally high between 2023 and 2026.[106]

The amount of ETS revenues also depends on how they are allocated to covered operators. From phase 3 of the ETS (2013), auctioning is the default method for allocating emission allowances to companies participating in the EU emissions trading system. However, in sectors other than power generation, the transition to auctioning is taking place progressively. Some allowances continue to be allocated for free until 2020 and beyond.[107] The gradual elimination of free allowances and eventual phaseout, particularly in sectors falling within the scope of the CBAM[108] and their conditional allocation based on decarbonization efforts,[109] combined with the tightened overall cap, is expected to increase decarbonization efforts in ETS sectors, as well as revenue stemming from ETS auctioned allowances.

As to the use of auctioned revenues, the revised ETS, combined with the proposal on the Next Generation ORs, alter their use by (a) increasing the amounts that will be allocated to the ETS funds; (b) accruing 25 per cent of most revenues from ETS allowances to the EU budget as a new OR, a nominal share of which will be used to finance the Social Climate Fund (through the

[104] Regulation 2023/955 (n 51).
[105] See recital 80 of Directive 2023/959 (n. 83).
[106] Ibid. recital 92 and Art. 1(29) inserting Art. 30k to Directive 2003/87/EC (n. 73).
[107] In the current period, the target is to auction 57 per cent of allowances available and a separate target of auctioning 15 per cent of aviation allowances (allocated on the basis of historical emissions).
[108] The allocation of free allowances to deal with the risks of carbon leakage to sectors and subsectors covered by the proposed CBAM (discussed below) will be gradually phased out from 2026 to 2034, leading to an increase of revenue from the ETS as more allowances will be auctioned: see recital 46 and Art. 1(13) of Directive 2023/959 (n. 83) inserting para. 1(a) to Art. 10a(b) of Directive 2003/87/EC (n. 73). Free allowances for aviation are to be gradually phased out by 2026: see recital 14 of Directive 2023/958 (n. 87).
[109] See Art. 1(13) of Directive 2023/959 (n. 83) amending Art. 10a(1) of Directive 2003/87/EC (n. 73).

EU budget) while the rest is not earmarked for climate-related purposes; and (c) creating a legal obligation for Member States to use the rest of the revenues from ETS allowances that accrue to them for climate-related purposes.

Currently, the largest share of revenue from auctioned allowances accrues to the Member States, who may decide on how to use them subject to a recommendation under the ETS Directive that 50 per cent should be used for climate-related purposes, emissions mitigation, and adaptation measures and technologies, including renewable energy, energy efficiency, and carbon capture and storage.[110] Member States received EUR 42 billion in auction receipts between 2012 and June 2019. According to the Commission, on the basis of reporting from the Member States, while approximately 80 per cent of ETS revenue is used for these purposes therein, the management decisions rest with the Member States.[111] The 'Fit for 55' revision of the ETS provides that all revenues from auctioned allowances[112] that are not attributed to the EU budget *shall* be used for climate-related purposes listed in the directive.[113] This is now to be turned into a legal obligation for the total amount of revenue from auctioned allowances accruing to the Member States from the ETS. A legal obligation is also established for Member States to use revenues from the new ETS on road transport, buildings, and other sectors (apart from revenues constituting external assigned revenue or ORs) for climate and social purposes.[114] Therefore, even though the ETS revenues accruing to the EU budget may not be earmarked for climate purposes, the revenue accruing to the Member States is to be used for climate purposes. Combined with spending targets under funding instruments including the RRF, they can mitigate any mismatches arising from the fact that the ETS OR funds are not earmarked, at least relating to operators based in the EU.

A small portion of the revenue from auctioned ETS allowances is currently reserved for two EU funds (ETS funds). In particular, 2 per cent of the total quantity of allowances between 2021 and 2030 is allocated to the Modernisation Fund, a dedicated funding programme to support 10 lower-income EU Member States (with a GDP that is 60 per cent below the EU average) in their transition to climate neutrality by helping them to

[110] See Art. 10(3) of Directive 2003/87/EC (n. 73). Member States have to report to the Commission on how revenues are used.

[111] For an overview of how revenues were used in practice, see Santikarn et al., 'The Use of Auction Revenue from Emissions Trading Systems', International Carbon Action Partnership (2019).

[112] Except the revenues used to compensate the most electro-intensive sectors for indirect costs related to increases in electricity costs as a result of the EU ETS under Art. 10a(6) of Directive 2003/87/EC (n. 73).

[113] See Art. 1(12) of Directive 2023/959 (n. 83) amending Art. 10 of Directive 2003/87/EC (n. 73).

[114] See Art.1(29) of Directive 2023/959 (n. 83) inserting Art. 30d to Directive 2003/87/EC (n. 73).

modernize their energy systems and improve energy efficiency. Additionally, the Innovation Fund receives 450 million allowances, the proceeds of which are used for promoting innovation in carbon capture and storage technology and renewable energy in industrial low-carbon processes and technology (helps decarbonize industry). The 'Fit for 55' revision maintains and strengthens the ETS funds.[115] On the one hand, the Modernisation Fund will receive an additional 2.5 per cent of total amount of allowances from 2024 to 2030 to support Member States with a GDP 75 per cent below the EU average during the period 2016–2018.[116] The Modernisation Fund is thus expected to further contribute to ensuring solidarity between the Member States, thereby affecting the EU ETS OR's overall *fairness*. The revision also eliminates support for energy generation based on fossil fuels[117] and increases the portion of the fund that must be invested in priority investments (renewable energy, support of households to address energy poverty, and just transition in carbon-dependent regions) under Article 10d(2).[118] On the other hand, the Innovation Fund will be financed by additional sources.[119] Furthermore, its scope will be extended to support innovation in low-carbon technologies in the buildings and road transport sectors as well as in maritime transport. Notably, the revised ETS has also integrated the DNSH principle as a condition for the use of revenue under both the Modernisation and the Innovation Funds from 2025.[120]

Concerns relating to the revision of the ETS and its introduction as an OR relate to its social fairness and economic rationality, harming industries that have been significantly hit by the crisis (such as aviation and maritime) as well as vulnerable households and transport users. These impacts are meant to be mitigated through additional financial support.[121] How the incentivizing potential of putting a price on carbon in these sectors will be combined effectively and fairly through additional financial support of these same sectors (albeit at different levels of the production and distribution chain) is not straightforward. As a corollary to the new ETS on road transport and buildings, the 'Fit for 55' revision introduces the Social Climate Fund, which is meant to benefit

[115] See Art. 1(12) of Directive 2023/959 (n. 83) amending Art. 10 of Directive 2003/87/EC (n. 73).

[116] This includes the same ten countries as before, but now Greece and Portugal can also receive funding from the Modernisation Fund.

[117] Except as regards the support for such investments with revenue from allowances voluntarily transferred to the Modernisation Fund in accordance with Art. 10d(4) of Directive 2003/87/EC (n. 73).

[118] See recital 64 of Directive 2023/959 (n. 83).

[119] Ibid. Art.1(13) amending Art. 10a(8) of Directive 2003/87/EC (n. 73).

[120] Art. 1(18) of Directive 2023/959 (n. 83) inserting Art. 10f to Directive 2003/87/EC (n. 73).

[121] Through the FuelEU Maritime Initiative, in combination with the Innovation Fund, as well as through the Social Climate Fund.

vulnerable households, micro-enterprises, and transport users in order to mitigate the effects of ETS 2 and is considered an 'important piece of the Fit for 55 jigsaw puzzle'.[122] It seeks to mitigate impacts of this regime for vulnerable households and urge investments in cleaner mobility. In the Commission's Proposal on Next Generation ORs, the Commission indicated that the financial envelope of the Social Climate Fund would correspond to 25 per cent of expected revenues from the ETS on road transport and buildings.[123] Pending discussions on the adoption of a new OR based on the ETS, the fund will initially be financed by revenues from the ETS and from the new ETS on road transport, buildings, and other sectors,[124] on an 'exceptional and temporary' basis, in the form of external assigned revenue.[125] A maximum amount of EUR 65 billion should be made available for its implementation in the period 2026–2032.[126] In the event that revenue from ETS allowances is established as an OR, the continuity and effectiveness of the fund will be ensured through appropriate proposals in the post-2027 MFF.[127] The fund will become operational in 2026, one year before the new ETS enters into force. Member States would have to prepare social climate plans, and the money would go towards compensation (direct payments to citizens through temporary income support) and investment in climate measures such as insulating buildings. Member States should finance at least 25 per cent of the total costs of the social climate plans.[128] As the RRF financial disbursements are meant to end by 2026, this fund would complement it in time and scope. The introduction of the Social Climate Fund can potentially achieve *fairness* internally in redistributing funds to those most acutely affected by ETS 2. Similar efforts (e.g. by allocating proportional funds to international funding mechanisms) are not reflected in the proposal in relation to operators established outside the EU to which the ETS will apply.

122 MEP Petros Kokkalis in an interview with Evi Kiorri, 'Climate Social Fund: Crucial for the Fit for 55 Jigsaw Puzzle' (2022), https://www.euractiv.com/section/energy-environment/podcast/climate-social-fund-crucial-for-the-fit-for-55-jigsaw-puzzle (last visited 18 January 2024).

123 An equivalent amount to this share will be available under the MFF to support the fund. To this end, the Commission proposed a targeted revision of the MFF, COM(2021) 569 final.

124 The Social Climate Fund will be financed by 50 million allowances from the ETS (previously allocated for free or auctioned) pursuant to Art. 10a(8b); 150 million allowances from ETS 2 on buildings, road transport, and additional sectors; and additional revenue generated from auctioned allowances from ETS 2 up to the maximum of 65 million euros by 2032: recital 84 and Art. 1(29) of Directive 2023/959 (n. 83) inserting Art. 30d to Directive 2003/87/EC (n. 73).

125 See recital 84 of Directive 2023/959 (n. 83); recital 30 of Regulation 2023/955 (n. 51).

126 Maximum annual amounts allocated to the fund are provided in the directive, and adjustments are made in case the ETS 2's start date is postponed to 2028: Art. 1(29) of Directive 2023/959 (n. 83) inserting Art. 30d to Directive 2003/87/EC (n. 73).

127 Regulation 2023/955 (n. 51) Art. 27(4).

128 Ibid. Art. 15.

Neither the Commission's proposal on Next Generation ORs nor the revised ETS indicate any further how the money accruing to the EU budget from the ETS or corresponding shares from the EU budget will be used.[129] The European Parliament had been more explicit, particularly regarding revenues from maritime and aviation allowances, including for the international aspects of their coverage. Regarding maritime allowances, the Parliament proposed for 75 per cent of revenues to be put into an Ocean Fund to support the transition to an efficient and climate-resilient EU maritime sector.[130] It also called for the Commission to engage with third countries about exploring options as to how they could also make use of the Ocean Fund. In addition, a corresponding share of the Ocean Fund is to be made available for those countries outside the Union, in particular LDCs and SIDS, whose voyages from or to a port outside the jurisdiction of a Member State are covered 100 per cent by measures aimed at adapting to climate change and decreasing their emissions in the maritime sector. As for aviation allowances, the European Parliament proposed that part of revenues should be allocated to the Climate Investment Fund to support innovations to reduce climate and environmental impact of the aviation sector. According to the Parliament, 15 per cent of revenues from flights leaving the EEA should be allocated to the UNFCCC climate funds to advance international action to mitigate climate change impacts on the most vulnerable communities. The Member States should use the rest for climate purposes and particularly for social dialogue and just transition. The revised ETS does not indicate any specific use for revenues attributed to the EU budget, but revenues that accrue to the Member States shall be used for climate-related purposes provided in the ETS Directive.[131]

Finally, concerns may be raised about the long-term stability and contribution of ETS-based revenue to the EU budget. As more emissions are included in the ETS, including maritime emissions and emissions from the new ETS for road transport, buildings, and other sectors, and as more allowances are auctioned in the aviation sector and in CBAM sectors, more revenue from the ETS is expected. At the same time, as the cap is reduced based on a more demanding linear reduction factor and more emissions are placed in the Market Stability Reserve (MSR), future revenues will also be reduced. However, overall, the operation of

[129] Except for the funds raised by ETS allowances in CBAM sectors, previously allocated for free, which will accrue to the Innovation Fund as discussed further below: recital 46 and Art. 1(13)(h) of Directive 2023/959 (n. 83) amending Art. 10a(8) of Directive 2003/87/EC (n. 73).

[130] Amendments adopted by the European Parliament, P9_TA(2022)0230 (n. 90).

[131] See Art. 1 of Directive 2023/958 (n. 87) amending Art. 3d(4) of Directive 2003/87/EC (n. 73).

Table 5.4 The ETS as a New Own Resource

Criterion	Assessment
Genuine	Emissions are attributed to individual Member States, but the damage on climate and in light of EU-wide mitigation targets does not create externalities to a particular Member State. It is truly based on EU policy addressing the global problem of climate change and affecting the internal market. The incentivizing potential stems mainly from the reduction of free allowances and the tightening of the cap and not necessarily from its designation as an OR. European Added Value is inherent in the ETS, which enabled the creation of an EU-wide carbon market.
Suitable	The long-term stability of revenue will be reduced as climate mitigation targets are met, but this will be gradual, and the MSR and the elimination of free allowances will increase revenue. Fresh revenue will be raised through the tightening of the cap, the inclusion of additional emissions, and the elimination of free allowances. Its main legal complexity relates to the global scope of coverage of emissions from aviation and maritime and its coexistence with the CBAM, which also raises international implications.
Fair	Solidarity among the Member States is meant to be ensured through the temporary solidarity adjustment mechanism, the Modernisation Fund, the Social Climate Fund, and the Just Transition Fund. These dedicated funds may address concerns about the non-allocation of revenues from auctioned allowances accruing to the EU (except for allowances in CBAM sectors previously allocated for free, which will accrue to the Innovation Fund with special attention to CBAM sectors). International distributive justice concerns are not directly and sufficiently addressed, although suggestions have been made by the European Parliament, particularly about the intended uses of the revenue raised.

the MSR, which is strengthened in the revised ETS,[132] renders the system more resilient to economic shocks and stabilizes the revenue coming from the system. As the EU moves towards reaching its carbon dioxide neutrality objective, revenues from auctions will fall. But during a time of transition that will likely last until at least 2050, the ETS will continue to generate revenue (see Table 5.4).

C. The Carbon Border Adjustment Mechanism as a Source of EU Revenue

Closely linked to the ETS is the introduction of a new, controversial EU policy aiming to regulate the carbon content of imports. The introduction of a carbon

[132] The MSR will be strengthened in the revised ETS for the period 2023–2030, including by restricting the number of allowances that can be held in the reserve to 400 million, with any surplus being permanently cancelled: Art. 2(1) of Directive 2023/959 (n. 83) amending Art.1(5a) of Decision 2015/1814.

border adjustment, while discussed in the past, resurfaced in the European Green Deal in late 2019 and was reinforced in the European Council's conclusions on the EU budget and recovery fund in July 2020. It consists of a new source of funding on the basis of a policy that is not yet agreed upon and which gained increased momentum after its identification as a new OR to be used partly to repay NGEU. The proposal for the CBAM Regulation was announced as part of the 'Fit for 55' package on 14 July 2021,[133] and its identification as a new OR followed up in the new ORs package proposed on 22 December 2021.[134] The CBAM Regulation entered into force in May 2023 and will enter into force in its transitional phase on 1 October 2023 and in its permanent phase on 1 January 2026.[135] Overall, the CBAM is a controversial policy, both internally and externally, initially proposed for selected sectors and with a gradual implementation schedule and a transition period that will take some time before it produces funds for the EU budget (if it ever does), which is one, and not the primary, of its many purposes.

The CBAM is meant to serve multiple purposes, which reflect different kinds of motives behind the EU's unilateral move and 'translate into different choices in terms of legal design'.[136] The multiple purposes also demonstrate different degrees of alignment between the EU's revenue and the underlying policy objective. The primary objective of the CBAM is to address GHG emissions embedded in imports that may undermine the EU's efforts to reduce its global carbon footprint. Putting a price on carbon for products imported to the EU, with the aim of enhancing the EU's climate action, incentivizes producers in third countries to modernize their operations and reduce the emission intensity of industries, as well as incentivizing third-country governments to ratchet up their efforts in the fight against climate change. It also aims to reduce carbon leakage and protect EU manufacturers from unfair competition.[137] Carbon leakage refers to the situation that may occur if, for reasons of costs related to climate policies, businesses transfer production to other countries with less stringent emission reduction requirements, or EU products are replaced by carbon-intensive imports. This could lead to an increase in emissions. Currently, the EU addresses concerns about carbon leakage (and

[133] Commission Proposal for a Regulation establishing a carbon border adjustment mechanism, COM(2021) 564 final.

[134] COM(2021) 566 (n. 53).

[135] Parliament and Council Regulation 2023/956, OJ 2023 L 130/52.

[136] Pirlot, 'Carbon Border Adjustment Measures: A Straightforward Multi-Purpose Climate Change Instrument?' 34 *Journal of Environmental Law* (2022) 25, at 27.

[137] Preventing the risk of carbon leakage identified as the primary aim: Art. 1 of COM(2021) 564 (n. 133).

competitiveness impacts) through free allocation (in the case of direct emissions for covered installations)[138] and indirect cost compensation (for the cost of carbon emissions related to electricity procured by covered installations).[139] According to the Court of Auditors, these mechanisms slowed down decarbonization and did not take into account the ability of industry to pass on costs to consumers.[140] The CBAM is an alternative to these mechanisms and would replace them over time,[141] recognizing that free allowance mechanisms under the ETS weaken the price signal of the system for those sectors.[142]

Addressing the risks of carbon leakage is served in a different way than that provided in the EU ETS and would create the need and impetus for eliminating free allowances to sectors covered by the CBAM, which have proven to threaten the environmental integrity and the decarbonizing potential of the system. At the same time, the revenues generated from the CBAM are then to be used for multiple purposes: repaying the recovery instrument, contributing to the just transition, and towards digitalization. While, according to the European Parliament, the budgetary role of the CBAM should only be a 'by-product' of the instrument,[143] proceeds from the CBAM (and its impact on ETS revenues) would significantly boost the EU's revenue.

Closely related to arguments about avoiding carbon leakage are motives to protect the competitiveness of domestic producers, which would face additional costs compared to their international counterparts. When unilateral measures are used primarily to protect domestic competition, significant questions from the perspective of third countries are raised as to the unilateral distribution of responsibilities relating to international climate externalities. The ways in which domestic producers are protected through such unilateral measures may also raise questions of compatibility with WTO principles, given that they are prone to give rise to protectionist abuse.

The CBAM Regulation consists of an extension of the ETS to imported products, with importers having to surrender CBAM certificates (outside the ETS pool). The choice of sectors and emissions to be covered has been the subject of intense negotiation and disagreement. Eventually, the CBAM will, at least initially, cover steel, iron, cement, fertilizers, aluminium, electricity,

[138] See Art. 10b of Directive 2003/87/EC (n. 73).

[139] Ibid. Art. 10a(6).

[140] Court of Auditors Special Report, 'The EU's Emissions Trading System: Free Allocation of Allowances Needed Better Targeting' (2020).

[141] Recital 12 and Art. 1(3) of Regulation 2023/956 (n. 135).

[142] Ibid. recital 11.

[143] Parliament Resolution of 10 March 2021 towards a WTO-compatible EU CBAM, P9_TA(2021)0071.

and hydrogen, with the possibility of adding further sectors at a later stage. A simplified CBAM system, where importers will have to report emissions embedded in their goods without paying a financial adjustment, was applied from 2023 to facilitate a smooth rollout and to facilitate dialogue with third countries. Once the definitive system becomes fully operational in 2026, EU importers will have to declare annually the quantity of goods and the amount of embedded emissions in the total goods they imported into the EU in the preceding year and surrender the corresponding CBAM certificates.

The CBAM will apply to direct emissions of GHGs emitted during the production process of the products covered as well as indirect emissions (i.e. carbon emissions from the electricity used to produce the good) in relation to cement and fertilizers. By the end of the transition period, the Commission will evaluate how the CBAM is working and whether to extend its scope to more products and services, including further down the value chain, and whether to cover indirect emissions in relation to additional products in the future.[144]

The CBAM will mirror the ETS in the sense that the system is based on the purchase of certificates, the price of which will be calculated based on the weekly average auction price of EU ETS allowances. A CBAM certificate, similarly to a European Union Allowance, corresponds to one tonne of carbon dioxide. Importers will need to acquire sufficient certificates to cover the embedded emissions of their imported goods. In this manner, imported goods would be priced as if they had been produced in the EU. For this adjustment to be applied fairly and without favouring domestic producers, it has to coordinate with existing mechanisms under the ETS to address the risks of carbon leakage, particularly through free allocation of allowances.

The CBAM will thus have an indirect effect on ETS revenues. The introduction of the CBAM requires the reduction—and ultimately abolition—of free allowances currently allocated to industries facing a high risk of carbon leakage due to international competition under the EU ETS. This would, in turn, increase revenues from the EU ETS as more allowances would be auctioned. Unilateral measures that aim to influence external developments can thereby create momentum to increase ambition internally, potentially including more sectors and expanding auctioning of allowances to sectors that currently receive most of their allowances for free. The CBAM's incentivizing potential for contributing to achieving climate change objectives thereby lies largely in its impact on the ETS, leading ultimately to the elimination of free allowances, which have hindered decarbonization efforts.

[144] Art. 30 of Regulation 2023/956 (n. 135).

To increase international acceptability, including from a WTO perspective, and ensure the environmental integrity of the measure, free allowances must be reduced hand in hand with the introduction of the CBAM. EU producers must not enjoy 'double protection'; that is, they cannot be simultaneously protected from carbon leakage through free allocation and an adjustment at the border. While there were hopes from environmental groups that free allowances would be abolished (at least from 2026) and both domestic and foreign producers would have to pay for the full amount of carbon, double protection is instead avoided by adjusting the amount of CBAM certificates in light of the number of free allowances accorded to EU domestic producers.[145] Free allowances will continue being allocated for a while. They are set to reduce over a nine-year period from 2026 until they are phased out completely by 2034.[146] This allows producers, importers, and traders to adjust to the new regime, while ensuring that free allowances and the CBAM are not cumulative. The CBAM will thus progressively apply proportionately to the reduction of free allowances under the ETS to ensure that imported and domestic products are treated even-handedly.

The CBAM, both as a policy and as a new OR, partly depends on its international acceptability by the EU's trading partners, which is complicated by the extraterritorial reach embedded in its legal design. The EU has increasingly resorted to internal environmental measures with extraterritorial implications (IEMEIs) to address pressing global problems, including climate change, that are insufficiently regulated at the international level.[147] One of the most well-known examples of such regulatory activity is the directive that first included international GHG emissions from aviation in the EU ETS.[148] This required all airlines arriving at or departing from EU airports to surrender allowances, including for emissions occurring outside EU airspace. Subsequently, it was provisionally restricted to intra-EEA flights, largely due to strong political opposition from many third countries. The introduction of the CBAM represents one of the latest examples of an IEMEI approach to regulating climate change. It aims to reflect the true carbon content of products coming from third countries by putting a price on imported products reflecting the GHG emissions caused by their production in third countries. It thereby exhibits what Scott

[145] Art. 31(1) of COM(2021) 564 (n. 133).

[146] See Art. 1(13)(b) of Directive 2023/959 (n. 83) amending Art. 10a by inserting para. 1a to Directive 2003/87/EC (n. 73). The phase-out will start at a slow rate and will accelerate towards the end of the period.

[147] Hadjiyianni (n. 92).

[148] Parliament and Council Directive 2008/101/EU, OJ 2018 L 24/8.

identifies as 'territorial extension', whereby the EU regulates activities with a territorial link to the EU, while taking into account (as a matter of law) conduct and circumstances beyond its borders.[149] Such measures create incentives for third-country companies to adjust their practices and third-country governments to emulate the EU's policies, sometimes giving rise to what Bradford identifies as the 'Brussels Effect'.[150] They often implicate significant legal complexities as well as political reactions by the EU's trading partners.

International reactions to the EU's proposal to introduce the CBAM, which can influence its *suitability* as an OR, have been mixed.[151] Depending on the sectors included, different countries are affected to different degrees. For example, the sectors of cement, aluminium, and steel would be greatly affected in Turkey, and the 'threat' of the CBAM pushed it to ratify the Paris Agreement and announce the introduction of a national ETS. In the United States, an initial negative reaction was followed by a softer reaction combined with discussions for the United States to set up its own carbon border adjustment measure. Moreover, the EU and the United States issued a joint statement to cooperate on arrangements for trade in the sectors of aluminium and steel, taking into account and reducing the carbon intensity of production. In any case, the introduction of a carbon border adjustment measure in the United States would require setting up an ETS in the first place, and the EU has declared that it is not willing to wait for a climate club combining carbon border adjustment measures before it introduces its own unilateral CBAM. US reactions may have been somewhat contained in relation to the Commission's proposal, which would not have included sectors in which the United States is a predominant exporter to the EU. If the sectoral coverage changes before the end of the transition period, particularly including chemicals as the European Parliament insisted, the reaction is likely to change. BASIC countries (Brazil, South Africa, India, and China) expressed 'grave concerns', while negative reactions were reported in African countries. Regarding LDCs, as the European Commission's impact assessment has noted, the emissions generated from imports to the EU are relatively limited compared to other EU trading partners.[152] However, the economies of certain LCDs substantially rely on exports to the EU. Mozambique is one of the most affected countries in relation to exports

[149] Scott (n. 92) 87.

[150] A. Bradford, *The Brussels Effect, How the European Union Rules the World* (2020).

[151] P. Pauw, L. van Schaik, and G. Cretti, 'The CBAM Effect: How the World Is Responding to the EU's New Climate Stick', *Clignedael Alert* (May 2022).

[152] 'Impact Assessment Report Accompanying the Proposal for a Regulation Establishing a Carbon Adjustment Mechanism', SWD (2021) 643, Part 2/2, 19.

of aluminium, and Senegal is most affected in relation to fertilizer. Generally, as regards LDCs, capacity constraints and additional costs are also expected. Notably, the EU's CBAM did not receive much attention at recent global climate summits. This may be partly explained by the fact that third countries are waiting to see how the CBAM will eventually be designed before reacting more forcefully. It can also be attributed to the fact that it might be possible to escape the CBAM through 'resource shuffling', exporting less carbon-intensive products to the EU while continuing with carbon-intensive materials and products domestically and in exports to other parts of the world.[153] Overall, despite an initial pushback, reactions have been less hostile to the EU's proposal to include global aviation emissions in the ETS back in 2008.

The *suitability* of the CBAM as a new OR depends on how its incentivizing potential to urge third countries to increase climate ambitions is realized. If incentivizing effects occur by the mere proposal, used as a lever to push countries in climate negotiations, then the CBAM may never deliver any revenues. As noted by Timmermans in November 2021, in response to the Turkish minister's comment on ratifying the Paris Agreement partly as a response to the EU's CBAM proposal, the incentivizing effect is materializing before its finalization. A different way in which EU revenue becomes a policy-steering mechanism is by convincing the Member States to agree to it (at least initially) and then using it as a potential 'stick' in international negotiations. Its external incentivizing impact may be symbolic rather than substantive by raising additional revenues for the EU budget swiftly. Furthermore, in terms of providing fresh revenue, the CBAM will only start producing revenue from 2026 onwards, and this will take place incrementally, hand in hand with the gradual reduction of free allowances under the ETS. Nonetheless, the CBAM is expected to create new and fresh revenue for the Member States and the EU, both through the CBAM certificates and its indirect impact on ETS revenues.

As to its *genuine* nature as an OR, the CBAM as an EU-wide instrument serving the common objective of reducing GHG emissions at the lowest cost, requires EU-level action, exhibiting clear European Added Value. While the surrender of CBAM certificates can be attributed to individual Member States, this does not necessarily diminish its pan-European nature. Similar to customs duties, the initial market in which products are placed on the EU market does not necessarily determine the final destination of the products or relate to the particular Member State's contribution. Its pan-European nature is also

[153] See n. 151.

evident through its close links to the EU ETS, which is itself a pan-European instrument, both by reflecting the ETS price and by leading to a reduction of free allowances under the ETS.

As to its likelihood of offering long-term *stability* of revenue, if successful, more countries will raise their ambitions and implement carbon-pricing policies, in which case, CBAM revenues will be reduced or the CBAM will not be required. In relation to green sources of revenue, the greater and more successful their incentivizing effect is in achieving the green transition goals (genuineness as OR), the less likely it is to offer a long-term, stable source of revenue for the EU budget (stability as OR), thereby demonstrating an inherent tension between the different criteria underlying EU ORs. Furthermore, CBAM revenues would be similarly volatile to ETS revenues as they reflect the ETS price. Nonetheless, given that carbon-pricing policies are not that widespread and that the ETS will continue to play a critical role in meeting the EU's climate ambitions at least until 2050, revenues emerging as a result of the CBAM would make a substantial contribution to the EU budget as a new OR, partly to be used to repay the NGEU debt.

Legal complexities influence the potential of the CBAM to contribute to the EU's climate mitigation efforts as well as its potential to be adopted, thereby influencing both its *genuineness* as a purposeful OR and its long-term *suitability* to provide a steady flow of income to the EU budget. The final design of the CBAM had to be carefully crafted, taking into account both internal legal complexities, relating to the competences and decision-making procedures of the EU, as well as external legal requirements stemming from the EU's international commitments. The fact that the CBAM 'taxes foreigners' raises distinct international legal implications. Achieving compatibility with WTO law, an explicit commitment by the Commission in the European Green Deal[154] and by the European Parliament,[155] largely influences the legal design of the EU's CBAM. The CBAM's flexibility in recognizing third-country efforts to address climate change will also determine its acceptability from the perspective of the bottom-up regulatory approach, reflecting CBDRRC in light of national circumstances, embedded in the Paris Agreement.

Starting from WTO law, CBAM measures are not inherently incompatible with WTO rules, but they need to be designed carefully to avoid violation of relevant WTO principles.[156] Among others, these include non-discrimination

[154] COM(2019) 640 final (n. 40) 5.

[155] Parliament Resolution P9_TA(2021)0071 (n. 143).

[156] Mehling et al., 'Designing Border Carbon Adjustments for Enhanced Climate Action', 113(3) *American Journal of International Law* (2019) 433.

among trading partners, the so-called most-favoured-nation (MFN) principle, and non-discrimination between domestic and imported products, the so-called national treatment principle. Exceptions about the country of origin of imported products and the extent to which a particular country has taken comparable climate action could be problematic from a WTO perspective, at least at first sight. If the CBAM violates one of the relevant substantive WTO obligations, it could potentially be justified under Article XX of the General Agreement on Tariffs and Trade (GATT) as necessary to protect the life and health of humans and/or animals or as relating to the protection of exhaustible natural resources. The CBAM also has to be designed and implemented in a way that avoids protectionism and demonstrates that it is not a disguised restriction to international trade or an arbitrary or unjustified discrimination among countries where the same conditions prevail, in accordance with the chapeau of Article XX. This has often been the case and is anticipated to be the most challenging aspect of the use of GATT exceptions in relation to the CBAM.[157] Both the type of instrument and the sectors and products need to be carefully selected and justified. Starting with some selected sectors (e.g. cement, steel) in order to test and prove the mechanism before expanding to other sectors could be problematic from a WTO perspective, particularly if the EU makes exceptions for certain carbon-intensive domestic sectors, while applying a CBAM for products largely produced abroad.[158]

Additionally, at the international level, the EU's unilateral action through the CBAM could be accused of interfering with the sovereignty of third countries, coercing foreign companies to comply with more ambitious climate policies than those applied domestically. Arguably, this could be seen as contrary to the Paris Agreement, which is founded on nationally determined and differentiated contributions to the overall temperature goal. However, in light of the Paris Agreement's provisions on increasing ambition and the shortcomings of current commitments to meet the temperature goal, the EU could hardly be accused of acting against the Paris Agreement.[159] At the same time, the bottom-up approach of the Paris Agreement and the importance of CBDRRC implications at the very least point to the necessity for the EU to carefully design such a unilateral measure in an effort to support, and not undermine, global efforts on climate change. While the EU claims that the CBAM is an important tool in

[157] Tamiotti, 'The Legal Interface between Carbon Border Measures and Trade Rules', 11(5) *Climate Policy* (2011) 1202.

[158] Horn and Sapir, 'Border Carbon Tariffs: Giving Up on Trade to Save the Climate?', 6 *Bruegel Policy Brief* (2013) 7.

[159] See n. 156.

achieving climate neutrality in line with the Paris Agreement, the CBAM does not foster compliance with the Paris Agreement but aims to allow the EU to deal with the risk of carbon leakage so that it can increase its own ambitions.[160] The inter-relationship between the EU's unilateral move and international commitments under the Paris Agreement is thus more complicated than it may initially seem.

Following previous practice in IEMEIs, the CBAM includes clauses that respect and anticipate action by third countries in the form of 'contingent unilateralism'.[161] The CBAM Regulation provides for contingent unilateralism in the form of exceptions and equivalence in two main ways. First, to avoid treating imports no less favourably than domestic products, Article 9 of the Regulation provides for a reduction of the number of CBAM certificates taking into account the carbon price paid in the country of origin. It provides for a deduction in the number of CBAM certificates to be surrendered corresponding to the carbon price paid in the country of origin for declared emissions, subject to verification that declared emissions are subject to carbon price and that they were paid. This contingency clause is relatively narrow, in the sense that it does not provide the possibility of adjusting the number of CBAM certificates in light of compliance with regulatory requirements in third countries but only in light of a carbon price paid in the country of origin. The CBAM is, therefore, coercive in a way that would make it hard to justify under GATT Article XX. Its incentivizing potential for third countries to ratchet up their climate policies is therefore narrow in terms of incentivizing the introduction of carbon-pricing measures while failing to recognize other kinds of regulation. This can be particularly controversial for countries at different stages of development. The narrow scope of equivalence built into the CBAM proposal, limited to carbon-pricing policies and no other kinds of regulatory approaches, indicates that the EU is putting all its eggs into one policy basket, convinced that this is the right way to reduce GHG emissions in specific sectors of the economy while not allowing sufficient flexibility for other kinds of policy approaches to flourish.[162]

Second, a different kind of country-level contingency is provided through the possibility for the Commission to conclude agreements with third countries with a view to taking their carbon-pricing mechanism (ETS or carbon tax) into account and adjusting the carbon charge accordingly in the application of Article 9 of the Proposal (i.e. reducing the number of CBAM certificates

[160] Pirlot (n. 136).
[161] Scott and Rajamani (n. 92).
[162] Prins and Rayner (n. 42).

to take into account the price paid in the country of origin).[163] The conclusion of bilateral agreements emerges as a different kind of equivalence through cooperation that allows room for negotiation with the third country and implicates state consent that ultimately renders the unilateral measure less problematic in principle. The explanatory memorandum to the CBAM proposal indicated that such agreements to take into account the carbon-pricing mechanisms of third countries are to be considered an alternative to the CBAM in case they ensure a 'higher degree of effectiveness and ambition to achieve decarbonization of a sector'.[164] Equivalence determinations at country level are always complex political determinations, and this formulation seems problematic both from the perspective of WTO flexibility[165] and the differentiated approach of the Paris Agreement in line with the CBDRRC in the light of national circumstances.

In relation to IEMEIs, their international acceptability, and ultimately their legitimacy, is partly determined on the basis of efforts taken to anticipate, factor in, and mitigate impacts on developing countries in line with the principle of CBDRRC, which governs the international climate regime. Given that the underlying policy objective, fighting climate change, is a global collective action problem with close links to international law, the EU's unilateral action may be partly justified. At the same time, its impacts on the poorest and most vulnerable have to be sufficiently taken into account and mitigated. The interests of developing countries were arguably ignored in the design of the initial Aviation Directive, which required all airlines to surrender allowances to EU Member States, irrespective of whether they originated from developing countries.[166] As Young put it, 'the EU was forcing behavioural change in other states but also distributing a burden that it would otherwise have to meet'.[167] Such outsourcing of responsibilities could raise international distributive justice questions as to the fair allocation of costs and benefits from environmental protection. As mentioned above, the revised ETS exempts extra-EEA flights to/from most LDCs and SIDS from the scope of the ETS (and CORSIA), thereby more concretely incorporating differentiation, at least in relation to countries falling under these classifications.

[163] Art. 2(12) of Regulation 2023/956 (n. 135).
[164] Explanatory Memorandum to Commission Proposal for a Regulation establishing a carbon border adjustment mechanism, COM(2021) 564 final.
[165] Marín Durán, 'EU Carbon Border Adjustment Mechanism: Key Issues Going Forward', 26(4) *European Foreign Affairs Review* (2021) 499.
[166] Scott and Rajamani (n. 92).
[167] Young, 'Trade Measures to Address Climate Change: Territory and Extraterritoriality', in P. Delimatsis (ed.), *Research Handbook on Climate Change and Trade Law* (2016) 343.

The CBAM Regulation does not move forward from the approach embedded in the initial aviation directive as there is no exception for LDCs or progressive inclusion of imports. The impact assessment recognized that in some sectors, exports from LDCs to the EU significantly contribute to their economies, and compliance costs are expected to be relatively higher. The EU should therefore carefully assess risks and support the transformative process of these countries in adjusting to the CBAM.[168] In the final version of the CBAM Regulation, two preambular paragraphs somewhat provide a weak incorporation of CBDRRC.

First, the EU reiterates its commitment to work with and support low- and middle-income third countries towards decarbonization as part of the external dimension of the Green Deal and in line with the Paris Agreement.[169] Support towards these countries, especially LDCs, should continue through the EU budget to ensure their adaptation to the CBAM Regulation and, more generally, for their climate mitigation and adaptation within the ceiling of the MFF and the financial support provided by the EU to international climate finance.

Second, the Commission is to 'strive to engage in an even-handed manner and in line with the international obligations of the Union with the third countries whose trade to the Union is affected by this Regulation, in order to explore the possibility for dialogue and cooperation'.[170] Alongside this qualified commitment to international cooperation, '[t]he Union should provide technical assistance for those purposes to developing countries and to least developed countries'. Such preambular commitments to assist poor countries do not leave it up to the expectations of the EU acting as an agent of global climate justice, leaving no one behind in the transition to a carbon-neutral economy. Also, the fact that the impact of the Regulation on and of any technical assistance provided to these countries forms part of the reviewing process of the CBAM Regulation[171] does not commit the EU to mitigating the effects of the CBAM in line with CBDRRC. The European Parliament's position in June 2022 was more demanding, requiring the Commission to regularly monitor changes in trade flows from LDCs attributable to CBAM as well as to monitor technical assistance provided to LDCs to evaluate the effectiveness of the measure to contribute to the decarbonization of those countries.[172]

[168] 'Impact Assessment Report', SWD (2021) 643 (n. 152) Part 2/2, 19.
[169] See recital 74 of Regulation 2023/956 (n. 135).
[170] Ibid. recital 71.
[171] Ibid. Art. 30(2)(f).
[172] See recital 57a new of Amendments adopted by the European Parliament on 22 June 2022 on the proposal for a regulation of the European Parliament and of the Council establishing a carbon border adjustment mechanism, P9_TA(2022) 0248.

Furthermore, no CBDRRC considerations in the allotment of CBAM revenues are currently included in the CBAM Regulation or in the proposal on Next Generation ORs. While the EU is committed to continue supporting low- and middle-income third countries, this is to be achieved through the EU budget, the MFF, and the EU's contributions to international climate finance, and it is not linked to the introduction of a new OR based on CBAM revenues or a related increase of support through established mechanisms in an effort to mitigate the impacts of the CBAM.[173] It could be argued that CBDRRC concerns are reflected by way of the choice of sectors to be included, which do not significantly affect developing countries and LDCs (but rather predominantly influence countries like Russia, the United Kingdom, Norway, and Turkey). However, this is not a satisfactory way of incorporating CBDRRC, given that there are provisions for including additional sectors in the future. In any case, even if developing countries and LDCs may not be currently classified among the top exporters of CBAM-covered products, their inclusion will hinder their ability to expand trade in those sectors. A more targeted and complete integration of CBDRRC is also required, given that it is less likely and notably more challenging for such countries (particularly LDCs) to put a carbon-pricing mechanism in place that would reduce the amount of CBAM certificates to be surrendered, insufficiently accounting for other, non-carbon-price-based efforts to address climate change. Designing the CBAM flexibly to reflect the different adjustments needed in relation to products coming from countries with different climate policies and at different stages of development might pose challenges for its WTO justification. Still, these are not insuperable and are needed to enhance the legitimacy, fairness, and environmental integrity of the measure.

Finally, the use of CBAM revenues and the associated ETS revenues in CBAM sectors is one of the most controversial decisions influencing both its internal and external acceptability. As noted by Marcu and colleagues, 'from a political perspective, retaining the revenues would be far more popular domestically, and far less popular internationally'.[174] The CBAM is estimated to generate additional revenue for 2030 at EUR 2.1 billion. Most revenues, that is 75 per cent of revenue generated by the CBAM, will accrue to the EU budget as one of the new ORs to fund the related expenditure for repayment of NGEU.[175]

[173] See recital 74 of Regulation 2023/956 (n. 135).

[174] A. Marcu, M. Mehling, and A. Cosbey, 'CBAM for the EU: A Policy Proposal', ERCST Roundtable on Climate Change and Sustainable Transition (2021).

[175] COM(2021) 566 (n. 53).

However, the proposals do not indicate that any part of CBAM revenues will be earmarked for climate change purposes either within or outside the EU. As indicated in the revised ETS, the allowances no longer allocated for free will should be auctioned and the revenues should accrue to the Innovation Fund so as to support innovation in low-carbon technologies, carbon capture and utilization, carbon capture and geological storage, and renewable energy and energy storage, in a way that contributes to mitigating climate change.[176] Special attention should be given to projects in CBAM sectors[177] that can raise concerns from the perspective of third countries and negatively affect the international acceptability of the measure, given that it will be used to support the domestic industries required to adjust the carbon intensity of their operations. Additionally, Member States are allowed to use auction revenues to address any residual risk of carbon leakage in CBAM sectors.[178] Notably, the use of revenue from allowances under the ETS previously allocated for free in CBAM sectors can be problematic from a WTO perspective and its likelihood to be justified under chapeau of Article XX GATT. Funds targeted to support covered firms provide evidence that the CBAM is more about protecting competitiveness than it is about protecting the environment. If a portion of CBAM revenues is earmarked for climate purposes, it would increase its chances of not being regarded as a disguised protectionist measure to help domestic industry and assist the EU to repay its recovery debt.

The Interinstitutional Agreement indicates that all new ORs should be used towards recovery of NGEU, with any excess going to the EU budget. Still, as part of the revenues from the ETS is earmarked for climate purposes at the EU and national levels, a similar approach could be applied to the CBAM, potentially by earmarking revenues through 'assigned revenue' under the Financial Regulation. While the European Parliament highlighted the need to repay NGEU and the importance of the principle of universality, it also committed to CBAM revenues not being used to subsidize policies or actions that run counter to the Paris Agreement and the objectives of the European

[176] See recital 46 and Art. 1(13) of Directive 2023/959 (n. 84) amending Art. 10a(8h) of Directive 2003/87/EC (n. 73).

[177] See recital 46 and Art. 1(13) of Directive 2023/959 (n. 84) amending Art. 10a(8h) of Directive 2003/87/EC (n. 73).

[178] See recital 47 of Directive 2023/959 (n. 84):

> Where allowances coming from a reduction of free allocation in application of the conditionality rules are not fully used to exempt the installations with the lowest greenhouse gas emission intensity from the cross-sectoral correction, 50per cent of those residual allowances should be added to the Innovation Fund. The other 50per cent should be auctioned on behalf of Member States and they should use the revenue therefrom to address any residual risk of carbon leakage in CBAM sectors.

Green Deal.[179] Different options for the use of the CBAM revenue had been discussed and put forward—including covering the administrative cost of CBAM, defraying the certification costs for importers who challenge default carbon intensity value and are successful, and funding mitigation actions in trade partner countries affected by the CBAM—while it would be politically necessary to assign some part of it to the EU budget.[180]

The credibility of the use of CBAM revenues should also be viewed in the broader context of the EU budget's green conditionalities. It could be argued that the climate spending target of 30 per cent across the MFF and the Recovery Instrument, as well as the horizontal principle of DNSH, which applies both to the RRF and funds under the cohesion policy governed by the Common Provisions Regulation,[181] contribute to ensuring that both some portion of the money is devoted to climate objectives and to ensuring that climate mitigation and adaptation are not undermined. However, much depends on how rigorously these 'green strings' will be applied in practice and, in any case, they do not address the international implications of raising money from imported products and not allocating funds to international climate funding.

There are also distinct concerns as to the equitable use of CBAM revenue, particularly given that no exemption is provided for LDCs. The emergence of purposeful green ORs cannot ignore the demands of international distributive justice related to the green transition. Part of the revenue could be used through devoted funds to help developing country producers, such as through the Adaptation Fund, the Special Climate Change Fund administered by the Global Environmental Facility, or the Green Climate Fund. Such an earmarking provision of parts of the CBAM revenue would amount to a more structural commitment to providing the necessary assistance to developing countries and a stronger incorporation of CBDRRC concerns in the design of the CBAM. To this effect, the European Parliament's position in June 2022, while indicating that CBAM revenues should go to the EU budget as general income and not be earmarked as such, in line with the principle of universality, is that the EU should finance LDCs efforts towards decarbonization at least to the level of revenues generated by the sale of CBAM certificates.[182] This support should be provided through the EU's international climate finance and relevant geographic programmes. Earmarking or otherwise adjusting budgetary appropriation to reflect equivalent amounts towards support of

[179] Parliament Resolution (n. 143).
[180] Marcu, Mehling, and Cosbey (n. 174).
[181] Parliament and Council Regulation 2021/1060, OJ 2021 L 231/159.
[182] See recital 55 of Amendments adopted by the European Parliament on 22 June 2022 (n. 172).

Table 5.5 The CBAM as a New Own Resource

Criterion	Assessment
Genuine	While the initial entry point of products and the surrender of CBAM certificates can be easily attributed to individual Member States, this does not influence its genuineness as an OR that is based on a truly EU policy with European Added Value linked to the ETS and driving the EU's role as an international climate actor. The incentivizing potential of the CBAM depends on its eventual design prior to the end of the transition period and its interaction with the ETS.
Suitable	Once operational, the long-term stability of revenue raised by the CBAM will gradually reduce as climate targets under the ETS are met and the cap is tightened and as third countries raise their climate ambitions and introduce carbon pricing policies equivalent to those of the EU. In the meantime, the CBAM will raise fresh revenue both through CBAM certificates and by indirectly increasing ETS revenues in CBAM sectors. The legal complexity surrounding the CBAM, particularly in light of its international implications, is significant and limits the regulatory scope available to the EU in introducing such a unilateral measure.
Fair	Solidarity among the Member States and fairness concerns are meant to be ensured through the operation of specialized ETS funds (such as the Modernisation Fund, the Social Climate Fund, and the Just Transition Fund). International distributive justice concerns are acute in light of the CBDRRC principle and may be partly addressed through the allocation of CBAM funds to purposes favouring LDCs and SIDSs.

LDCs may reduce the *sufficiency* of new ORs to repay NGEU, but it does influence *fairness* and the acceptability of ORs.

The decision about the use of CBAM revenues and related ETS revenues has been repeatedly postponed and forms one of the most contentious aspects of trialogue discussions. Ultimately, this decision will determine the international credibility and acceptability of the measure. 'Taxing foreigners' and only allowing for consideration of carbon-pricing mechanisms in third countries acutely demonstrates the difficulty of reconciling internal and external concerns in the formulation of IEMEIs. The use of the CBAM revenues may influence its WTO compliance and raise concerns in relation to international justice (see Table 5.5).

5. Conclusions

In light of the need to repay NGEU, there is a noticeable shift in the EU's funding strategy, providing economic incentives to achieve EU common policies, thereby achieving agreement among Member States on key policy areas while simultaneously urging third countries to adjust their regulatory approaches to the EU's priorities. The strategic use of EU funding to promote priorities agreed by the EU presents a significant tool for furthering EU integration and achieving common policies. However, introducing new ORs based on controversial underlying policies is not straightforward. The policy instruments that will generate new proceeds for the EU budget have been subject to intense negotiations within the EU, affecting different Member States to different degrees. Their designation as new ORs does not necessarily render the internal negotiations less contentious. At the same time, from the perspective of the rest of the world, while the EU emerges as a leader on pressing global issues that are insufficiently regulated at the global level, going it alone through the unilateral use of economic instruments can raise concerns as to the true motives behind the EU's action and the extent to which the impacts on foreign interests are sufficiently taken into account.

In combination, the reform of the EU's ORs and the need to cover the repayment of NGEU have led to a fast-moving shift to European integration that raises significant issues both internally, relating to solidarity and distributive fairness among Member States, and externally, relating to the EU's role as a global actor. Furthermore, a mismatch between the policy-orientated character of new ORs and the way the funds will be spent, primarily repaying the EU's debt for the COVID-19 pandemic recovery, further accentuate these concerns. Particularly, ORs that largely aim to tax foreign companies and operators with the purpose of using those monies to promote the EU's green transition goals at a level and pace set unilaterally by the EU, as well as repaying the recovery debt, have to be carefully designed in order to address legitimacy concerns raised.

This chapter has organized the different kinds of features and concerns associated with the introduction of new ORs into three key criteria (genuine, suitable, and fair), defined and adapted in light of the distinctiveness of green sources of revenue. The plastic levy emerges as less genuine, particularly given that its incentivizing potential in reducing plastic pollution and delivering a circular economy approach is not systematically embedded in its design and depends on how Member States exercise their discretion. At the same time, it is the OR with the least controversial external implications, which emerges as incidental and not as part of the legal design itself. In this respect, the legal considerations for its introduction were less controversial, allowing for its early inclusion in the 2020 ORD. The climate-related ORs, on the other hand, present truly genuine ORs, with clear European Added Value, but raise significant fairness concerns among Member States. Also, due to their close links to international law, they present significant legal complexities, implicating the EU's obligations under multiple international fora and raising distinct distributive justice concerns as they involve direct financial obligations on foreign actors.

Individually, each of the new green ORs may fall short on the basis of the benchmarks of genuineness, suitability, and fairness as adopted in this chapter. In combination however, and despite the expected reduction of their calculation base as environmental targets are met, the three green ORs offer promising sources of revenue, serving as the starting point for a more long-term shift in the operation of the EU's OR system, moving away from a *juste retour* logic and more visibly exhibiting the benefits of pooling resources at the EU level. A mixture of different green ORs ensures the diversification of revenue sources, which would enable a better focus on priority areas and more independence and stability, as well as fairness.

Overall, this chapter has demonstrated how green sources of EU funding could potentially lead to a win–win situation, serving policy objectives for which the EU has a clear mandate and which are characterized by deep integration among the Member States. With the emergence of green ORs, environmental protection requirements are integrated more systematically in the EU's funding, with EU revenue serving as a significant policy-steering mechanism. At the same time, this integration is not straightforward. Concerns have been raised about the capacity of the new green ORs to deliver the underlying objectives, the external and extraterritorial implications of the EU's policies, and the fairness of their impacts. To ensure a win–win, policy measures serving as the basis for green ORs have to be monitored and regularly reviewed not only as to whether they provide stable and sufficient proceeds into the EU's coffers but also as to whether they achieve the underlying policy objective without reversing the logic of the 'polluter pays' principle by providing a way for operators to 'buy out' environmental externalities and pass the cost to consumers without implementing the infrastructure and technology adjustments needed for a green and just transition. Furthermore, the overall integration of environmental requirements in EU funding is multifaceted. It also depends on how other horizontal mechanisms, such as spending targets in EU funding instruments, the DNSH principle, and policy-specific funds, operate in practice. Research on the practical implementation of these 'green strings' attached to EU funding can further reveal the extent to which green sources of revenue and their associated purposes provide a good fit for strengthening the EU budget and furthering EU integration.

6
Accountable National Governance of European Union Funds

*Emilia Korkea-aho**

1. Introduction

Accountability is a crucial concept to understanding and assessing the workings of public law and governance. At its core is the idea that those who wield power should be made responsible for using this power. Since power can be exercised in many ways, activities through which accountability works have also proliferated and can be carried out by many people at different places and in contrasting positions. Scholars have identified actors who are held accountable, different institutions (legal, political, judicial, social, and financial) to which accountability must be rendered, and the processes of accountability, as well as the various levels of accountability.[1] What cuts through its many dimensions is the view that 'accountability requires government actors to justify their positions for others to evaluate, challenge, or override'.[2] It is fundamentally a multi-party and deliberative notion.

Accountability is also a key concept for discussions about public spending. At a time when the Next Generation EU (NGEU) funds channel billions of European Union (EU) money to individual Member States (in addition to more traditional EU funds), setting up a credible accountability system not only for outcomes but also for actual monetary disbursement seems both urgent and beneficial for the EU's overall ambition to renew its democratic system. In Citizens' Panels organized during the Conference on the Future of

* This chapter builds on my lectures at the Academy of European Law (AEL) Course 'New Frontiers of EU Funding: Law, Policy, Politics' in the summer of 2021, as well as the draft paper I presented virtually at the workshop with the same title on 18 March 2022. I thank Markus Sairanen for his excellent assistance with collecting and reviewing the literature and Joanne Scott for helpful comments.

[1] Curtin and Nollkaemper, 'Conceptualizing Accountability in International and European Law', 36 *Netherlands Yearbook of International Law* (2005) 3.

[2] Bernstein and Rodriguez, 'The Accountable Bureaucrat', 132 *Yale Law Journal* (2022), https://ssrn.com/abstract=4067359 (last visited 22 January 2024).

Emilia Korkea-aho, *Accountable National Governance of European Union Funds*. In: *New Frontiers of EU Funding*. Edited by: Claire Kilpatrick and Joanne Scott, Oxford University Press. © Emilia Korkea-aho 2024.
DOI: 10.1093/oso/9780198940319.003.0006

Europe, the participants called for investments in Europeans' quality of life, augmenting their call with ideas of radical accountability for budget spending, noting 'the need to ensure supervision, transparency and effective communication towards citizens in the implementation of public investment (on the part of the EU)' and 'to allow citizens to track the entire process of investment'.[3]

Citizens' demands for a radical accountability overhaul suggest that the current system has been found wanting. Perceptions (and indeed, evidence) of misconduct by officials and fraud by those in receipt of funds from the EU budget are important factors behind such dissatisfaction. With the deterioration of rule of law conditions in Poland and Hungary and the EU's efforts to get these Member States in line by adding elements of conditionality into funding arrangements and threatening to delay or withdraw funding, citizens—perhaps rightly so—think that if there are any forms of accountability for public spending, they do not work.

Devising and implementing accountability has proved difficult in complex institutional environments; a case in point is the shared management of EU funds. Such a system means that the Commission and Member States are together responsible for the management of funds from the EU budget. However, it is not just management that is shared; accountability for public spending is also split between the Commission and Member States. Yet, scholarly consensus has long held that split accountability is impossible. Neither the Commission nor Member States are accountable to the people whose money they use, nor to each other. If anything, shared management has led to an 'accountability gap', where one governmental entity (in this case, the Commission) is made responsible for the use of funds that are authorized by other independent governmental entities (in this case, Member States), whose interests do not always coincide with those of the Commission.[4] This gloomy view is echoed across the scholarship. For Hansen, there cannot be any real accountability, because each Member State modifies the goals agreed on at EU level to better suit the preferences of the implementing actors at national level.[5] Porras-Goméz describes how the model of '"shared management" does not rest on "shared interests"'.[6] To inject some accountability into the implementation of EU funds, scholars

[3] Alemanno and Nicolaïdis, 'Citizen Power Europe: The Making of a European Citizens' Assembly', 3 *Revue Européenne du Droit* (2022), https://geopolitique.eu/en/articles/citizen-power-europe (last visited 22 January 2024).

[4] G. Cipriani, 'The EU Budget. Responsibility without Accountability?', Centre for European Policy Studies (2010), https://www.ceps.eu/ceps-publications/eu-budget-responsibility-without-accountability (last visited 22 January 2024).

[5] Blom-Hansen, 'Principals, Agents, and the Implementation of EU Cohesion Policy', 12 *Journal of European Public Policy* (*JEPP*) (2005) 624.

[6] Porras-Gómez, 'Metagovernance and Control of Multi-level Governance Frameworks: The Case of the EU Structural Funds Financial Execution', 24 *Regional & Federal Studies* (2014) 173, at 179. See also Porras-Gómez, 'The Evolution of the Internal Control System for the Structural Funds: Between

have sought to operationalize the concept of a formal vertical accountability structure, with the Commission as principal and the Member States as agents.

My exploration of the national governance of EU funds—the concept I use to name the array of roles, rules, and processes dedicated to aligning national practices with the shared management of EU funds—comes to a different conclusion. Shared management does not do away with accountability, but it changes the way in which accountability is produced. Following the 'pragmatic turn' in the regulatory governance studies,[7] in this chapter, I ask how accountability is pragmatically produced in the specific context of the shared management of EU funds. Using the national implementation of the European Regional Development Fund (ERDF) as a concrete example, I describe the practices, relationships, and structures that underlie the national governance of EU funds. Through this examination, I show how national funds officials engage in highly routinized processes that contribute to accountable funds decision-making, which is deliberative, inclusive, and adaptive.

I capture the type of accountability emerging from everyday routine governance practices under the concept of 'bottom-up' accountability. This accountability type is tailored to a governance model that rests on inclusive planning, deliberative monitoring, and programme evaluation through learning and adaptation. These positive governance practices do not, however, flourish without effort. I argue that the anti-corruption agenda, which is obviously a worthy goal in itself, is a threat to them, with national governance processes of EU funds management needing to be actively defended against their colonization by an emerging 'penal rationality' in this area.

This chapter provides an overview of many crucial issues of shared management, especially how national governance practices concretely operate at the Member State level. The national governance of EU funds is not adequately recognized and analysed in research, and in legal research in particular.[8] Political scientists have studied the Member States and how they administer EU funds, but their focus is often, although not exclusively, on Central and Eastern European (CEE) countries.[9] Recent debates on conditionality and rule of law

the European Commission and National Authorities', in P. Stephenson, M.-L. Sánchez-Barrueco, and H. Aden (eds), *Financial Accountability in the European Union* (2020) 145.

[7] Huising and Silbey, 'Accountability Infrastructures: Pragmatic Compliance inside Organizations', 15 *Regulation and Governance* (2021) 540.

[8] For exceptions, see e.g. Scott, 'Law, Legitimacy and EC Governance: Prospects for "Partnership"', 36 *Journal of Common Market Studies (JCMS)* (1998) 175.

[9] Charasz and Vogler, 'Does EU Funding Improve Local State Capacity? Evidence from Polish Municipalities', 22 *European Union Politics* (2021) 446; Surubaru, 'European Funds in Central and Eastern Europe: Drivers of Change or Mere Funding Transfers? Evaluating the Impact of European Aid on National and Local Development in Bulgaria and Romania', 22 *European Politics and Society*

compliance as a condition for EU funding are important but fall as anomalies outside the scope of this chapter.[10] In the vast majority of Member States, the governance of EU funds involves a series of routinized, well-functioning practices, which deserve dedicated attention from EU law scholarship. The chapter thus invites a further exploration of what public law and governance research of EU funds may and should involve, to enable a future systematic exploration of one of the most critical issues of EU integration.

Section 2 briefly describes the legal framework and policy objectives, with section 3 introducing the concept of governance in the shared management of EU funds. Section 4 outlines the five stages of the national ERDF governance. Section 5 portrays the model of national funds governance and the 'bottom-up' accountability that goes with it. Section 6 describes the increased call for criminal law enforcement and anti-corruption mechanisms, and section 7 problematizes their application to national funds governance. Section 8 concludes.

2. The Legal Framework and Policy Objectives

This chapter concretely focuses on EU structural funds and, more specifically, the ERDF. The treaty basis for EU structural funds is laid down in Articles 174–178 of the Treaty on the Functioning of the European Union (TFEU). Other important articles of EU primary law are Articles 310–325 TFEU on the establishment and implementation of the budget. Secondary law covers both general legislation and specific pieces of law that apply to a particular fund or a group of funds. Relevant general legislation includes the Multi-Annual Financial Framework (MFF) Regulation 2020/2093[11] and the Financial Regulation (FR) 2018/1046.[12] The central piece of specific

(2020) 203; Yesilkagit and Blom-Hansen, 'Supranational Governance or National Business-as-Usual? The National Administration of EU Structural Funds in the Netherlands and Denmark', 85 *Public Administration (PA)* (2007) 503; Polverari, 'The Multiple Accountabilities of EU Cohesion Policy. Wicked Problem or North Star?', in P. Stephenson, M.-L. Sánchez-Barrueco, and H. Aden (eds), *Financial Accountability in the European Union* (2020) 111; Damen-Koedijk, 'The Implementation and Accountability of EU Cohesion Policy in the Netherlands', in P. Stephenson, M.-L. Sánchez-Barrueco, and H. Aden (eds), *Financial Accountability in the European Union* (2020) 176.

[10] For an analysis of conditionalities in EU funds management, see Viorica Viță, Chapter 4, '(Un) Constitutional Conditions: A European Perspective' in this volume.

[11] Council Regulation (EU, Euratom) 2020/2093 of 17 December 2020 laying down the multiannual financial framework for the years 2021 to 2027. OJ L 433I (22 December 2020) 11–22.

[12] Regulation (EU, Euratom) 2018/1046 of the European Parliament and of the Council of 18 July 2018 on the financial rules applicable to the general budget of the Union, amending Regulations (EU) 1296/2013, (EU) 1301/2013, (EU) 1303/2013, (EU) 1304/2013, (EU) 1309/2013, (EU) 1316/2013, (EU) 223/2014, (EU) 283/2014, and Decision 541/2014/EU and repealing Regulation (EU, Euratom) 966/2012, PE/13/2018/REV/1, OJ L 193 (30 July 2018) 1–222.

secondary law for the current budget period 2021–2027 is the Common Provisions Regulation (CPR) that covers the ERDF.[13] The MFF and the CPR are amended for each seven-year budget cycle, which is also called the programming period in the context of EU funds. There is also a wide range of soft law documents, such as the European Code of Conduct on Partnership, which sets out minimum requirements to ensure that the partnership principle is respected in the context of the EU funds;[14] Guidance on ensuring the respect for the Charter of Fundamental Rights of the European Union;[15] and Guidance on the avoidance and management of conflicts of interest.[16]

The ERDF forms part of the EU cohesion policy, the objective of which is to support the Member States in promoting economic development, reducing unemployment, and improving the competitiveness of national territories and the EU as a whole.[17] The key rationale for the cohesion policy is to even out incomes and wealth, not only between Member States but also between regions within and across Member States. The cohesion policy is delivered through four specific funds: the ERDF, the Cohesion Fund (CF), the European Social Fund Plus (ESF+), and the Just Transition Fund (JTF). In the programming period 2021–2027, EU funds allocated to the cohesion policy amount to EUR 392 billion. With a total of EUR 313 billion, the ERDF and the ESF+ together account for the majority.[18]

As a policy area, economic, social, and territorial cohesion is a shared competence between the EU and the Member States, and the implementation of the cohesion policy takes place in the context of shared management, which, as explained, means that the Commission and the Member States collaborate in executing policy measures. The principle and rules of shared management are a fund-specific interpretation of shared competence that underlies the entire

[13] Regulation (EU) 2021/1060 of the European Parliament and of the Council of 24 June 2021 laying down common provisions on the European Regional Development Fund, the European Social Fund Plus, the Cohesion Fund, the Just Transition Fund and the European Maritime, Fisheries and Aquaculture Fund and financial rules for those and for the Asylum, Migration and Integration Fund, the Internal Security Fund and the Instrument for Financial Support for Border Management and Visa Policy PE/47/2021/INIT, OJ L 231 (30 June 2021) 159–706.

[14] Commission Delegated Regulation (EU) 240/2014 of 7 January 2014 on the European code of conduct on partnership in the framework of the European Structural and Investment Funds, OJ L 74 (14 March 2014) 1–7.

[15] Commission Notice, Guidance on ensuring the respect for the Charter of Fundamental Rights of the European Union when implementing the European Structural and Investment Funds ('ESI Funds'), C 269/1.

[16] Commission Notice, Guidance on the avoidance and management of conflicts of interest under the Financial Regulation, 2021/C 121/01.

[17] See Art. 176 TFEU.

[18] See European Commission, 'Available Budget of Cohesion Policy 2021–2027', https://ec.europa.eu/regional_policy/en/funding/available-budget (last visited 22 January 2024).

cohesion policy. The contours of the principle of shared management are described in the recitals of the CPR:

> In accordance with the principle and rules of shared management, Member States and the Commission should be responsible for the management and control of programmes and give assurance on the legal and regular use of the Funds. Since Member States should have the primary responsibility for such management and control and should ensure that operations supported by the Funds comply with applicable law, their obligations in that regard should be specified. The powers and responsibilities of the Commission in that context should also be laid down.[19]

While responsibility is, in principle, shared, Member States are given the primary role of managing and controlling the use of EU funds. The principle of shared management seems to involve one fundamental relationship, that is the one between the Commission and the Member State. Yet, the principle involves at least three important relationships. The first is between the Commission and an individual Member State, which tends to be the relationship we think about when considering shared management. The second concerns the relationship between an individual Member State and the Member States as a collective, and the third relates to power-sharing within the Member State. All three provide different yet complementary interpretations of how powers are exercised in the shared management of EU funds.

In the first relationship, a Member State can choose not to (fully) abide by EU norms and can benefit, if it so chooses, from a situation of highly asymmetrical information.[20] Yet, the Commission is not completely stripped of power and can effectively influence Member State implementation, as I explain in section 4.[21] The second relationship prompts a question of whether the CPR gives the primary role for managing and controlling the use of EU funds to a collective of Member States or an individual Member State. Currently, any ideas of a collective of Member States as a responsible agent are theoretical at best, because shared management is not usually captured in horizontal terms, and instances of information-sharing or peer monitoring between Member States are rare.

[19] See recital 55 CPR.

[20] Porras-Gómez, 'Metagovernance and Control of Multi-level Governance Frameworks' (n. 6) 178.

[21] Given the direct effect of EU law, a non-compliant Member State may be taken to court, as happened in Case C-321/95, *P Greenpeace* or Case T-461/93, *An Taisce*, even though the non-governmental organizations did not succeed in those cases. See Scott, 'Environmental Compatibility and the Community's Structural Funds: A Legal Analysis', 8 *Journal of Environmental Law* (1996) 99.

Whereas the first two relationships portray the Member State's relational individuality (vis-à-vis the Commission or a collective of other Member States), the third important relationship concerns the relations between central authorities and regional authorities or central authorities and stakeholders within a Member State. The cohesion policy constitutes a typical example of European governance that is both integrated and highly diffused at the same time, which means that decision-making powers are diffused not only from the supranational to the national level but also from the national level to regional and local levels and to private actors and other stakeholders on different territorial levels. In the third relationship, the fundamental question concerns the administrative identity of a Member State: who is, and speaks as, the Member State?

This mapping demonstrates how the principle of shared management does not involve just one but rather several fundamental relationships that are crucial to understanding the workings and production of accountability within shared management and how the Member State, not the Commission, is at the crux of these intersecting relationships. Prior to examining the actual decision-making in the ERDF, I will briefly discuss the concept of governance in EU funds management.

3. The Concept of Governance and Its Application to EU Funds Management

As a term, governance is used in diverse ways. However, it usually refers to issues of decision-making and prompts questions about how, and at what level, decisions are made; who has a voice in making them; and who is accountable for these decisions. Governance is also associated with soft law instruments and policy values such as learning, deliberation, and participation.[22]

In the specific context of EU funds, one quickly notices that governance has no official or fixed meaning. The first mention is in the context of 'sound economic governance', a phrase used in the MFF,[23] the CPR,[24] and the Recovery

[22] In the context of EU funds, see Porras-Gómez, 'Metagovernance and Control of Multi-level Governance Frameworks' (n. 6) 175: 'From a policy perspective (considering the coerciveness of the modes of political steering), government is connected with hard instruments such as command and control, while governance is connected with soft instruments such as incentive and supply, information, deliberation and persuasion.'

[23] See Art. 6 MFF.

[24] See Art. 19 CPR.

and Resilience Fund Regulation (RRFR).[25] The concept of sound economic governance is not specified further. The second reference is to 'multi-level governance' found in Article 8 CPR: 'The partnership ... shall operate in accordance with the multi-level governance principle and a bottom-up approach.'[26] Neither multi-level nor bottom-up are elucidated further. The CPR also includes the third meaning of governance, namely the Member States' 'administrative capacity and governance'.[27] Finally, for the European Parliament (EP), 'governance' in the context of EU funds means respect for the institutional balance and its co-legislative prerogatives.[28]

Of the possible meanings given to the notion of governance in the context of EU funds, multi-level governance is possibly the most common. The multi-level governance model is sometimes portrayed as the 'traditional approach to EU cohesion policy'; however, there is no consensus as to what this governance model is. Instead, there are commonly shared views on what it lacks or what is wrong with it. In Craig's view, 'there may well be evidence of multilevel involvement in the implementation of EU regional policy, but less of a case for multilevel governance as such'.[29] Hansen argues that the multi-level governance model has led to Member States running wild, and the whole system thus needs to be replaced with the principal–agent framework.[30] For them, and indeed many others, the multi-level governance model has failed to ensure that there is sufficient accountability about how and where EU funds are spent.

In this chapter, the concept of governance underpins and informs all aspects of my analysis. This 'governance perspective' is used both as an analytical tool and as a concept with substance. Its usefulness as an organizing principle to analyse the law and policy of EU funds makes sense, given the cacophony of technical details in this area. As Paul Craig, one of the rare legal scholars to ever examine EU funds in any close detail, writes,

> The legal regime governing regional policy is daunting in its complexity. It cannot, however, be ignored by anyone seriously interested in law and administration within the EU, because expenditure in this area still consumes a

[25] See Art. 10 of Regulation (EU) 2021/241 of the European Parliament and of the Council of 12 February 2021 establishing the Recovery and Resilience Facility. OJ L 57 (18 February 2021) 17–75.
[26] See Art. 8(2) CPR.
[27] Ibid. Art. 22(3)(a)(v).
[28] Annex I, point 40 of the Interinstitutional Agreement of 16 December 2020 between the European Parliament, the Council of the European Union and the European Commission on budgetary discipline, on cooperation in budgetary matters and on sound financial management, as well as on new own resources, including a roadmap towards the introduction of new own resources.
[29] P. Craig, *EU Administrative Law* (2nd edn, 2019) 80.
[30] Blom-Hansen (n. 5).

large part of the EU budget, and because the regime of shared management poses unique problems and challenges.[31]

Legal scholars often assume the view of a judge, looking at and organizing the material on the basis of case law. This is not, however, the organizing principle adopted here, and a concerted effort is made to shift the perspective away from courts.

To use the notion of governance as a concept with theoretical 'baggage' means that I position myself, and this chapter, in the law and (new) governance literature.[32] Pursuant to this positioning, the concept of governance connects to the above-mentioned idea of governance as 'multi-level governance'; yet, the governance idea adopted in this chapter is broader than just this principle. The governance perspective (both in its organizing and substantive dimensions) adopted in this chapter incorporates three themes derived from the law and governance scholarship.

First, as explained in more detail in section 4, decisions are taken and implemented in a multi-level network of public and private actors that come from different cultural backgrounds and have different grounds of legitimacy.[33] This comes closest to the idea of multi-level governance as enshrined in Article 8 CPR. Second, EU funds management has been approached and analysed from the legal perspective of administrative cooperation and composite procedures with issues such as auditing, (judicial) control, and legal accountability highlighted.[34] The law and governance perspective brings in alternative perspectives of deliberation, inclusiveness, and adaptability and uses them to understand how accountability works in practice. This second theme is closely aligned with the 'bottom-up approach' of the same CPR article. Third, the benefit of the governance perspective is that it helps appreciate and focus on normal, routine governance. Lawyers are typically needed when things go wrong, which explains why legal research also tends to direct its attention to

[31] Craig (n. 29) 100.

[32] G. de Búrca and J. Scott (eds), *Law and New Governance in the EU and the US* (2006); Trubek and Trubek, 'New Governance & Legal Regulation: Complementarity, Rivalry, and Transformation', 13 *Columbia Journal of European Law* (2007) 539; Cottrell and Trubek, 'Law as Problem Solving: Standards, Networks, Experimentation, and Deliberation in Global Space', 21 *Transnational Law & Contemporary Problems* (2012) 359.

[33] Porras-Goméz, 'Metagovernance and Control of Multi-level Governance Frameworks' (n. 6) 175. See also Domorenok, 'Financial Accountability and the Quality of Performance in the EU Cohesion Policy. The Case of Italy', in P. Stephenson, M.-L. Sánchez-Barrueco, and H. Aden (eds), *Financial Accountability in the European Union* (2020) 160.

[34] Meuleman and Brenninkmeijer, 'How to Deal with Legal Uncertainty: Managing and Audit Authorities in Cohesion Policy', 2 *European Structural and Investment Funds Journal* (2017); Brenninkmeijer, 'Audit and Administrative Law', in C. Harlow (ed.), *Research Handbook on European Administrative Law* (2017) 344; Craig (n. 29).

situations where problems have occurred and where courts have stepped in to fix things (just think of the conditionality debates in the EU).[35] While this may be an organic way of prioritizing research needs, such focus makes legal research blind to, or unappreciative of, situations when things go as planned and when they do so because of well-established routines.

A decade ago, a group of governance scholars highlighted the plight of state child protective services in the United States. After careful consideration of various causes of the problems associated with child protective services, they concluded how the work of frontline administrators had managed to prevent a total collapse of the system, with their efforts resulting in what the authors described as 'accountable administration that strives to reconcile programmatic flexibility with rule-of-law values'.[36] The article is a result of the time that the authors spent observing state administrators in Utah and Alabama. The ethnographic approach of this article is valuable, yet its enduring value lies in its interest in the importance of context-sensitive routines as a condition of accountable governance.

Another important work relevant here is a recent article on accountable bureaucrats. Drawing on in-depth interviews with officials from US regulatory agencies, Bernstein and Rodriguez show how US regulatory agencies' work facilitates continued justification and negotiation among officials with different roles inside the state. In their analysis, the standard principal–agent model gives way to the dispersion of decision-making power, which promotes the pluralistic inclusivity of views also from outside state administration. Numerous administrative routines 'connect agencies directly to the people and situations they regulate'.[37] Routines as conditions for accountability are also highlighted by regulatory governance literature. Huising and Silbey note that 'because the ostensible goal of regulation must surely be to transform legislated expectations into normalized routines and taken-for-granted habits', we should understand accountability not as 'a singular alignment in a specified chain of action connecting rule to implementation on the ground but instead as the mutual constitution of expectations and performances that become securely integrated into taken-for-granted organizational routines'.[38]

[35] Of the tendency to see the courts as 'the star of the show', see also C. Abbot and M. Lee, *Environmental Movements and Legal Expertise. Shaping the Brexit Process* (2020).

[36] Noonan, Sabel, and Simon, 'Legal Accountability in the Service-Based Welfare State: Lessons from Child Welfare Reform', 34 *Law & Social Inquiry* (2009) 523.

[37] Bernstein and Rodriguez (n. 2).

[38] Huising and Silbey (n. 7) 543. For a discussion of the manifestation of accountability as routines in closed, hierarchical organizations, see also Olsen, 'Democratic Order, Autonomy, and Accountability', 28 *Governance* (2015) 425.

Building on this literature, this chapter posits that the model of governance and accountability are coupled at the fundamental level. Accountability is not something that is imposed top-down on actors but rather emerges from bottom-up and is nested in various practices, relationships, and structures, indeed routines, of any given governance regime. Using the national implementation of the ERDF as a concrete example, I next proceed to show how national funds officials are embedded in deliberative, inclusive, and adaptive processes that facilitate accountability. I identify and describe a bottom-up model of 'accountable funds governance' that incorporates the tenets of law and governance philosophy: inclusive planning, programming through iteration and adaptation, and the execution of programmes through deliberation.

While the notions 'multi-level governance' and 'bottom-up approach' are mentioned in legal regulation, their concrete manifestations in the 'real life' of the CPR are difficult to observe, at least for legal scholarship. To gain some idea of how national funds officials work, I conducted a qualitative document analysis, as well as five semi-structured interviews with central and regional administrators, business interests, and non-governmental organization (NGO) representatives in the summer of 2021.[39]

4. The National Governance of EU Funds

In this section, I discuss the ways in which actors orchestrate their steps when deciding on the implementation of EU funds. I describe the ERDF decision-making process, starting with Member States identifying national authorities and arriving at the stage where Member States execute payments to beneficiaries and annually report on progress. At each stage, I highlight how the specific governance features manifest in the work that national funds officials do (see Table 6.1). I also show how the implementation of the ERDF is increasingly aligned with the EU strategic long-term governance in the Europe 2020 Strategy.

[39] The interviews took place in Helsinki via Zoom or Teams. These interviews were not recorded and were exploratory in nature, which is why I do not use extensive direct quotations when reporting on the interviews. All the interviewees have had the opportunity to comment on the final text, including how their own contributions have been used.

Table 6.1 Key features and instruments of the national governance model

Governance stage	Governance features	Key instruments
Pre-management	Participation and inclusiveness	National bodies Partnership principle
Programming	Adaption and learning	Partnership agreement Operational programmes
Selection and monitoring	Deliberation	Projects Project committees Enhanced proportionate arrangements
Administrative enforcement and protection	(Negative) adaptation	Recovery Reimbursement
Evaluation	Learning and effectiveness	Project audits Indicators European Added Value (EAV)

A. Pre-Management: Participation and Inclusiveness

Member States' work towards a new funding programme commences while the implementation of the previous programme is still underway. The Commission began preparations for the currently applicable MFF 2021–2027 in 2018. Member States were not much further behind, starting their respective preparations at the turn of the year 2018–2019. Administratively, the idea is not that Member States revamp their national management and control systems with every new MFF but rather that they preserve most of it across successive MFFs. Such 'roll-over' enables Member States to build on those elements of the current programme period that are functioning well.[40] The EU does not, however, 'recycle' information from the previous MFFs, and Member States need to provide an up-to-date description of the management and control system by the time the request for payment of the balance for the first financial year is submitted to the Commission and, in the context of the current MFF, by 30 June 2023 at the latest.

[40] European Court of Auditors, Opinion 6/2018 (pursuant to Arts 287(4) and 322(1)(a) TFEU) concerning the proposal for a Regulation of the European Parliament and of the Council laying down common provisions on the European Regional Development Fund, the European Social Fund Plus, the Cohesion Fund, and the European Maritime and Fisheries Fund and financial rules for those and for the Asylum and Migration Fund, the Internal Security Fund and the Border Management and Visa Instrument, para. 98.

Member States are responsible for 'identifying' national and sub-national authorities to carry out specific tasks. While they have some discretion in establishing the national system, two authorities 'shall' be identified.[41] Managing authorities are at the apex of the national management system. They are authorities with the responsibility for planning, including drafting and preparation of all programmatic policy documents and reports. In addition, these bodies oversee the application of EU rules nationally, including the so-called horizontal priorities, such as gender equality and non-discrimination, and, most importantly, the partnership principle (more on this below).[42] Usually, ministries assume the role of the managing authority, but EU law does not mandate a one-size-fits-all approach and endorses functional equivalence whereby many models are possible.[43] There must also be an independent audit authority. Auditing cannot be delegated to private actors, and the CPR specifically states that the audit authority must be a public authority. As a general rule, it examines the audit documents at least once a year and meets with the Commission on a regular basis.[44]

The managing authority may 'identify' intermediate bodies that, under its supervision, translate general policy priorities into concrete actions and policies, select eligible projects for funding, monitor their implementation, and undertake financial reporting.[45] Intermediate authorities operate at the regional levels.[46] Finally, a mention must be made of the monitoring committee. Unlike the managing and audit authorities, the monitoring committee is not a programme authority, yet the Member States must still create it. The committee meets at least once a year, providing an avenue for a wide range of national (both central and regional level) authorities to discuss and make recommendations to the managing authority.[47] The representatives of the Commission participate in the monitoring committee both 'in a monitoring and an advisory capacity',[48] which indicates the Commission's growing hands-on involvement in ensuring governance on the ground.

The composition of the monitoring committee must reflect a balanced representation of actors.[49] This is a specific application of the partnership principle

[41] See Art. 71 CPR.
[42] Ibid. Arts 49, 72–75.
[43] Ibid. Art. 71(2).
[44] Ibid. Arts 77–79. The audit authority is also responsible for more comprehensive system audits, to be undertaken within 21 months of the approval of the programme (see ibid. Art. 78).
[45] Ibid. Art. 71(3).
[46] See also ibid. Art. 29(5).
[47] Ibid. Arts 38–40.
[48] Ibid. Art. 39(2).
[49] Ibid. Art. 39(1).

that applies to the implementation of the EU cohesion policy. Its main goal is to engage and involve, throughout all stages, different actors at both EU and national levels in order to (a) ensure respect for the principles of 'multi-level governance and a bottom-up approach', (b) take into account the particularities of different institutional and legal frameworks in Member States, and (c) ensure the ownership of the programme by stakeholders and build on the experience and knowledge of relevant actors.[50] Due to its importance, Member States' discretion regarding its composition has been limited, and the committee 'shall include' at least the following actors:

(1) regional, local, urban, and other public authorities;
(2) economic and social partners;
(3) relevant bodies representing civil society, such as environmental partners, NGOs, and bodies responsible for promoting social inclusion, fundamental rights, rights of persons with disabilities, gender equality, and non-discrimination;
(4) research organizations and universities, where appropriate.

The chosen actors are involved from the preparation of the partnership agreement (see subsection B on this topic) and programmes to the implementation and evaluation of programmes.[51]

EU law is vague regarding the procedural aspects of the partnership principle, apart from the provisions on the monitoring committee.[52] Moreover, the CPR refers to Member States' legal and administrative traditions as guiding principles for the involvement of actors. The degree to which the partnership principle is implemented effectively depends on the institutional background and administrative system of each Member State and the different national cultures regarding the representation and participation of various socio-economic interest groups in decision-making procedures. The research has highlighted how the participation of socio-economic interest groups is less about having a voice in the democratic sense and more about acting in expert capacity. NGOs are expected to focus on providing expertise to support the national decision-making process and refrain from making political claims that are interpreted by funds officials as attempts to 'politicize' the process and as

[50] Ibid. Art. 8. See also Pantazatou, 'European Union Funds', in H. C. H. Hofmann, G. C. Rowe, and A. H. Türk (eds), *Specialized Administrative Law of the European Union: A Sectoral Review* (2019) 532, at 537.

[51] See Art. 39(2) CPR.

[52] Note, though, Commission Delegated Regulation (EU) 240/2014 (n. 14) on the European code of conduct on partnership.

a betrayal of national interests.[53] The Finnish interviews also point to the fact that NGOs feel that their contributions should focus on technical aspects–to the extent that national planning and monitoring work is inaccessible to outsiders because of the funds-related jargon.[54]

Participation in the EU cohesion funds governance contains many typical features identified across EU governance instruments over the years.[55] While the (EU-level) goals are ambitious, ambiguity plagues (national) implementation. As the partners are the same in the programming and monitoring stages, the possible unrepresentativeness, as well as the good practices, spreads easily across many levels of governance.[56]

B. Programming: Adaptation and Learning

Each Member State prepares a partnership agreement for the programming period. The main purpose of this agreement is to transpose the Common Strategic Framework, the strategic guiding principles for the EU funds established by the Commission, into the national context.[57] Member States also draft operational programmes for each fund and submit both the agreement and the operational programmes for Commission approval. Previously, the partnership agreement was made for the whole seven-year programme. While the agreement technically covers the whole period in the new MFF, in practice only the first 5 years will be programmed. Allocations for the last 2 years will be made on the basis of a substantial and in-depth mid-term review, leading to corresponding reprogramming ('amending') in 2025.[58] From the governance perspective, the new MFF's change encourages learning and adaptation and underlines the iterative nature of the programming.[59]

[53] Demidov, 'Efficient Implementers and Partners. What Do We Miss in Our Understanding of How Cohesion Policy Administrators Work?', in J. Bachtler et al. (eds), *EU Cohesion Policy. Reassessing Performance and Direction* (2016) 206, 211–12. See also Batory and Cartwright, 'Re-visiting the Partnership Principle in Cohesion Policy: The Role of Civil Society Organizations in Structural Funds Monitoring', 49 *JCMS* (2011) 697.

[54] Interview 5, 21 June 2021.

[55] Smismans, 'New Modes of Governance and the Participatory Myth', 31 *West European Politics* (*West Eur. Polit.*) (2008) 874.

[56] Pantazatou (n. 50) 539.

[57] See Arts 10–13 CPR; Pantazatou (n. 50) 540.

[58] See Art. 13 CPR.

[59] On learning as a governance feature and a condition for problem-solving, see e.g. Sturm, 'Gender Equity Regimes and the Architecture of Learning', in G. de Búrca and J. Scott (eds), *Law and New Governance in the EU and the US* (2006) 323–61; Sabel, 'Learning by Monitoring: The Institutions of Economic Development', in N. J. Smelser and R. Swedberg (eds), *The Handbook of Economic Sociology* (1996) 137–65.

Member States have a wide margin of independence to nationally translate the Commission's Common Strategic Framework. This margin exists, however, only in principle, because the interviewed actors noted the Commission's growing input in the substance of national plans. The interviewees took note of 'something quite massive' changing in the cohesion policy, with one describing this as the shifting of 'the tectonic plates'.[60] They described how the Commission is dictating the substance of programmes and raised the question of whether digitalization and the green transition as new horizontal policy aims are doing away with the traditional objectives of the cohesion policy of reducing regional disparities.[61]

There are two potential reasons that may have led to this stronger Commission presence. The first relates to the changes in mindset that are paving the way to new or adjusted cohesion policies. For instance, the structural funds have links to the Green Agenda and long-term and globally critical aims such as climate change mitigation, and the Commission is trying to find ways to make these global aims feel relevant and acted on at the local level. One way to do so is to closely observe that, in their programme documents, Member States create links to, for instance, climate policies. The resulting more interventionist Commission is not necessarily welcomed by Member States, who may, in the first place, have reservations about the new directions of the cohesion policy. While generally sympathetic to the Green Agenda, digitalization, and innovations, the interviewed national actors are also unsure how regional projects can be concretely linked to what they described as global aims.[62]

The second reason for the Commission's strong position vis-à-vis Member States is explained by increased policy alignment in EU funds governance. The Commission's approval of the partnership and operational agreements is conditional not only on compliance with EU law and fund-specific considerations but also on the European Semester requirements. In an effort to connect the Member States' budgetary performance to EU funds, the Commission's assessment takes into account national reform programmes and country-specific recommendations of the European Semester in accordance with Article 12(1) CPR: 'In its assessment, the Commission shall, in particular, take into account how the Member State intends to address relevant country-specific recommendations.'[63] Due respect is also paid to integrated national energy and climate plans as well as the European Pillar of Social Rights.

[60] Interview 5, 21 June 2021.
[61] Ibid. See also Interview 4, 18 June 2021 and Interview 1, 3 June 2021.
[62] Interview 1, 3 June 2021.
[63] See also Art. 23 CPR.

This alignment of national agreements and programmes with various ambitious policy goals not only reduces national discretion but also poses problems for Member States that try to ensure coherence between different governance instruments. Alignment may lead to a situation in which policy instruments become overly complicated as they attempt to deliver economic and social convergence, tackle business cycles, safeguard fiscal discipline, and sanction rule of law backsliding. Overly zealous policy alignment may also negatively affect adaptation capacity.

The Commission cannot request a reprogramming of the partnership agreement, but Member States may be required to 'review' the agreement, taking into account the observations made by the Commission.[64] Once the Commission is satisfied with national programmes, it makes an implementing decision on each partnership agreement.[65] Here, the question then relates to the extent to which the Commission is capable of thoroughly examining national programme documents. The number of relevant reports that circulate between the Commission and Member States is impressive, with the average length of a partnership agreement being around 150 pages and that of an operational programme between 150 and 200 pages.[66] Programme documents therefore amount to tens of thousands of pages. The new MFF restricts the length of a partnership agreement to 35 pages, yet the Member State can 'at its own initiative, decide[s] to extend the length of the document'.[67] If the Commission cannot engage with the documents, the potential for learning and adaptation on the basis of feedback is not adequately realized.[68] There is no element of

[64] The Commission has the ability to request a reprogramming of operational programmes.

[65] See Art. 12(4) CPR. Planning does not stop with the Commission's approval of the partnership agreement and operational programmes. There is a wide range of national policy documents, from regional development decision to regional programme and implementation plans, to prepare and implement.

[66] These come on top of other existing reporting obligations. See C. Charveriat and E. Bodin, 'Delivering the Green Deal: The Role of a Reformed Semester within a New Sustainable Growth Strategy for the EU', Institute for European Environmental Policy (2020), https://ieep.eu/wp-content/uploads/2022/12/Delivering-the-Green-Deal-through-the-European-Semester-Final_compressed.pdf (last visited 22 January 2024) at 22:

> Member States have to submit a wide range of reports and evaluations to the European Commission in areas covered by EU legislation. At the moment, it is quite difficult to make sense of the different, partly overlapping timelines of these processes. Examples of key processes include reporting for 2020 targets, National Energy and Climate Plans (NECPs), national long-term strategies (LTS), river basin management plans, Birds and Habitat directive implementation, the forthcoming Common Agricultural Policy's (CAP) strategic plans.

For the same issue in the relation to the Water Framework Directive, see E. Korkea-aho, *Adjudicating New Governance. Deliberative Democracy in the European Union* (2016).

[67] See Art. 10(5) CPR.

[68] Member States do not fully implement country-specific recommendations, and the Commission has not always (or not sufficiently) used its powers to recommend specific measures where Member States have not addressed the recommendations: see Bekker, 'Hardening and Softening of Country-Specific Recommendations in the European Semester', 44 *West Eur. Polit.* (2011) 114.

peer review in the programming stage, underlining the vertical dimension (Commission–Member State) of the principle of shared management.

C. Selection and Monitoring: Deliberation

Once the national plans are approved by the Commission, Member States proceed to open calls for projects, select eligible projects, allocate funds to the beneficiaries, and generally take care of all the actions connected to the implementation phase. This is where intermediate bodies come into the picture.

It is crucial to understand the importance of a 'project' because, ultimately, EU funds are channelled into these. A project is a unit of life in funds governance. According to the interviewed authorities, four key criteria stand out in the context of project selection, with this stage not being significantly guided by EU law. First, the eligible project must be linked to a Member State programme, as well as to a regional programme if one exists. Second, the project must be financially viable in the sense that the project has a fair chance to succeed and deliver results. Third, EU funds must have an impact (more about the concept of European Added Value below), the project outputs must be published, and there must be a plan of how the further utilization of project outputs can be facilitated after the project comes to an end. Fourth, the projects eligible for support must comply with the objectives of the Paris Agreement and the principle of 'no harm' under the European Green Development Programme.[69] As recalled in subsection B, the authorities interviewed recognize the tension between the local and global as they work to select projects that would realize the aims of national programmes (interpreting the Commission's Common Framework Strategy) and those of regional programmes.

After the selection of projects to be funded, national authorities adopt single-case decisions, with the Commission reimbursing eligible costs.[70] Beneficiaries are diverse, ranging from small NGOs or single universities to large consortiums involving a host of actors. All beneficiaries need to draw up a project plan and acknowledge and communicate, in their activities, the support they have received from EU funds.[71] Securing and managing funding requires professionalism, and in many countries, programme authorities speak of 'serial applicants' who are professionally capable of applying for and managing

[69] Interview 1, 3 June 2021; Interview 3, 7 June 2021. For the fourth point see also Art. 9(4) CPR.

[70] Crowe, 'The Union Budget', in H. C. H. Hofmann, G. C. Rowe, and A. H. Türk (eds), *Specialized Administrative Law of the European Union: A Sectoral Review* (2019) 598.

[71] See Art. 50 CPR.

EU-funded projects. In order to train successful candidates and widen the pool of applicants, some Member States are known to organize study trips: 'the initiatives of state officials to train partners, including sending them abroad to "learn how to be a partner"'.[72]

Beneficiaries are monitored through the entire life cycle of the project. In practice, this means that beneficiaries submit payment requests every six months and report on progress. In Finland, beneficiaries also need to set up 'project committees' involving the representatives of programme authorities. While the project committee is not mandated by EU law, the authorities interviewed noted that its existence is conducive to deliberation and mutual learning, assisting both them and the beneficiary in ensuring that the obligations under the CPR are fulfilled.[73] The findings of the monitoring of each individual project then feed into the annual review by the managing authority. Every year, a review meeting is organized between the Commission and each Member State to examine performance.[74] CPR provisions are not specific about the participants, the content, or the consequences of such meetings.

Previously, national programme authorities were also required to prepare an annual implementation report, but this requirement was abolished in favour of more frequent and up-to-date submission of data and an ongoing policy dialogue. The new policy dialogue style is underpinned by the fact that the CPR obliges Member States to transmit information on the financial and performance implementation of each programme nearly every two months via an electronic system.[75] The idea is that performance is reflected almost in real time. However, as the European Court of Auditors (ECA) noted, this real-time monitoring is a significant increase over the reporting requirements in the 2014–2020 period and makes little sense given that review meetings between the Commission and Member States, as well as monitoring committee meetings, will only take place once or twice a year.[76]

Member States carry out a mid-term review of each programme supported by the cohesion policy funds. That review should provide a fully fledged adjustment of programmes based on programme performance, while also providing an opportunity to take into account new challenges and any relevant country-specific recommendations.[77]

[72] Both quotations are Demidov (n. 53) 215. Interestingly, this reminds an observer of role-playing exercises used in Alabama and Utah child services to train caseworkers to make contextual judgments: see Noonan, Sabel, and Simon (n. 36) 537.
[73] Interview 3, 7 June 2021.
[74] See Art. 41 CPR.
[75] Ibid. Art. 42(1).
[76] ECA, Opinion 6/2018 (n. 40), paras 66–67.
[77] See Art. 18 CPR. The mid-term review was in 2024.

Finally, Member States must annually examine audits. The Commission has emphasized that the internal audit process is not only about verification but also a learning process.[78] Audit requirements have been relaxed over time because auditing has involved much double work.[79] The so-called 'single audit concept' was introduced in the previous programme periods but was limited to the relationship between national audit authorities and the Commission. The innovation of the current CPR is that single-audit arrangements should be extended to cover the relationship between audit and management authorities nationally: audit authorities should no longer ask for documents from beneficiaries but use those available from managing authorities.[80]

The CPR also introduced another major audit reform. The so-called 'enhanced proportionate arrangements' under the CPR allow a Member State to apply simplified procedures for the certification and verification of expenditure, a change the ECA calls 'radical'.[81] For those Member States with a 'good' track record, the Commission will substantially reduce its supervision and rely largely on national audits, the number of which is also reduced.[82] The Member State may apply the enhanced proportionate arrangements where the Commission has confirmed that the management and control system of the programme is functioning effectively and that the total error rate for each year is 2 per cent or below for the preceding two years. The Commission shall take into account the participation of the Member State in the enhanced cooperation on the establishment of the European Public Prosecutor's Office.[83]

While the Commission reduces and refocuses the administrative burden of auditing, it takes the prevention and detection of conflicts of interest as one of its future priorities.[84] In future audits, more attention will be paid to conflicts

[78] ECA, Opinion 6/2018 (n. 40).

[79] Mendez and Bacthler, 'Administrative Reform and Unintended Consequences: An Assessment of the EU Cohesion Policy Audit Explosion', 18 *JEPP* (2011) 746.

[80] See Art. 80(1) CPR. See also ECA, Opinion No 6/2018 (n. 40), para. 103. The use of simplified cost models is also hoped to reduce the administrative burden.

[81] ECA, Opinion 6/2018 (n. 40), paras 112 and 139. The ECA has, however, supported the introduction of enhanced proportionate arrangements, arguing that complexity is a particular issue in EU-15 countries where EU funding is relatively smaller, suggesting a need for proportionality. This is correct, because the ERDF funds are quite large, for instance in Poland, while funds, for instance in Austria, Belgium, or the Netherlands, are comparatively small: see European Commission, 'Cohesion Open Data Platform, Funding Period 2014–2020', https://cohesiondata.ec.europa.eu/funds/erdf (last visited 22 January 2024).

[82] See Art. 83(1)b CPR: 'the audit authority may limit its audit activity to audits of operations covering a sample based on a statistical selection of 30 sampling units for the programme or group of programmes concerned', and ibid. Art. 83(3): 'the Commission shall limit its own audits to a review of the work of the audit authority through re-performance at its level only, unless available information suggests a serious deficiency in the work of the audit authority'.

[83] Ibid. Art. 84.

[84] The Commission has issued more than 40 pages of guidance: see 2021/C 121/01 (n. 16).

of interest, fraud, and double financing. The Commission anticipates that increased funding in the coming years will increase risks associated with corrupt practices, and intermediary (regional) bodies will need to step up control measures to combat them. It remains to be seen whether auditing arrangements can be simultaneously streamlined and strengthened to root out corruption.

D. Administrative Enforcement and Protection: (Negative) Adaptation

Under shared management, the Member States are responsible for investigating any irregularities,[85] and for recovering, where needed, any amounts improperly paid. As Crowe points out, the Court of Justice long used the duty of mutual sincere cooperation as a legal basis to oblige the Member States to take all effective measures to penalize conduct harmful to the financial interests of the Union. That obligation is now laid down in the Treaties, notably in Article 325(2) TFEU, and in the Financial Regulation, which obliges Member States to 'take all necessary measures, including legislative, regulatory and administrative measures, to protect the Union's financial interests'.[86] In other words, the Commission must rely on national authorities for frontline enforcement vis-à-vis final beneficiaries.[87]

When the amount incorrectly paid to a beneficiary cannot be recovered, and this is a result of fault or negligence on the part of a Member State, the latter is responsible for reimbursing the amount to the Union. Since the detection of financial irregularities may result in financial penalties and the withholding of further disbursements to particular projects, individual Member States have a strong incentive to avoid these consequences in relation to projects conducted in their territory and a disincentive to investigate irregularities. This may explain why the evolution of legislation as far as administrative enforcement is

[85] See Art. 2(31) CPR: The term 'irregularity' means 'any breach of applicable law, resulting from an act or omission by an economic operator involved in the implementation of the Funds, which has, or would have, the effect of prejudicing the budget of the Union by charging unjustified expenditure to that budget'.

[86] Crowe (n. 70) 600.

[87] Pantazatou (n. 50) 545. All the official exchanges of information between national authorities, the Commission, and the European Anti-Fraud Office are carried out by electronic data exchange systems, notably by the Irregularity Management System (IMS) and the Early Detection and Exclusion System (EDES): see also Crowe (n. 70) 599. EDES, also known as the EU blacklist for fraudsters, is not working as well as it could according to a report by the ECA: see ECA, 'Special Report 11/2022: Protecting the EU Budget—Better Use of Blacklisting Needed' (23 May 2022), https://www.eca.europa.eu/en/Pages/DocItem.aspx?did=61175 (last visited 22 January 2024).

concerned has progressively strengthened the power of the Commission in relation to investigating and penalizing irregularities.[88]

E. Evaluation: Learning and Effectiveness

Evaluation has been traditionally concerned with the tendency of EU funding to allocate funds to projects where funds are likely to be fully spent rather than where they address key needs and produce results. For example, in the cohesion policy, funds must be spent by the end of the third year after their allocation. The concentration of spending towards the end of the MFF poses the risk that Member States may prioritize the absorption of funds at the expense of performance.[89] However, the use of EU funds is no longer only followed for the ability of national authorities to make sure that the money is spent (absorption capacity), or spent correctly, but also for results; that is, how effective are EU-funded projects at achieving the agreed targets? This change in emphasis from verifying receipts to inspecting results is evident at the level of *individual* projects and the *system* as a whole.

Attention is paid in project audits to establishing that the agreed objectives have been achieved and that the project indicator data are correct.[90] For this reason, national authorities have insisted on project committees through which they can monitor progress at the *individual project* level. In order to guide the evaluation process and ensure that it is underpinned by expert knowledge,[91] the programme authorities devise indicators. The previous programme period resulted in over 9,000 indicators, which obviously is a problem, as overall evaluation becomes impossible.[92] The torrent of indicators and effectiveness

[88] See Arts 95–97 CPR.

[89] Cipriani, 'Improving the Accountability of the EU Budget's Multi-level Implementation: Strengthening the Contribution of the European Court of Auditors', 22 *German Law Journal* 466.

[90] Interview 3, 7 June 2021; Interview 4, 18 June 2021.

[91] Vesan, Corti, and Sabato, 'The European Commission's Entrepreneurship and the Social Dimension of the European Semester: From the European Pillar of Social Rights to the Covid-19 Pandemic', 19 *Comparative European Politics* (2021) 277, at 280 (arguing that the European Semester is 'an evidence-based policy process ... To be effective, the Semester has to percolate into the language of bureaucracy and the semantics of indicators in order to affect the EU coordination of national social and employment policies').

[92] European Court of Auditors, Opinion 4/2020 (pursuant to Arts 287(4) and 322(1)(a), TFEU) concerning the proposal 2020/0101 (COD) for a Regulation of the European Parliament and of the Council amending Regulation (EU) 1303/2013 as regards exceptional additional resources and implementing arrangements under the Investment for growth and jobs goal to provide assistance for fostering crisis repair in the context of the COVID-19 pandemic and preparing a green, digital and resilient recovery of the economy (REACT-EU); and on the amended proposal 2018/0196 (COD) for a Regulation of the European Parliament and of the Council laying down common provisions on the European Regional Development Fund, the European Social Fund Plus, the Cohesion Fund, the Just Transition Fund and the European Maritime and Fisheries Fund and financial rules for those and for

criteria is also felt at the regional level in the work of intermediate authorities. When choosing the eligible projects, these authorities need to pay simultaneous attention to several possibly conflicting criteria.

Evaluation applies to the *systems level* too. Both managing authorities[93] and the Commission[94] are required to assess the programme's effectiveness, efficiency, relevance, coherence, and European Added Value (EAV) with the aim of improving the quality of the design and implementation of programmes. These assessments feed into the Article 318(2) TFEU obligation, according to which the Commission is required to submit each year to the EP and to the Council 'an evaluation report on the Union's finances based on the results achieved'.[95] As an external auditor, the ECA also evaluates the performance of EU funds. In accordance with Article 27 of the Financial Regulation, it assesses whether the audited entities have used EU funds in terms of value for money–economy, efficiency, and effectiveness. The results of audit findings are published by the ECA in its special reports.[96] From the perspective of national governance, the ECA's reports include valuable information, but their impact on frontline administration in the Member States is uncertain.

As a process, evaluation is politically charged, and much of the tension relates to the concept of EAV. Used in different contexts and with distinct meanings, the concept of EAV is unspecified. There is no EU-level political understanding of what it means, with Member States resisting its further operationalization. In the current framework, where the MFF represents a compromise between different rationales and national stances, with funding spread across a large number of policy areas and spending programmes, a firm definition of EAV could be seen by political authorities as a constraint rather than an opportunity.

5. The National Governance of EU Funds: An Evaluation

This account of the national governance of EU funds masks the complexity of processes and interactions. To illustrate this: one interviewee gave me four

the Asylum and Migration Fund, the Internal Security Fund and the Border Management and Visa Instrument, para. 18.

[93] See Art. 44 CPR.

[94] Ibid. Art. 45.

[95] See also Art. 29 of the Interinstitutional Agreement (n. 28), which stipulates that the Commission 'shall use more performance information, including performance audit results, to evaluate the finances of the Union based on the results achieved' in its evaluation report in accordance with Art. 318 TFEU.

[96] ECA's audit reports, reviews, and opinions can be found at https://www.eca.europa.eu/en/multiple-reports (last visited 22 January 2024).

pages of organizational charts depicting the allocation of responsibilities, with boxes and lines marking channels of communication and reporting obligations! And yet we know that the real accountability work is messy and cannot reasonably be captured or limited within such a stylized account or the neat design of boxes and lines.

At the risk of simplifying, this account manages to highlight how national funds officials are embedded in routinized processes. These processes are not 'informal' in the traditional sense of the word used in legal scholarship, which assumes decoupling between a legal norm and an informal norm.[97] Rather, many of the routinized processes, such as appointing relevant committees or organizing mid-term reviews, are required by law. The national governance of EU funds implements the design laid down by the Common Provisions Regulation, although implementation is very different from the clean, ordered designs presented in the regulation. The fact that national governance systems derive their concrete manifestations from the law does not diminish their contextual, adaptive nature or devalue their ability to navigate uncertain and fluid circumstances. It should be kept in mind that funds legislation is also the product of continuous adaptation. Both the CPR and the MFF are amended for each seven-year budget cycle, but the well-functioning processes are 'rolled over' to a new cycle to support the routinization of national governance arrangements beyond budget cycles.

These everyday, routinized processes facilitate deliberation, inclusiveness, and adaptation. Deliberation is visible, for instance, in the development and utilization of a policy dialogue to check performance almost in real time, or in the use of 'project committees' that assist both national programme authorities and the beneficiary in staying in regular contact throughout the implementation of a project. Inclusiveness is evident in the use of monitoring committees, the members of which should represent civil society organizations and groups as well as the funds administration. Yet, inclusiveness is an important policy value also at the evaluation stage, when broader public-policy considerations (of citizens as taxpayers) are internalized to evaluate what it is that the projects have delivered. Finally, adaptation is integral to several processes. Within the current MFF, for instance, partnership programmes are planned for the first five years instead of the first seven years of the budget cycle, requiring national funds officials to constantly react and adapt to changes in the external

[97] Ní Aoláin, '"Soft Law", Informal Lawmaking and "New Institutions" in the Global Counter-Terrorism Architecture', 32 *European Journal of International Law* (2021) 919 (arguing that 'human rights norms are not meaningfully included in the creation and implementation of these [soft, informal] norms').

environment. Adaptive tendencies have also found their way into auditing, a phase that usually sends shivers down the spine of national officials and beneficiaries. The so-called 'enhanced proportionate arrangements' under the CPR allow a Member State to apply simplified procedures for the certification and verification of expenditure. The Commission adapts its supervision to the individual performance of a Member State, considering past (good) performance as a signal for a future where less scrutiny is warranted.

I capture the type of accountability that these routine governance practices produce under the concept of 'bottom-up' accountability. Such accountability type is tailored to a governance model that rests on projects, programme evaluation, and formative reviews. In this version, 'accountability is an ongoing process that does not merely swoop in to exact penance for done deeds, but influences and shapes the doing of deeds all along'.[98] The utilization of 'projects' illustrates how accountability gets produced now, not once a programme or budget cycle has been completed. The project is, as described in section 4, the most basic 'governance' unit of EU funds.[99] Beneficiaries create a project for which they seek funding from national programme authorities. Once selected for funding, the project becomes the main unit of organization for distributing money, monitoring its use, managing and conducting activities, reporting results, and verifying accounts. National authorities insist on 'project committees' through which they can monitor progress at the level of an individual project. The findings of the monitoring of each project then feed into the annual review by the managing authority. But 'projects' have relevance for facilitating accountability further down the line as well. As explained below when discussing Transparency International's Integrity Pact projects, even ethics and good governance are produced and negotiated through 'projects'.

This sketchy portrayal of the national governance model points to the Commission's strong and growing presence in the governance of national funds. Its role is muscular in the early stages, in particular pre-management and programming, while diminishing somewhat towards the end of the governance process.[100] Does this not contradict the idea that there is a strong case

[98] Bernstein and Rodriguez (n. 2) 64.

[99] For the project logic of EU funding, see Büttner and Leopold, 'A "New Spirit" of Public Policy? The Project World of EU Funding', 3 *European Journal of Cultural and Political Sociology* (2016) 41.

[100] Nastase, 'Catering to Organizational Needs in Ethics Management: The Case of the European Commission', 37 *IJPA* (2014) 93 (arguing that 'In many ways, in the discourse of REGIO [Directorate-General for Regional and Urban Policies] officials the relationship between the Commission and the Member State is portrayed as a connection between teacher and students'). The authorities interviewed noted that, over time, Finnish authorities and stakeholders have gained self-confidence, and meetings with the Commission are conducted in the spirit of mutual learning and collaboration: see Interview 4, 18 June 2021 and Interview 5, 21 June 2021.

for everyday administrative practices contributing to accountability? If the Commission is effectively in control, one could argue that small step efforts at 'bottom-up' accountability are being supplanted. However, my exploration of the national governance funds management shows that the relationship between the Commission and Member States does not function on a hierarchical command-and-control basis. The previously described governance model relieves the Commission of much of its commanding authority and shifts the burden (and costs!) of checking and monitoring to the national level. Further, the fact that the Commission assumes a stronger (although not prescribing) role when the common goals are defined, and fades into the background when it is the time to execute and review, is indicative of the governance model also used in the Open Method of Coordination (OMC) and framework directives.[101]

While the Commission's role in relation to Member States is not premised on the concept of command-and-control, the way in which it operates prevents the Member States from being more active and, subsequently, the emergence of peer review for funds management.[102] The meetings that national actors have with the Commission to discuss partnership agreements have the advantage of exchanging information on how a Member State is performing and what challenges the Commission anticipates for the Member State, but such bilateral meetings do not engender learning from errors or inspire the development of alternatives on the basis of what others are doing in similar situations.[103] Similarly, while the feedback from the Commission may prompt Member States to review their operational programmes, the law and governance approach would emphasize the importance of governance structures that enable civil society to provide 'bottom-up' and real-time feedback on national programmes and their execution.[104]

[101] Korkea-aho (n. 66).

[102] Note, though, that to help Member States manage and use cohesion policy funds, the Commission has provided administrative support frameworks to enable administrations to share experiences and good practices, such as TAIEX–REGIO Peer2Peer and REGIO Communities of Practitioners, the Integrity Pacts, the Transnational ESF+ Platform, online videos on how to prevent and identify fraud and corruption, and transnational cooperation networks: see Commission Staff Working Document, 'Supporting Public Administrations in EU Member States to Deliver Reforms and Prepare for the Future', SWD (2021) 101.

[103] See the discussion in Noonan, Sabel, and Simon (n. 36) (533) (arguing how an 'effective monitoring regime needs both outcome information that indicates how effective the system is in achieving its goals and diagnostic information that indicates the locales and practices that are responsible for failures').

[104] Apart from participatory structures, such 'bottom-up' feedback would also require transparency, the fact to which the European Ombudsman has drawn attention in the case of EU recovery funds: see Decision on how the European Commission dealt with two requests for public access to documents concerning the Swedish and Danish Recovery and Resilience Plans (Case 925/2022/LDS).

Thus far, I have identified and described a set of routinized processes that contribute to accountable funds decision-making, which is deliberative, inclusive, and adaptive. As routines, these processes are hardly perfect, and any progress is piecemeal at best. For instance, there are serious and substantiated doubts about whether participation mechanisms deliver their inclusive potential, whether national processes are echo chambers closed to those who do not speak the esoteric 'language' of funds, or whether interactions between the Commission and a Member State result in 'diagnostic' information needed to improve performance. Yet, the processes that I have discussed do have value as imperfect routines feeding into accountability; it is in these everyday processes that accountability gets produced. It is, of course, possible, and even likely, that the process may, at various points, become stuck or derailed, and officials may decide to act in a way that contravenes the CPR and the governance model built on it. There is no guarantee that national funds decision-making *is* accountable, but there is evidence that funds governance comes with tools for accountability.[105]

These positive governance practices do not, however, flourish without efforts to support and—in some cases—protect and defend them. In sections 6 and 7, I first describe how the good governance of funds has become a European and global concern and discuss the institutional framework for addressing corruption concerns in the EU. I then explain why and how the recent anti-corruption agenda, which is an obviously worthy goal in itself, is a threat to national funds governance and why governance processes need to be actively supported against their colonization by an emerging penal rationality.

6. The Emerging Penal Rationality

EU cohesion policy and, perhaps more broadly, EU funds seem to be afflicted with bad management practices and corruption.[106] Even a brief glance at audit reports, public statements, or research literature gives an idea that EU funds governance is flawed and inefficient. It is either excessively entangled in

[105] Similarly in the US context, see Bernstein and Rodriguez (n. 2).

[106] Batory, 'A Free Lunch from the EU? Public Perceptions of Corruption in Cohesion Policy Expenditure in Post-Communist EU Member States', 43 *Journal of European Integration* (2021) 651 (arguing that 'Popular narratives indicate that citizens perceive cohesion policy implementation as intertwined with grand corruption. While national political elites are considered as the main culprit, EU institutions are also seen as failing in their duties'); Fazekas and Toth, 'Corruption in EU Funds?: Europe-Wide Evidence of the Corruption Effect of EU-Funded Public Contracting', in J. Bachtler et al. (eds), *EU Cohesion Policy. Reassessing Performance and Direction* (2016) 186.

bureaucratic red tape, leading to waste and inefficiency, or in need of improved regulatory oversight to prevent fraud and illegality. Despite numerous waves of administrative reforms aimed at rectifying the system, they have yielded minimal success.[107]

There is no question that money gets lost in the implementation of EU funding programmes. According to the 2021 Annual Report on the protection of the Union's financial interests, approximately EUR 1,605 million were lost due to fraudulent irregularities in 2020 in the context of cohesion and regional policies alone, with the number and financial amounts reported as fraudulent being the highest in the ERDF.[108] It is feared that sums lost to bad practices and criminal activities will only grow in the coming years. In 2020, Europol launched the new European Financial and Economic Crime Centre, warning that 'Economic stimuli such as those proposed in the wake of the COVID-19 pandemic will be targeted by criminals seeking to defraud public funding.'[109] The Group of States against Corruption (GRECO), established in 1999 by the Council of Europe, has recommended streamlining anti-corruption measures in pandemic-related processes, such as the allocation and disbursement of recovery funds, emergency legislation, and medical care.[110] In 2023, GRECO announced that it will devote its next evaluation round to the sub-national level, highlighting the crucial role of local authorities in preventing corruption and promoting integrity in EU funds management.[111] There are worries that COVID-19 has added to corruption risks not only because of the unprecedented sums of the RRF (and of the other temporary emergency packages)

[107] For the history of administrative reforms in the EU, see Cini, 'Change and Ethics in the EU Commission', 16 *British Journal of Politics & International Relations* (2014) 479. Cini reminds readers that the Commission has been required to reform its internal procedures, because ill-functioning Commission procedures have been identified as facilitating fraudulent activity at the domestic level, noting the interdependent synergies of administrative reforms.

[108] European Commission, 'The 33rd Annual Report on the Protection of the European Union's Financial Interests. Fight against Fraud 2021', https://anti-fraud.ec.europa.eu/system/files/2022-09/pif-report-2021_en_0.pdf (last visited 22 January 2024) 36. See also at 39 (bold font removed): 'The most frequent fraudulent irregularities were the use of false or falsified documents … Most fraudulent irregularities concerning ethics and integrity were about conflicts of interests. Infringements of public procurement rules were the most reported of non-fraudulent irregularities, but only in 4% of these cases was fraud detected.' According to the report, there is a significant reduction in non-fraudulent irregularities in cohesion policy: see at 38.

[109] Europol, 'Europol Launches the European Financial and Economic Crime Centre', Press Release (5 June 2020), https://www.europol.europa.eu/newsroom/news/europol-launches-european-financial-and-economic-crime-centre (last visited 22 January 2024).

[110] Greco 2020, 'Corruption Risks and Useful Legal References in the Context of COVID-19' (15 April 2020), https://rm.coe.int/corruption-risks-and-useful-legal-references-in-the-context-of-covid-1/16809e33e1 (last visited 22 January 2024).

[111] Greco 2023, '94th Green Plenary Meeting, Strasbourg, 5–9 June 2023', https://rm.coe.int/greco-2023-9-eng-decisions-greco-94-2786-5003-4696-1/1680ab8d38 (last visited 22 January 2024).

but also because COVID-19 has directed attention away from anti-corruption efforts, with transparency measures being neglected or rolled back.[112]

Ensuring good funds management has become a global concern. The Organisation for Economic Co-operation and Development (OECD) has warned that integrity violations and corrupt practices could undermine recovery, flagging in particular the need to address immediate risks in emergency procurement and integrate anti-corruption risk assessments in economic recovery measures.[113] Besides giving rise to concerned statements on a global scale, corruption is seen as an existential threat to the democratic order and decision-making. President Biden's address illustrates the hardening logic: 'Fighting corruption is not just good governance. It is self-defense. It is patriotism, and it's *essential to the preservation of our democracy and our future*.'[114]

Against this background, it is not surprising, then, to find that the fight against fraud affecting the Union's finances has become 'fertile grounds for institutional innovation over the years, with a clear trend towards strengthening the central institutional framework'.[115] This is consistent with the bolstering of the legal framework governing the protection of the Union's financial interests in the Member States.[116] The EU relies on three main institutions to defend its budget, each building on the work of the other. The ECA carries out the external audit of Union revenue and expenditure by examining the reliability of accounts and the legality and regularity of the underlying transactions.[117] Its work, as previously explained, builds on that done by national audit authorities. When the ECA suspects fraud, corruption, or other illegal activity, it must report it to the European Anti-Fraud Office (OLAF), which 'investigates fraud against the EU budget, corruption and serious misconduct

[112] V-Dem, 'Pandemic Backsliding: Democracy during COVID-19 (March 2020 to June 2021), http://www.v-dem.net/pandem.html (last visited 22 January 2024).

[113] OECD 2020, 'Policy Measures to Avoid Corruption and Bribery in the COVID-19 Response and Recovery' (26 May 2020), https://www.oecd-ilibrary.org/governance/policy-measures-to-avoid-corruption-and-bribery-in-the-covid-19-response-and-recovery_225abff3-en (last visited 22 January 2024).

[114] White House, 'Statement by President Joseph R. Biden, Jr. on the National Security Study Memorandum on the Fight against Corruption' (3 June 2021), https://www.whitehouse.gov/briefing-room/statements-releases/2021/06/03/statement-by-president-joseph-r-biden-jr-on-the-national-security-study-memorandum-on-the-fight-against-corruption (last visited 22 January 2024) (emphasis by author).

[115] Crowe (n. 70) 591.

[116] A. Sandulli et al. (eds), 'The Protection of EU Financial Interests across Four National Legal Systems: A Comparative Perspective' (2021), https://betkosol.luiss.it/wp-content/uploads/2021/07/D1-BETKOSOL-final-26-June-2021-def.pdf (last visited 22 January 2024); A. Bernardi and D. Negri (eds), *Investigating European Fraud in the EU Member States* (2017).

[117] See Art. 287 TFEU.

within the European institutions'.[118] OLAF can open administrative investigations and issue administrative, financial, disciplinary, or judicial recommendations addressed to EU or national authorities. Yet, because OLAF can only refer the results of its administrative investigations to the competent national authorities who then independently decide whether or not to initiate criminal proceedings, a new EU-level body with a wider remit was deemed necessary.[119]

The groundwork for such an EU body was laid down by the Lisbon Treaty, with the legal basis and rules for the creation of the European Public Prosecutor's Office (EPPO) enshrined in Article 86 TFEU.[120] The EPPO was established via the enhanced integration procedure,[121] with 22 out of 27 Member States participating in its activities. Among the non-participants are, inter alia, Hungary, Poland, and Sweden. Beginning its operations in 2021, the EPPO acts as an independent body with competence for directing, coordinating, and supervising criminal investigations and for prosecuting suspects in national courts in accordance with a common prosecution policy. It has uniform investigation powers throughout the Union based on, and integrated into, the national systems of the Member States.

The first European Chief Prosecutor was Romanian Laura Kövesi, working with 22 nationally appointed European Prosecutors, and close to 100 European Delegated Prosecutors. In November 2021, six months into its existence, the EPPO announced that the Special Penal Court of the Slovak Republic had issued the first conviction in an EPPO investigation concerning the use of falsified documents in order to illegally obtain financial support from the European

[118] In 2021, there were 15 such cases (in 2020, there were 6 and in 2019, there were 9). OLAF usually opens investigations in all cases flagged by the ECA. Out of 15 cases, the ECA reported one case both to OLAF and the European Public Prosecutor's Office: see ECA, '2021 EU Audit in Brief', https://www.eca.europa.eu/Lists/ECADocuments/auditinbrief-2021/auditinbrief-2021_EN.pdf (last visited 22 January 2024).

[119] The research on the need of a central authority such as the European Public Prosecutor's Office was intense. For instance, Gómez-Jara argued that EU funds are to be treated as US federal funds, and any mismanagement should be prosecuted and punished by the EU: see Gómez-Jara, 'European Federal Criminal Law: What Can Europe Learn from the US System of Federal Criminal Law to Solve Its Sovereign Debt Crisis?', *European Criminal Law Review* (2012).

[120] See Art. 86 TFEU. See also Council Regulation (EU) 2017/1939 of 12 October 2017 implementing enhanced cooperation on the establishment of the European Public Prosecutor's Office, OJ L 283 (31 October 2017) 1–71. The definition of criminal offences affecting the Union financial interests is provided in Directive (EU) 2017/1371 of the European Parliament and of the Council of 5 July 2017 on the fight against fraud to the Union's financial interests by means of criminal law, OJ L 198 (28 July 2017) 29–41.

[121] According to Art. 20 TEU, a minimum of nine EU Member States are allowed to set up advanced integration or cooperation in a particular field within the EU, when it has become clear that the EU as a whole cannot achieve the goals of such cooperation within a reasonable period. Authorization to proceed with the enhanced cooperation is granted by the Council as a last resort, on a proposal from the Commission and after obtaining the consent of the Parliament.

Social Fund for co-financing of local services.[122] Two other indictments were announced on the EPPO website in January 2022, one concerning tobacco smuggling in Lithuania and the other bribery of a state Agricultural Fund official in Bulgaria.[123] The EPPO's first conviction and indictments underline the importance of the robust national judiciary and the EU's role in defending and fortifying it in the face of national competences. The Commission is already signalling that domestic legal systems need to invest more in investigating and prosecuting cases because 'the proportion of cases of suspected fraud that have not led to conviction remains very high, while the proportion of cases in which fraud is established is low'.[124]

In addition to strengthening the central institutional framework, the EU is streamlining the existing policy instruments to give more attention to anti-corruption efforts and align the EU financial framework with the rule of law agenda. When evaluating the European Semester, the ECA noted that it 'found a limited number of cases where Country Reports point out rule of law related issues such as judicial independence, corruption, conflict of interest, and media freedom. These are good examples of the contribution the European Semester can make to the rule of law.'[125] The ECA recommended the inclusion of a chapter specifically devoted to corruption in country-specific recommendations. In January 2022, Commissioner Věra Jourová described corruption as 'a cancer for democracy' and announced that, for the first time, the 2022 edition of rule of law reporting includes recommendations on anti-corruption.[126] Moreover, the new EU's anti-corruption agenda, a key policy after Qatargate (the European Parliament's corruption scandal in 2022–2023), emphasizes how action to combat fraud and people trying to 'secure illicit gains from the EU budget' also helps action against corruption more broadly.[127]

[122] EPPO, 'First Conviction in EPPO Case: Former Slovak Mayor Sentenced to 3 Years of Conditional Imprisonment' (23 November 2021), https://www.eppo.europa.eu/en/news/first-conviction-eppo-case-former-slovak-mayor-sentenced-3-years-conditional-imprisonment (last visited 22 January 2024).

[123] For the Lithuanian case, EPPO, 'Tobacco Smuggling Case Leads to First EPPO Indictment in Lithuania (28 January 2022), https://www.eppo.europa.eu/en/news/tobacco-smuggling-case-leads-first-eppo-indictment-lithuania (last visited 22 January 2024), and for the Bulgarian case, EPPO, 'First EPPO Indictment in Bulgaria: Bribery of a State Fund Agriculture's Official' (20 January 2022), https://www.eppo.europa.eu/en/news/first-eppo-indictment-bulgaria-bribery-state-fund-agricultures-official (last visited 22 January 2024). In its first 7 months of activities in 2021, the EPPO investigated 40 cases of corruption affecting the EU budget. In 2022, the number increased to 87.

[124] See the European Commission's 33rd protection of financial interests report (n. 108) 40.

[125] ECA, Special Report 16/2020 'The European Semester—Country Specific Recommendations' addresses important issues but needs better implementation.

[126] Politico, 'Brussels Playbook: Ukraine Fears—Corona Corruption—Ariane's Success' (25 January 2022), https://www.politico.eu/newsletter/brussels-playbook/ukraine-fears-corona-corruption-arianes-success (last visited 22 January 2024).

[127] Joint Communication to the European Parliament, the Council and the European Economic and Social Committee on the fight against corruption, Brussels (3 May 2023), JOIN(2023) 12 final, 10.

Civil society is also contributing to 'cleaning' the management of EU funds.[128] An integrity pact is a mechanism, launched by Transparency International EU, through which a public entity or a group of entities can collaborate with civil society. The purpose of collaboration is to ensure that authorities and bidders act within the constraints set out by the law, address corruption risks, and foster public trust in a given contracting project.[129] Through public agreement, the parties involved commit to refrain from any corrupt behaviour and to enhance transparency and accountability throughout the process. An independent mechanism led by civil society to monitor compliance is embedded in the agreement. An integrity pact can be tailored to specific markets, sectors, and legal frameworks, but usually they are implemented in the planning or pre-tendering stages of high-value projects with large budgets. The increased involvement of civil society has proven useful in reducing issues with public procurement.[130] In collaboration with the Commission, integrity pacts have been piloted in 18 contracting projects across 11 EU Member States from 2015 to 2021. Civil society actors must have proven expertise in anti-corruption, public contracting, or related fields, and can be funded through the project by the contracting authority in question. In other cases, contributions from external institutions or donors have covered the monitoring costs. This was the case with the Integrity Pacts EU project, where the Commission provided the necessary funding.[131]

Ensuring good funds management has quickly become a global concern, and a multitude of reforms have been proposed or put in place to translate the commitment into reality. The EU's defence of its budget has also grown discernibly more robust, with the tools provided by criminal law at the forefront of the fight against fraud. Besides the EPPO, the growing importance of the criminal law toolbox has percolated into the language of various policy instruments, such as the European Semester and the rule of law reporting. The EU's anti-fraud policy, aimed at protecting its budget, is 'criminal law-oriented'.[132]

[128] See also the Open Spending EU Coalition, a collaboration between various national NGOs, to advance the principles of openness in spending of funds, procurement, and company ownership within the EU, https://www.open-spending.eu (last visited 22 January 2024).

[129] Transparency International, 'Safeguarding EU-Funded Investments with Integrity Pacts. A Decision-Maker's Guide to Collaborative Public Contracting Monitoring' (2021), https://www.transparency.org/en/publications/integrity-pacts-safeguarding-eu-investments-decision-makers-guide-collaborative-public-contracting (last visited 22 January 2024).

[130] See the European Commission's 33rd protection of financial interests report (n. 108) 38.

[131] Transparency International (n. 129).

[132] Kuhl, 'The Future of the European Union's Financial Interests. Financial Criminal Law Investigations under the Lead of a European Prosecutor's Office', 3–4 EUCRIM (2008) 186, https://eucrim.eu/articles/the-future-of-the-european-unions-financial-interests (last visited 22 January 2024).

However, as the recap of new policy reforms shows, the EU today prefers to use a broader term—'anti-corruption efforts'—rather than just 'anti-fraud'. While both the EU and Member States agree that 'the issue of corruption should not be limited to a purely criminal interpretation and should therefore also cover administrative law tools',[133] the EU continues its fight against fraud and, more generally, corruption through the repertoire of criminal law.[134] I explain below why this emerging penal rationality—the concept I use to name the series of criminal (and administrative) law policy reforms aiming to protect the EU's financial interests—is, however, incompatible with the funds decision-making, which is deliberative, inclusive, and adaptive.

7. Criminal Law and the Governance of EU Funds: A Fundamental Mismatch?

There are justified (and indeed, substantiated) policy concerns about fraud by the recipients of EU funds. However, the argument I present here, in six steps, is that the criminal law-orientated anti-fraud approach chosen by the EU does not provide the appropriate framework to address corruption concerns in national funds management and may even be counterproductive to existing accountability tools.[135]

First, national funds governance is fluid and flexible, emphasizing learning while doing. The current MFF is set to increase this flexibility, allowing Member States to adjust programme objectives and resources in light of changing circumstances. Criminal law thinking, for its part, operates more from a binary logic of legal/illegal that is ill suited for recognizing and accommodating learning and the potential for correction. It is thus unclear how to attain flexibility within a framework that forcefully emphasizes the protection of EU interests from abuse. The difficulties in reconciling these two fundamentally different mentalities are already manifest in the ECA's work. Cipriani notes

[133] Peirone, 'Another Brick in the Building of the EU Rule of Law: Anti-Corruption', *Italian Review of International and Comparative Law* (2023) 1–26, at 5.

[134] Proposal for a Directive of the European Parliament and of the Council on combating corruption, replacing Council Framework Decision 2003/568/JHA and the Convention on the fight against corruption involving officials of the European Communities or officials of Member States of the European Union and amending Directive (EU) 2017/1371 of the European Parliament and of the Council, COM/2023/234 final.

[135] See in a different context, Klein, 'Criminal Law, Public Health, and Governance of HIV Exposure and Transmission', 13 *International Journal of Human Rights* (2009) 251 (arguing that 'the principal human rights and policy concerns that have been raised over criminalization of HIV exposure or transmission since the early days of the epidemic cannot be neatly addressed within the traditional criminal law framework').

that, since 2014, the number of transactions tested by the ECA has been reduced significantly, and its assessments do not contain qualitative data on the frequency of errors or their nature, or indications as to their appropriate treatment to avoid errors in the future.[136] There is no evidence that the ECA would have reduced its testing *because of* the orientation towards criminal law, but the criminal law mindset may discourage the ECA from identifying mistakes and presenting them as necessary building blocks of any learning process, thus impeding learning.

Second, the enhanced proportionate arrangements model, another innovation of the current MFF, seems ill advised when set against the EU's criminal law-orientated anti-fraud policy. As a concept, the enhanced proportionate arrangements model rewards countries that have done the right thing in the past (countries with a 'good' track record) and which participate in the EPPO's work. In criminal law, prudent behaviour in the past is seldom rewarded by the promise of less control in the future.[137] For instance, two years of sober driving is not rewarded by the promise that in the future there will be fewer breathalyser checks. It is important to note that I do not assume that the application of the enhanced proportionate arrangements model leads to a situation where well-performing Member States abuse the period of fewer controls, but rather it again shows the fundamental mismatch of the governance model and criminal law.[138]

[136] Cipriani (n. 89) 474.

[137] My argument here is simply that the ehanced proportionate arrangements model and criminal law mindset are not compatible in a single system. The idea of 'responsive regulation', coined by Ayres and Braithwaite, helps clarify the point I am making. Responsive regulation suggests criminal law should be the last resort, forming the tip of the regulatory pyramid. The presumption is to employ lower-level strategies from the pyramid first, only resorting to criminal enforcement when these strategies prove ineffective: see I. Ayres and J. Braithwaite, *Responsive Regulation: Transcending the Deregulation Debate* (1992). This pyramid, however, does not incorporate incentives for good behaviour; such elements are part of a separate system known as the 'pyramid of supports'. This positive pyramid includes components like 'informal praise for progress' or 'prizes or grants'. For the pyramid of supports, see G. Dukes, J. Braithwaite, and J. P. Moloney, *Pharmaceuticals, Corporate Crime and Public Health* (2014). In contrast, the pyramid of supports does not offer the option of reducing controls in line with the enhanced proportionality arrangements model in EU funds governance. In other words, the introduction of enhanced proportionality arrangements introduces elements that regulatory theory does not acknowledge, attempting to merge two distinct 'pyramids', which is bound to fail. Thanks to Joanne Scott for helping me to flesh out my argument more fully here.

[138] This cannot, of course, be ruled out entirely. In the United Kingdom, water companies are responsible for self-monitoring water recycling sites, while the Environment Agency carries out audits and inspections of waste water treatment works. Anglian Water was fined £2.65 million for failing to manage and monitor effluent at the Jaywick Water Recycling Centre in Essex, leading to sewage being discharged into the sea. It seems, however, that the failures resulted from the company not having the effective monitoring system in place, rather than the company ditching its formerly good monitoring system as a reaction to fewer inspections: see https://www.gov.uk/government/news/anglian-water-fined-265m-after-sewage-discharged-into-north-sea (last visited 22 January 2024).

Third, criminal law emphasizes those instruments through which individual responsibility can be realized. It overlooks systemic corruption and problems at the level of the system that may lead to funds going missing, instead focusing on instances of falsified documents and other individual beneficiary misconduct in the context of single projects. It is questionable whether establishing who is to blame leads to improved learning about what is good governance of EU funds or increased citizen trust in government. Writing in the national context of France, Antoine Vauchez and Pierre France critically assess anti-corruption tools, which they argue disproportionally 'focus on corrupt practices or on individual circumstances. They thus underestimate the systemic dimension, and the more diffuse corruption of the "public spirit".'[139]

Fourth, it seems difficult to reconcile the stronger criminal law orientation with an increasing emphasis on evaluation. As recalled above when discussing evaluation, it is important for the EU to be able to demonstrate that resources from EU funds are spent correctly and effectively and that EU funds make a difference on the ground. However, as one of the interviewees noted, 'It is easier to monitor euros than results.'[140] In other words, while the criminal law approach may be suited to tracking euros, it is definitely at odds with the current governance model that emphasizes the importance of evaluating whether or not the project has an impact on society and results in an added value for the EU.

Fifth, it is unclear how well civil society participation works within broader criminal law architecture. The emphasis on criminal law could potentially act as a deterrent to civil society actors, who may grow reluctant to innovate and participate in activities such as an integrity pact if there is a risk that doing so may result in a situation where the EPPO starts investigating a large building project in which a certain civil society organization has participated in monitoring activities. Although the investigation may not have anything to do with the organization, the EPPO's involvement can tarnish the expert reputation of participating civil society actors more broadly.[141]

Sixth, the reliance on criminal law is likely to pose problems also in the sense that the landscape of EU criminal law is complex and contains both intergovernmental and supranational structures and activities. Whatever the the EU's

[139] A. Vauchez and P. France, *The Neoliberal Republic. Corporate Lawyers, Statecraft, and the Making of Public–Private France* (2020) 142.

[140] Interview 4, 18 June 2021.

[141] Creating the EPPO was described as also sending a signal of mistrust to the national administrative level and decreasing the interest of acting as an 'EU agent': see Interview 1, 3 June 2021.

efforts to ensure that EU funds are used responsibly and honestly, in the context of the EPPO and the OLAF or otherwise, it has to take into account the fact that, in some sense, EU criminal law does not exist but could be rather described as 'piggybacking on existing national criminal law and procedures'.[142]

My argument, as outlined in these six steps, is that the emerging penal rationality is a problem because it is fundamentally misaligned with the basic tenets of the governance model that relies on inclusive planning, programming through iteration and adaptation, and the execution of programmes through deliberation. It is the implications of this mismatch that should worry us. The penal rationality risks overriding and weakening the accountability tools that are built into the national governance model. A similar logic has also been identified by others. Analysing data from over 100,000 public procurement contracts in the Czech Republic and Hungary in 2009–2012, Fazekas and King concluded that EU funds increase the risk of corruption by up to 34 per cent. The negative effects are largely attributable to 'overly formalistic compliance and EU Funds overriding domestic accountability mechanisms in public organizations entirely dependent on external funds'.[143] While my argument is focused on the emerging penal rationality of EU funds and its implications for accountable funds governance, theirs claims that EU funds come with excessive red tape, interfering with domestic accountability mechanisms. What connects both is the view that devising workable accountability mechanisms is important, but so is protecting and defending them.[144]

One final issue needs consideration. Recent socio-historical research has analysed 'the legal, political and professional practices that helped define and transform the spaces of European and international criminal law'.[145]

[142] Harding and Öberg, 'The Journey of EU Criminal Law on the Ship of Fools—What Are the Implications for Supranational Governance of EU Criminal Justice Agencies?', 28 *Maastricht Journal of European and Comparative Law* (2021) 192.

[143] Fazekas and King, 'Perils of Development Funding? The Tale of EU Funds and Grand Corruption in Central and Eastern Europe', 13 *Regulation & Governance* (2019) 405.

[144] This connects to discussions in charity governance. The Economist's Special Report on Philanthropy highlights the emergence of a new model of 'no-strings philanthropy' that empowers NGOs to determine how funds are best spent without the 'hoop-jumping and form-filling' that have become the hallmarks of 'philanthrocapitalism'. This influential model, which described charity governance for the best part of 20 years, brought market logic to NGOs, requiring them to plan and measure key performance, but it also burdened them with bureaucracy in the process. The no-strings approach sees donors giving out unrestricted grants that do not specify how they need to be used or impose reporting requirements. See the January 2024 report by Avantika Chilkoti, 'The Super-Rich Are Trying New Approaches to Philanthropy', *The Economist* (10 January 2024), https://www.economist.com/special-report/2024/01/10/the-super-rich-are-trying-new-approaches-to-philanthropy (last visited 1 February 2024).

[145] Christensen, 'Reunited Europe and the Internationalization of Criminal Law. The Creation and Circulation of Criminal Law as an International Governance Tool', in M. J. Christensen and R. Levi (eds), *International Practices of Criminal Justice. Social and legal perspectives* (2017).

Dismantling the idea that criminal law just spontaneously emerged as a tool of international governance, the research has highlighted how criminal law was consciously 'activated as a potential European and international governance technology in an atmosphere characterized by social and political restructuring. The specific political circumstances allowed for specific forms of governance mechanism to become politically viable.'[146]

The EU's struggle with its Eastern Member States has been clearly central to creating 'an atmosphere' for a stronger criminal law orientation. What is interesting is that this activation of criminal law as a viable governance mechanism also needs professionals who *create* the market for criminal law and *act* as drivers in the expansion of criminal law to new social and political contexts. Who could these professionals be in the context of EU funds management? With respect to France, Vauchez and France have noted the appeal of an 'ethical and transparent governance',[147] and the role of *law firms* specializing in the governance of compliance programmes and 'penal business law'.[148] Indeed, 'the exact shape of this new expertise is still in flux, but it is always a matter of advising companies on public regulations and criminal law related to tax fraud, discrimination, health and safety standards, environmental issues, personal data, corruption, and money laundering, business ethics and so forth'.[149] As far as I am aware, there is no research on the role of law firms in the markets created around EU funds governance. It would be important to shed light on different professional roles that EU funds management has created, and in particular on the question of whether law firms have contributed to creating the market for criminal law and a role in it for themselves as accountability entrepreneurs.

8. Conclusion

The national governance of EU funds is, as one of the interviewees described it, 'a tip of the elephant's tail'.[150] The sheer structure of the EU budget, not to mention its complex circuits and circulations, baffle and overwhelm, and national funds decision-making is, quite understandably, often overlooked. National

[146] Ibid.
[147] Vauchez and France (n. 139) 27.
[148] Ibid. 104 (my emphasis). The authors have added the French language term *droit pénal des affaires* in brackets.
[149] Ibid. 27. They trace the emergence of this new expertise to 'new forms of corruption' that flourish on the muddled public–private distinction: see ibid. 131.
[150] Interview 5, 21 June 2021.

governance is, however, the closest to citizens, and their negative views of EU public spending are not based on how the EU budget is negotiated in Brussels but on how national funds are governed at the local, regional, and government levels, which makes the 'tip of the tail' hugely important. In this chapter, I interrogated the relationships, structures, and practices that underlie the national governance of ERDF funds. By examining these processes, I showed how national funds officials are embedded in highly routinized processes that contribute, in a piecemeal fashion, to accountable funds decision-making, which is deliberative, inclusive, and adaptive. There is no guarantee that national funds decision-making is accountable, but there is evidence that the funds governance comes with tools for accountability.

The EU's ambitious anti-corruption agenda, which seeks to ensure that no funds are misused and that any misused funds can be claimed back to the EU budget and ultimately returned to the national level, has popular and political appeal. Yet, such an agenda may colonize the national governance process and supplant its accountability tools with criminal law's binary logic of black/white, legal/illegal, corrupt/non-corrupt. At the risk of romanticizing things, my exploration of the national governance process shows that while funds decision-making at that level is not perfect, it is not beyond repair either, and unscrupulous criminals, although posing a problem, should not exhaust our attention. Mixing governance and penal rationalities leads to unintended consequences that not only threaten the 'tip of the tail' but also the whole of an elephant—the operation of the shared management of EU funds.

Index

For the benefit of digital users, indexed terms that span two pages (e.g., 52–53) may, on occasion, appear on only one of those pages.